JOYCE between FREUD and JUNG

Kennikat Press
National University Publications
Literary Criticism Series

General Editor
John E. Becker
Fairleigh Dickinson University

JOYCE

BETWEEN

FREUD AND JUNG

SHELDON BRIVIC

National University Publications
KENNIKAT PRESS // 1980
Port Washington, N.Y. // London

To my brother
Irwin Jack Brivic

Manufactured in the United States of America

Published by
Kennikat Press Corp.
Port Washington, N.Y. / London

Library of Congress Cataloging in Publication Data

Brivic, Sheldon R   1943-
  Joyce between Freud and Jung.

  (Literary criticism series) (National university publications)
    Bibliography: p.
    Includes index.
    1. Joyce, James, 1882–1941–Criticism and interpretation. 2. Freud, Sigmund, 1856–1939. 3. Jung, Carl Gustav, 1875–1961. 4. Psychoanalysis and literature. I. Title.
PR6019.09Z526316   823'.9'12   79-22470
ISBN 0-8046-9249-1

CONTENTS

ACKNOWLEDGMENTS

I owe a great deal to many fine teachers. Arthur Waldhorn first got me interested in modern literature, and it was with Marvin Magalaner that I first became a Joycean. I studied psychoanalysis with Fred Crews and wrote my dissertation for him and Tom Flanagan. All of these have given me support over the years, and after I began teaching, I continued to learn from J. Mitchell Morse and Paula Robison.

The preparation of this book was made possible through two summer research grants from Temple University.

My greatest debt is to my wife, Barbara. I've been devoted to her and to Joyce for fifteen years without feeling any diminishment in either.

JOYCE between FREUD and JUNG

... the modern theme is the subterranean forces, those
hidden tides which govern everything and run humanity
counter to the apparent flood: those poisonous subtleties
which envelop the soul, the ascending fumes of sex.

... the inner construction, the pathological and
psychological body which our behaviour and thought
depend on. Comprehension is the purpose of literature,
but how can we know human beings if we continue to
ignore their most vital functions?

(Joyce during the twenties, quoted in
Arthur Power,
Conversations with James Joyce)

BIBLIOGRAPHIC ABBREVIATIONS

CW [Joyce]   *The Critical Writings of James Joyce*, ed. Ellsworth Mason and Richard Ellmann. New York: Viking Press, 1959.

CW [Jung]   *The Collected Works of C. G. Jung*, trans. R. F. C. Hull, ed. Sir Herbert Read, Michael Fordham, Gerhard Adler and William McGuire, Bollingen Series XX, in 19 vols. (Princeton: Princeton Univ. Press, 1953-1971): volume numbers in arabic numerals.

D   *Dubliners*, ed. Robert Scholes. New York: Viking, 1967.

E   *Exiles*. New York: Viking, 1951.

FW   *Finnegans Wake*. New York: Viking, 1939, 1958.

JJ   Richard Ellmann, *James Joyce*. New York: Oxford Univ. Press, 1959.

Letters, I, II, III   *Letters of James Joyce*, I, ed. Stuart Gilbert. New York: Viking, 1957; reissued with corrections, 1965. Vols. II and III, ed. Richard Ellmann. New York: Viking, 1966.

N   *Joyce's Ulysses Notesheets in the British Museum*, ed. Phillip F. Herring. Charlottesville: Univ. Press of Virginia, 1972.

P   *A Portrait of the Artist as a Young Man*, corrected from the Dublin Holograph by Chester G. Anderson, ed. Richard Ellmann. New York: Viking, 1964.

SE   *The Standard Edition of the Complete Psychological Works of Sigmund Freud*, trans. and ed. by James Strachey in collaboration with Anna Freud, assisted by Alix Strachey and Alan Tyson, 24 vols. (London: Hogarth Press, 1953-1974): volume numbers in roman numerals.

SH   *Stephen Hero*, ed. John J. Slocum and Herbert Cahoon. New York: New Directions, 1944, 1963.

U   *Ulysses*. New York: Random House, 1961.

INTRODUCTION

JOYCE IN PROGRESS

Although a continuous personal vision ties James Joyce's works together through shared concerns, patterns, techniques and characters, nevertheless no two books of Joyce resemble each other in form or manner. Most artists settle into one or two modes, but even without considering the experiments in verse, drama and memoir, Joyce's career may be traced as a relentless spiral of transformation. The mean *Dubliners* stories, the lush impressionism of *A Portrait of the Artist as a Young Man*, the polyphonic monumentalism of *Ulysses* and the dream collage of *Finnegans Wake* not only differ radically from each other, but each book changes nature from inception to conclusion, growing, among other tendencies, more subjective, experimental and expansive as it proceeds.

These transformations may be explained by viewing Joyce's canon dynamically as an ongoing process in which issues are worked out and possibilities created and lost as personality develops. Depth psychology will be needed to explain the reasons for these changes it helped reveal, but a few descriptive points are readily established. Contrasting *Dubliners* and *Portrait* to *Ulysses* and the *Wake*, I see sweeping movement from bitterness and rejection to good humor and acceptance. I also see a steady shift from naturalism and social criticism to symbolism and myth. These two trends parallel and reinforce each other in moving from a harsh view of empirical reality to a mellow view of a world defined in terms transcending realism—from unpleasant truth to pleasant creation.

The naturalistic *Dubliners* subordinates symbolism to an unsparing view of socially induced paralysis. Symbolic elements are more pronounced in *Portrait*, while in *Exiles* and *Ulysses* symbols and archetypes make up about half the substance of the work and play a more systematic role in shaping plot than they do in the autobiographical novel. Social reality in *Portrait* and later works remains as barren and corrupt as in *Dubliners*, but a myth of spiritual transcendence increasingly opposes this reality.

In *Exiles* and *Ulysses*, especially later in *Ulysses*, the myth of creativity gains enough power to compete with the brute world. This allows the possibility of love, which is, for Joyce at least, essentially a myth rather than an objective phenomenon. These works suggest that Richard Rowan and Leopold Bloom may win spiritual victories of communion even though they are both obstructed by social and psychic bindings. In the *Wake* it no longer matters who wins or loses, and objective reality is reduced to a shadow occasionally glimpsed behind a dream of immortal forms and magic language. *Finnegans Wake* is one of the most affirmative works since *The Divine Comedy*, but its cosmic affirmation deals with the problems of ordinary reality about as contextually as Dante does.

Reason for the shift from fact to myth must lie in Joyce's mind. Joyce believed his work expressed this mind, including the unconscious: ". . .do any of us know what we are creating?. . .Which of us can control our scribblings? They are the script of one's personality like your voice or your walk."[1] I see no reason to imagine a being who is not a narrator and separate from Joyce behind any of the decisions involved in his writing—Although I think the "arranger" David Hayman sees orchestrating the narrators of *Ulysses* is a sound step in the direction of doing justice to a function of authorial presence.[2]

Assuming that there is a mind behind the works and that it is Joyce's, my purpose is to understand the development of that mind as it went into and came out of the works. The main tool I use is Freudian psychoanalysis. Fortunately, Joyce's mind has been portrayed as thoroughly as any in literature and portrayed with singular concentration on the question Freud answers more effectively than anyone else—the why of mental motivation.

It may be emblematic that the two men who have contributed most in our century to the understanding of the mind—Joyce through art and Freud through science—had the same name in different languages. Both spent their careers mining the soul and drawing—or (in Joyce's phrase) "pressing out"—what was below the surface of life into words. Preoccupied with the meanings of language, both strove to bridge the great gap between what we feel and what we express, between the inner world of spirit and the outer one of matter. Their concern with the tie between subject and object concentrated the meticulous minds of both on the link between men and women: their works revolve around themes of love and sex. And in their treatment of sexual and mental life they revealed great tracts of reality that were usually ignored and are still often denied.

Finally, both Freud and Joyce settled on variations of the basic heuristic principle of following the mind in the process of its thought and judging its real reasons by the turns it took. Freud's version of this method has become linked to the term *free association,* Joyce's to *interior monologue.*

If both were concerned with bridging the distance between spirit and matter, it must be said that Freud was more consistent than Joyce in bringing them together so as to subordinate the spiritual to the material. Freud's science led him to a firm skepticism about the transcendent and the supernatural, and most of his work explains in physical terms feelings thought of as spiritual, sublime or terrible. He saw religion and love as products of instinctual drives modified by bodily experience. Joyce likewise often brought holy feelings down to earth by indicating with Swiftian acuity the physical realities behind what Stephen Dedalus calls "the spiritual-heroic refrigerating apparatus" (*P* 252). But there are also, increasingly after *Dubliners,* spiritual values in his work, as evident in sublime esthetic effects such as the lyrical conclusions of all of his works or the moment when Leopold Bloom has a vision of his son Rudy in Nighttown (*U* 609). Balanced between naturalism and symbolism, Joyce's writings move steadily from a world of frustration to one of transcendence. The ultimate uplift can be explained penetratingly by Freudian analysis, as we will see; but it will be comprehended more fully in its own terms by a psychology of the spirit. Carl Gustav Jung, who subordinated physical manifestations to a transcendent totality called the collective unconscious, has done most in our century to relate depth psychology to the spiritual realm.

In my effort to trace the nature and development of Joyce's mind as reflected in his work, I will first use Freudian insights to show how Joyce's mind was formed and to explore its unconscious aspect. Then I will show the relation between these influences and Joyce's conscious, mature ideas, which I'll explain partly in Jungian terms. After his youthful break with the Church, Joyce moved from an antipathy to religion (such as Freud felt) toward an attempt, in the *Wake,* to formulate his own universal mythic system based on psychology, as Jung did.

Mark Shechner's able psychoanalytic study of *Ulysses, Joyce in Nighttown*, provides a suggestion of why Jung's ideas are needed. Schechner applies ego psychology to show Joyce advancing toward mastery and control through art; but he makes it clear in Freudian terms that what Joyce gains control over is a process of self-satisfaction through fantasies. Shechner finds the fantasies he equates with inner life boringly redundant in themselves, but valuable insofar as they provide release through self-reflexive artistic gestures.[3] This is sound as far as it goes, but it leaves Shechner far from being able to give credence to many of Joyce's beliefs or to explain the enormous sense of the affirmation of human value and love that readers find in Joyce's later works. Jung provides the best means of comprehending the power of Joyce's vision beyond its narrow value as a game he played with himself.

An understanding of the psychological dynamic behind the shift from irony to myth in Joyce's canon will clarify crucial questions of how issues are resolved in each book. The central problem of Joyce's work may be described as one of relationship. The relations of Joyce's characters to each other and to their worlds are so rendered as to signify larger issues: connections between the artist and his object, spiritual and material things, man and woman, parent and child, one person and another. All of these problems revolve around the need to find a valid mode of relation.

S. L. Goldberg's distinguished study of *Ulysses, The Classical Temper*, points out that Stephen's description of the artist's relation to his subject late in *Portrait* quotes St. Thomas Aquinas on the relation of the soul to the universe. Goldberg sees Stephen's attempts to define the proper connection between artist and subject in *Stephen Hero, Portrait* and *Ulysses* as stages in the key Joycean quest for a fruitful, constructive mode of relation to the world. He describes the solution to this problem arrived at in *Ulysses* as an attitude of calm acceptance of reality, "the classical temper" opposed in *Stephen Hero* to the unrealistic romantic temper, which strives for what is unattainable (*SH* 78–79). Goldberg feels that stable contact with real people and objects solves the problem of alienation that *Ulysses* inherits from *Portrait*.[4]

The difficulty in finding such a solution in *Ulysses* is that relations remain sundered: Stephen is not reconciled to Ireland or to any parent or object of love, while Bloom does not appear to achieve meaningful contact with either Stephen or Molly. Youth and age, artist and object, man and woman seem at least as badly out of touch at the close of *Ulysses* as at the start, for Stephen gives up home, job and friends during the book, and Bloom is cuckolded. If Joyce wanted to show reconciliation or contact, why not do so? And yet many hints—mythic parallels, symbols, dreams, coincidences and others—suggest some sort of communion relating the characters to each other and to their world beneficially. The novel points toward a positive ending even though its action ends negatively.

This contradiction reaches to the roots of Joyce interpretation, for we must know how Joyce's works end to determine what they mean, and the sort of ambiguity present at the end of *Ulysses* is found at the ends of all the major works. Is Gabriel Conroy dead or reborn at the end of "The Dead"? When Stephen leaves Ireland and *Portrait*, is he liberating himself victoriously or compounding his alienation and soaring toward disaster? Is Richard Rowan triumphant or defeated at the end of *Exiles*?

And in *Finnegans Wake*, where the end is the beginning, the ambiguity is so pervasive and ingrained that attempts to solve it seem pointless.

While many critics regard *Portrait* and *Ulysses* as devastating satirical or tragic portrayals of the modern wasteland,[5] others have been reluctant to take the ending of *Ulysses* as a bleak vision of alienation which deflates *Portrait*. These others have seized on hints in the text to read a *Ulysses* that indicates Stephen, Molly and Bloom will somehow unite or reform as a result of their experiences with each other.[6] These theories are unsatisfactory contrivances of hopes and hints that can be sustained only by ignoring the bulk of negative indication in *Ulysses*.

Goldberg, the most systematic of the optimists, rejects certain episodes as Joycean oversights because they do not accord with Goldberg's conception.[7] Ellmann hails Bloom's masturbation as "heroic" because it defies "spatial separation" to join "ideal and real."[8] These examples show the options involved in interpreting *Ulysses* as a work of affirmation: either to avoid portions of the text or to elevate symbolic indications or imaginary possibilities in the novel at the expesne of basic human values. On the other hand, those who regard *Ulysses* as a sprawling nightmare of irony fail to do justice to the book's human warmth or to Joyce's expressed intentions. Likewise with *Portrait*—those who celebrate Stephen's departure from Ireland as an apotheosis overlook his offensive qualities and the ironies which brand him as Icarus; and readers who see a portrait of a damned soul or failed artistic impulse are missing central points the book makes about art and freedom. An indissoluble dispute among single-minded critics may cause art to look defective, and Wayne C. Booth's *The Rhetoric of Fiction* condemns *Portrait* as marred by lack of control because no clear, single meaning may be educed from it.[9] But why shouldn't art remain unresolved when life so often does?

Arnold Goldman's *The Joyce Paradox* comprehends both positive and negative views by saying that in *Dubliners, Portrait* and *Ulysses* two possibilities exist side by side: the characters may change and resolve their problems, or their personalities may be fixed so that they can never escape their conflicts and divisions. Goldman shows evidence for both of these conclusions in each text and argues that the view any reader chooses to take depends on his intellectual and literary allegiances. Among other distinctions, he says that the Freudian will see Joyce's figures as trapped, while the Jungian will perceive their capacity for change.[10] Several thoughtful books on *Ulysses* since Goldman's have followed his idea that there is more than one meaning in the book, tying the simultaneous opposed directions in Joyce's narrative to the open-minded complexity of modern philosophy.[11]

I apply Goldman's two intentions to the problem of relationship in

Joyce's work by saying that in *Portrait* and *Ulysses* the protagonist para-doxically achieves creative relation to the world by means of separation. Thus, Stephen confronts Ireland productively to create an artistic image of it by separating himself from it. As he puts it, ". . .the shortest way to Tara was via [out of the way] Holyhead" (*P* 250). Similarly, the cross-ing of Stephen and Bloom will have a positive effect on them because the two men part and go their ways in the "Ithaca" episode. And Bloom affirms his love for Molly and revives her love for him by permitting her to commit adultery with Blazes Boylan just as Richard Rowan renews his love for Bertha in *Exiles* by giving her to Robert Hand.

These paradoxes of creativity binding together the contradictions in Joyce's endings are supported not only by structures of action and image in the two books, but by parallels in Joyce's life: he left Ireland and broke with his parents only to return to nation and progenitors through art, and he seemed almost to cultivate the idea of yielding his beloved to another. Hélène Cixous, in *The Exile of James Joyce*, shows how Joyce and Stephen dealt with the world by a course of progress through conflict and relation through a voluntary exile which was really involuntary.[12] The union of connection and separation makes Joyce's works embody un-resolved conflict. This conflict is not merely between critics; it is built into the books as an expression of Joyce's mind. How can we explain such conflict?

The idea of union through separation is psychologically and culturally profound. It is stressed in some of Joyce's favorite writers: Ibsen's *Enemy of the People* concludes "the strongest man in the world is he who stands most alone," and Blake says "Opposition is true friendship." And it was and old idea when it serves as basis for the *Odyssey*. Reconciliation through sundering or death and rebirth is perhaps the most basic mythic pattern, as the Jungian Joseph Campbell demonstrates in *The Hero with a Thou-sand Faces* (Princeton: Bollingen, 1949), and it underlies the fall and redemption of Christian eschatology.

Whatever the traditional weight of the concept of union through separation, Joyce's idiosyncratic versions of this theme strike readers as odd, limited and defective. Perhaps this is because traditional myth in-cludes a supernatural power which imposes alienation from Eden, while Joyce, as modern man, appears to choose it voluntarily. As Edward Brandabur points out, the personal ties between Joyce's characters are virtually always indirect, vicarious or perverted.[13] Why does Joyce never portray positive, direct relationship? Are there no husbands who love wives directly? No people who love their parents, nations, societies or worlds? Why did Joyce take the indirection of art and meditation as his model for life? These questions led me to psychoanalysis as the most penetrating system by which to understand the motivations and values behind Joyce's peculiar, paradoxical formulations of experience. The link between the skeptic Joyce and tradition often makes one wonder about tradition rather than gaining faith in Joyce. Freudian analysis explains why Joyce saw life as he did in terms which match the asperity and self-consciousness of his vision while relating that vision to universal forces.

Another quality which invites analysis is the sexualization of his fiction. Cixous says a sexual level is always present in Joyce's metaphysics (*Exile*, p. 281), and Marilyn French describes a highly developed analogy in the "Oxen of the Sun" episode of *Ulysses* between stylistic blocks to objective perception and psycho-social blocks to sexual union.[14] In fact, Stephen's account of the process whereby the artist apprehends his object, the core of his esthetics theory, is analogous to the sex act. The main example of an esthetic object Stephen speaks of on this occasion is a beautiful woman. After seeing the object as a whole, "you feel the rhythm of its structure" (*P* 212) and analyze the relation of its parts. And the final stage of *claritas* or radiance is a luminous stasis of pleasure compared to a fading coal (*U* 213). Joyce describes orgasm vividly as fading fireworks in *Ulysses* (*U* 366-367). The phases that follow the ecstatic union of artist and object are "artistic conception, artistic gestation and artistic reproduction" (*P* 209), making the sexual analogy obvious.

Ellmann's study of *Ulysses* emphasizes Joyce's belief that "the sexual act is the essential act of artistic as of natural creation."[15] Like Freud, Joyce took sex as a standard of truth: Ellmann calls sincerity Joyce's "supreme virtue"[16] without mentioning that in his notes for *Ulysses* Joyce wrote, "Fuck only time people really sincere" (*N* 429). But sex is capable of many permutations and interpretations, and it often seems more like an ideal than a reality in Joyce's work. As in the esthetics theory, he often makes it a spiritual analogy rather than a physical fact. And Jung is the theorist of sex in its traditional religious function as abstraction.

Joyce's biography records his ironic and hostile comments on psycho-analysis, but these may have been reactions against exposure, competition and scientific rigor (*JJ* 393, 538, 642). He often argued that Freud's ideas were better expressed elsewhere, as by Vico or the Church (*JJ* 351, 486, 706), another matter than denying Freud's truth. Stephen favors Aquinas's theory of incest over Freud's, implying that the two economic views of emotion are not dissimilar (*U* 205). In gathering Joyce's critical remarks, Ellmann may have intended to correct the impression, prevalent during the forties, that Joyce was the most Freudian of novelists.

It has been conjectured that Joyce read *Die Traumdeutung* (1900; *Interpretation of Dreams*) during his visits to Paris to study medicine in 1902.[17]

This is unlikely, because Freud was scarcely known outside Vienna at the time. But Joyce was inclined to psychoanalytic insight before he knew Freud, as Stanislaus Joyce's description of his brother in 1901-1902 suggests: "He regarded psychology, which he was then studying, as the basis of philosophy, and words in the hand of an artist as the medium of paramount importance for the right understanding of the inmost life of the soul."[18] Shechner says Joyce's epiphanies always aimed at the revelation of unconscious material and describes Joyce's recording and analysis of his dreams and associations (*Nighttown*, pp. 17-18).

Dubliners, which grew out of the early "Epiphanies," is a series of clinically detailed studies of neurosis apparently written before Joyce knew of analysis. "A Painful Case" shows complex awareness of repression and the unconscious as Mr. Duffy avoids for years the awareness of the sexual sin of omission he performed on Mrs. Sinico—his essential insincerity—then remembers, then forgets again. "Eveline" and "Clay" are laden with the weight of impulse their neurotic heroines have repressed in their rejections of life. "Clay" has four Freudian slips or psychologically significant errors, while "Eveline" is knowing in its depiction of the girl's guilt toward her dead mother (the Electra complex). "An Encounter" ebbs craftily into an examination of how sadism works, and "Counterparts" shows how sexual frustration generates violence. Little Chandler in "A Little Cloud" hurts himself in the real world by his fixation on fantasies of poetry and romance, prefiguring Bloom. I will discuss "The Dead" in detail later.

It has long been known that *Finnegans Wake* is loaded with references to Freud and Jung, and Chester Anderson detects references to Freud in *Ulysses*.[19] But little indication of Joyce's interest in Freud before the *Wake* was available until recently. Then Arthur Power's *Conversations* presented Joyce's intention to "enlarge our vocabulary of the subconscious" (see epigraph) and "Wit. Read Freud" appeared on a notesheet for *Ulysses* (*N* 101). And Joyce's Trieste library was found to contain four psychoanalytic works in German, three of them apparently purchased before he left Trieste in 1915. Ellmann thinks Joyce bought them close to their dates of publication: "The Significance of the Father in the Destiny of the Individual" (1909) by Jung, *Leonardo da Vinci and a Memory of His Childhood* (1910) by Freud, *The Problem of Hamlet and the Oedipus Complex* (1911) by Ernest Jones and *The Psychopathology of Everyday Life*, a 1917 revision of a book Freud wrote in 1901.[20]

I will discuss the relevance of the da Vinci study to *Portrait* later, but start with the earliest and most unusual item on the list. Jung wrote this examination of a series of cases who were drastically controlled by their fathers when he was still Freud's leading disciple. Even then he emphasized the idea of destiny and saw the unconscious father images wreaking havoc on the lives of his patients as "demons." Revising the article after his break with Freud, he made them autonomous beings, possessors rather than possessions: "the power of the archetype is not controlled by us" (*CW*, [Jung] 4, p. 315). In giving up Freud's heroic effort to control the mind through reason, Jung gave power to unconscious mental forces, recognizing them as beings deserving life. This grant of authority to the unconscious is a crucial distinction between Freud's thought and Jung's; and also between Joyce's early works, where the prime issue is whether people can control their lives and the later ones in which they follow their destinies with growing dynamism.

Freud sees the male and female images that impose upon our lives from the unconscious as based on exaggerated infantile memories of parents, possibly influenced by other individuals. But Jung argues that these parental images are endowed with such power and universality in forms like God, Satan or the Blessed Virgin that memories of parents are not adequate to explain such gigantic spiritual entities any more than an animal's parents explain the instincts born in it. While Freud emphasizes individual experience as the source of the mind, Jung holds that each person has to realize his dependence upon a permanent collective unconscious that he can find represented in mythology and cultural tradition. In effect, Jung formulates a universal religion of archetypes based on recurring patterns in the minds (mainly dreams) of his patients and in the spiritual literature of the world.

His theory of the collective unconscious fails to convince me of the existence of the absolute system it postulates, and I often sense that Jung preferred to deal in sublime terms rather than facing the realities Freud stalwartly insisted on. Moreover, as Edward Glover points out, Jung's unconscious, being composed mainly of forms given at birth, is incapable of the dynamic interplay with consciousness exemplified by repression. As a result, Jung reverts to a conscious, descriptive psychology of edifying myths.[21] Glover pinpoints dangers in Jung's system, but he is as reductive as Jung's gibe that for Freud, civilization was a substitute for incest. For Jung's writings do provide revelatory sensations of penetrating the mystery of self. The material Jung focuses on is not sexual, but metaphysical; but it is barred from consciousness in the way thoughts of death are barred by our adjustment to ordinary reality.

Glover's objection applies more solidly to the ego psychologists and existential psychologists, who rose to prominence since Glover wrote and who tend respectively to neglect and to deny the unconscious. If the value of psychoanalysis lies in its clarifying of the irrational, it seems that no analyst since Jung has built up such a rich, complex understanding of unconscious patterns. Nor is this the only respect in which Jung was closer to Freud than later, more mechanical Freudians. Jacques Lacan has reason to insist that the history of analysis since Freud has been one of retreat. And a real parallel exists in literature, where William Faulkner and Virginia Woolf come closer to the psychological depth of Joyce and Lawrence than any writer since World War II.

Freud, in tracing the childhood roots of behavior, deals with causes, while Jung, in describing eternal symbolic patterns of value, deals with goals. And though Freudian analysis tells better than any other method where mental life comes from, it can't tell where it goes. The traditional analytic goal of making the unconscious conscious, the rule of reason, about which even Freud expressed misgivings in *Civilization and Its Discontents* (1930), is in itself less psychologically realistic than such mythic goals as paradise and transcendent love. For paradise is something to aim at, but whoever tries to make reason his goal is suppressing his desire. Working for fame, Freud sacrificed himself to afterlife as surely as any saint. William Blake said that reason needs energy to live, and Jung points out that life, conceived as a flow of energy, requires a goal of greater value than its cause in order to advance and that such goals are mythological symbols.[22]

It is innate in the human mind to require a purpose. And for this reason Jung's unconscious, though no scientific phenomenon, exists as a cultural entity: a body of spiritual facts there because men's minds have created and shared them, ideals and overvaluations. These facts can hardly be proven, but are central to the reality of life and will continue so. To ignore or dismiss them is to cripple one's apprehension of reality as surely as one does by trying to live wholly within them. Jung, then, is here because he had brilliant insights into the spiritual and transcendent, while Freud was limited in his ability to extend his thought into these areas. Just as a view tied to materialism can't do justice to values, so a view tied to causality is incapable of explaining how something new is created. As Molly points out at the end of *Ulysses*, something new must have been created at some point. It may be that something is created every day in countless lives which science and reason cannot perceive, and this may be the ironic theme of the "Ithaca" episode, with its patently reductive mathematical description of the meeting of Stephen and Bloom.

Joyce and Jung crossed paths, for Joyce lived in Jung's city of Zurich from 1915 to 1919 and Jung treated Joyce's disturbed daughter Lucia in 1934 (*JJ* 688-693). It's a pity the 1932 essay "Ulysses: A Monologue" by Jung was unable to surmount the initial difficulties of the text, for Joyce and Jung had much in common as thinkers, starting with the fact that both admired religious values without subscribing to a particular religion. Understanding transcendence in psychological terms, both saw life as conflict between matter and spirit or outer and inner worlds. Both were preoccupied by mythology, by self-realization and the unconscious, by the pattern of connection through distance or rising through falling.

The attraction of uplift, however, should not lead us to take Jung as a substitute for Freud; for the spiritual area of life is relatively marginal. Freud's discoveries about the unconscious, dreams, repression, psychic structure and childhood are more fundamental than those of Jung. Freud explored an expanse of mental activity comparable to the watery part of the earth and explained the operations of this area in the dry land terms of cause and effect. Next to this feat, the works of other analysts have been jetties, buoys and castles in the sand, or the work of disciples spreading an essentially Freudian word into new areas. One area Freud neglected was that of relationships: late in life he remarked to Theodore Reik, "We really know very little about love."[23] An important line of analysts, including Melanie Klein, Lacan and D. W. Winnicott, has pursued study of the operation of the unconscious between people, and many of their insights seem to me to follow Jung's ideas about projection, attitude, myth and sharing.

Freud, who opposed religion and was taught to adhere to scientific principles of "rigorous mechanism," may be said to have combined psychology with science.[24] (That these two tend to exclude each other is shown by the behaviorists, who carry scientific scruples to the point where they are unable to recognize the existence of the mind.) Jung considered a theological vocation in youth and was led to psychology by spiritualism.[25] He combined psychology with religion. Joyce was devoutly religious up to his fifteenth year and then became a skeptic and remained one; but he never lost the sense of values and spiritual order the Church had inculcated. His works, combining naturalism with myth, are built, like life itself, on both scientific and spiritual truths.

Only by using both a psychology of the body and a psychology of the spirit can I obtain a complete picture of the mental process in Joyce's work. In fact, while structuralism in the human sciences is emphasizing relations between systems, the physical sciences have now adopted a dualistic concept of the atom as at once both particle and wave—a concept resembling the old duality of matter and spirit that preoccupied Joyce. The need to accept simultaneous, opposing points of view is now as well established in the sciences as in society or art, as the physicist Werner Heisenberg indicates in his explanation of complementarity:

The concept of complementarity is meant to describe a situation in which we look at one and the same event through two different frames of reference. These two frames mutually exclude each other, but they also complement each other, and only the juxtaposition of these contradictory frames provides an exhaustive view of the. . .phenomena.[26]

I do not, however, expect my systems to be exhaustive. Elements of Joyce's thought and feeling are not explained by any analyst, and I should recognize them when I reach them. But the conjunction of Freud and Jung gives me a view broad enough to perceive solid Joycean reality.

As Freud tells how mental life originates, while Jung tells what it aims at, so Joyce's early works concentrate on where he came from and how it shaped him, while *Ulysses* and the *Wake,* both suggesting voyages in their titles, move toward concern with ultimate goals. The first third of this book will examine *Portrait* to show the origins of Joyce's obsessions from a Freudian perspective. The next third, starting from the recognition that personal mythology is a classic product of obsession, will attempt to connect the unconscious determinants of Joyce's personality to his conscious systems of meaning and value, which will be seen to resemble the thought of Jung. The final part will attempt to delineate the value Joyce found in life through his mythology and to examine the relation between Joyce's skeptical side and his affirmative side in *Ulysses* and the *Wake,* showing how the two sides promote each other and work together to see reality whole.

PART ONE

STEPHEN OEDIPUS

When someone told him that the account which he had given of his early life, so full of . . . the beginnings of sorrows, was wildly overstated and partly false, he answered—"Maybe I dreamed it." ("James Clarence Mangan" [1902] C.W. [*Joyce*] 77.)

Ma mère m'a mariée. (*U* 424)

I

THE GRAVE OF BOYHOOD

The problem of why Joyce sees connection as separation, which leads to analysis, also leads back to *Portrait*; for the genesis of later, more complex portrayals of relation through distance lies in Stephen's early alienations. And to understand the mind behind Joyce's works, it is logical to go back to the autobiographical novel that traces the development of a version of that mind almost from the beginning. The action of *Portrait* consists of Stephen sundering himself from his society, his Church, his beloved E. C. (Emmy Clery) and his nation. The novel justifies these sunderings by its derogatory portrayals of institutions and people and its presentation of concepts of freedom and esthetics. Stephen's concepts and his case against the establishment are effective, yet I doubt if they are at the root of his alienation. He is alienated before he has much chance to take critical stock of his environment. In the first brief section of the book he hides under a table while Dante Riordan threatens him. As Cixous points out, he already practices here the silence, exile and cunning he will advocate later (*Exile*, p. 287).

In the following scene on the football field, Stephen feels out of touch with his peers and threatened. Throughout the novel, except for brief, essentially delusive interludes of security, Stephen's isolation is consistent. He could not feel a sense of belonging in any group for long: his alienation is built in, and its basis must be assumed at the start. What causes it? The main reason Stephen gives is poor eyesight (*P* 41, 166–167), an explanation that leaves us to wonder why all boys with poor eyesight are not so alienated—or which of the two symptoms is causal.

Another cause the novel argues is preordination: destined to be an artist, Stephen is set apart from the first (*P* 165ff.). This is true in that

17

Joyce, as C. H. Peake indicates, selected material that illustrates artistic development from the longer *Stephen Hero* to frame his *Portrait of the Artist.*[1] The predestination of Stephen by Joyce as Providence brings us to the theater of teleology, illuminated by Jung, who tells us every "truly living thing" has a "final meaning" and is not "a mere leftover from antecedent facts" (*CW* [Jung], 7, p. 130). Stephen's apartness prefigures his destiny in a myth of artistic vocation; but God seldom seems present in *Portrait*, and myth only occasionally emerges from behind fastidious actuality. And predetermination does not explain Stephen's motives in causal terms—it is a subsequent rationalization. The more relevant question in *Portrait* is why alienation leads to art.

Stephen's problem has been explained by Joyce's biography. Ellmann suggests Joyce's lifelong effort to be unique was based on competition with his large family for the love of his mother (*JJ* 302-309). Cixous blames the early situation of Joyce's family, who were divided and went through many moves and setbacks: "The decline and displacement are the germs of that theme of exile which is, in Joyce's work, at the origin of every movement" (*Exile*, p. 4). Both explanations work, but seem thin motivation for "every movement" in Joyce's work or life. Moreover, the use of facts from the life to explain the work is questionable. We can't be sure Stephen is influenced by details of Joyce's life not in *Portrait*, but we can be sure everything in *Portrait* comes from or is selected by Joyce's mind. For this reason, I take virtually all evidence for analysis of Joyce's characters from the texts: where I cite biography, it serves to confirm what the text shows. But at the same time I see fit to take the texts as reflections of the development of Joyce's personality.

The question of relating Joyce's mind to those of his protagonists is a thorny one. New critics incline to find fallacy in any attempt to see the mind of an author in his work. Others, often with psychological orientation, object to analyzing a literary character as if he were a patient, though Freud analyzed Hamlet and da Vinci without meeting them. Both objections are useful as warnings against overinterpretation; if, however, both are taken as absolute rules, it actually becomes impossible to detect a full-fledged human consciousness anywhere in any work, thus reducing literature to a level of humanity near that of crossword puzzles. Insofar as the author's mind, the mind in his works and the minds of his characters correspond, seeing the connections between the three levels can help us to understand them.

As projections of Joyce, all of his protagonists share features of his personality and may be described as selves he left behind. But all are not equally autobiographical. Gabriel Conroy, Robert Hand of *Exiles* and Shaun of the *Wake* are firmly rejected examples of what Joyce might have become if he were not saved by his vision. Bloom and H. C. E. are viewed with more empathy, but the only figures who substantially represent Joyce are Stephen, Richard Rowan and Shem the Penman. In particular, Stephen has the potential to be Joyce and may be separated from him only by time, whereas Bloom, who has reached middle age without creating a son, a work of art or his destiny, does not have this potential.

Stephen is closest to Joyce's roots, and in *Portrait* Joyce precisely articulates the development of his personal vision of himself with a deep-reaching sense of the importance of each turn of thought and perception to the mental structure being built. I will examine the development of this mind in detail, defining Stephen's psychological situation as precisely as possible. My position is that Stephen's mind is contained in Joyce's much as past is in present. The feelings of school companions that Stephen differs, particularly in his alienation, from the "Sunny Jim" they knew, may well reflect the difference between external impressions and internal ones.[2] The irony with which Stephen is presented is covered by the title phrase "as a Young Man" and is consistent with Joyce's irony about himself. I will have to risk the wrath of those who deny that Joyce's first novel may be a portrait of the artist as a young man.

Joyce's literary criticism constitutes a defense of my method. The major critical effort of Stephen and Joyce, Stephen's discussion of Shakespeare in the library in *Ulysses*, identifies a central pattern in Shakespeare's mind which informs all of his work essentially. This crucial knot of feeling built into the bard's works is tied to father, mother, wife, brothers and children. Stephen's pattern that builds the works from the mind joins the individuality of Mr. William Shakespeare to a structure representative of universal responses to family ties. Joyce agrees with Freud that our human relations define our souls. Nor is this method reserved for Shakespeare. Of the man he regarded as Shakespeare's equal, Joyce remarked in 1908 that he wrote "essentially the same drama over and over again. I suspect that Ibsen met the four or five characters whom he uses throughout his plays before he was twenty-five" (*JJ* 276). Such a pervasive structure may not appear in the works of all artists, but it does in Joyce's. Stephen says a genius makes "his own image. . .the standard of all experience" (*U* 195). Goldberg adds, "We might restate his point by saying that the artist's self contains the forms or quidities he portrays in art, or that an artist's material is the activity of his own soul. . .a man understands only what he has a capacity to understand" (*Temper*, p. 74). The nature of the form of Joyce's soul built into his works can be understood through its origin.

I will indicate a few points where Joyce presents psychosexual material explained in the brief treatments of infantile sexual etiology and the oedipal complex by Freud and Jones he bought around 1911; and Hans Gabler believes he revised the first three chapters of *Portrait* extensively after this year.[3] But I will not limit myself to conscious influence. To get near the psychic life of Joyce's work, I will have to grasp two opposing principles: the extent of his knowledge of the mind and the limits of that knowledge. The first derives from the depth of probing and complexity of perception with which Joyce united with his objects—the souls of himself, his wife and those he knew.

Probing as he was, Joyce had to limit social ties, and his best friends after Nora were probably his characters. Even for ordinary folks, best friends resemble one because they entail projection. Giving her life to Joyce, Nora became enough like him to write letters in which he found matchless masterstrokes, a literary feat. Stephen and Bloom, though sprung from Joyce's brain, often seem more real than mere people. Stephen, for example, is able in *Ulysses* to put together thousands of associations he has "lived through" (though his life is a dream) to realize himself that he loves his mother sexually and hates his father mortally, and he realizes less than Joyce. The second principle, however, is the tough analytic observation that even a sophisticated, aware person will delude himself with partial, rationalized understanding to screen exactly what is most painful and crucial. By combining both these principles, I have a chance of distinguishing Joyce's psyche from his theory, unconscious from conscious.

Joyce had many diverse interests on both levels, but the major meeting place of his conscious and unconscious thought seems to have centered on a severe case of heterosexuality. And insofar as he was given to this prevalent problem, his central psychological pattern was the Oedipus complex of Freud, which has been observed in *Portrait*.[4] In fact, for reasons to be shown, Joyce was a doctrinaire heterosexual, redeemed only by the fact that what he was fanatic about was the confusion of human love. And so he inclined toward the doctrinaire view—not Freudian, but a common distortion of Freud—that all feelings which were not heterosexual were homosexual.

Even if he were not the sensitive son of a flawed family in a compromised country, Joyce's mere humanity entailed latent homosexual tendencies, as Freud and Joyce indicate. These tendencies corresponded to the gap of time it took him to connect with the opposite sex in spirit as well as body, the twenty-two years until the Bloomsday he met Nora Barnacle. And they corresponded also to the extent to which, as Stephen says of Shakespeare, he would "never be a victor in his own eyes after nor play victoriously the game of laugh and lie down" (*U* 196), or as the *Wake* puts it, his spark was beside the mark (*FW* 383)—the extent to which he did anything in life not aimed at a cervical bull's eye.

Joyce was always aware of active and passive roles in social situations. In a game played to win, aiming off target is aiming at yourself, and insofar as Joyce was perverted, he opted to be his own target. Joyce blamed the aggressive behavior of both sexes on the materialism inculcated by Church and State, but he moved toward the recognition that aggression was inevitable, while Church and State descend from mom and dad. In terms of the oedipal complex—the most all-embracing explanatory pattern in Joyce's work—Joyce's flaw was a replacing of the normal desire to kill father with a tendency to be threatened by him, a gap of neurotic guilt.

Stephen's first six years are represented in the section that takes up the first page and a half of *Portrait*, introducing many key images, including the looming, hairy father with his glass and the nicer smell of mother. The conclusion of this section, based on one of the earliest incidents in Joyce's life to be recorded in *Epiphanies*, poses a threat that echoes through *Portrait*:

> When they were grown up he was going to marry Eileen. He hid under the table. His mother said:
> —O, Stephen will apologise.
> Dante said:
> —O, if not, the eagles will come and pull out his eyes.
> *Pull out his eyes,*
> *Apologise,*
> *Apologise,*
> *Pull out his eyes.* (P8)

Robert Ryf points out that this passage threatens castration, though he sees this castration in non-Freudian terms as a symbol of social pressure.[5] Oedipus himself established eye loss as a classic castration image. Freud says the idea of emasculation starts to be important for children during the phallic or oedipal stage, around ages four and five, or just before Stephen's "Eagle" epiphany. Feelings previously invested in oral and anal areas become concentrated on the genitals in this stage, and the child develops intense desire for genital contact with parents, particularly the one of opposite sex. These desires and the masturbation and aggression they cause are forced out of consciousness, bringing on about six years of latency. And this repression is enforced by fear of castration: told that what he wants to do will be punished, the child comes to associate punishment with loss of the offending organ (*SE* XIX, pp. 174-176). This anxiety may attach itself to anything that denies, breaks or curtails being, but it has its most concrete basis in sexual desires and fears directed at parents, and an understanding of its origin helps to reveal how it operates.

The trigger of Stephen's fear is desire in that he is threatened for want-ting to play father: "When they were grown up he was going to marry Eileen." In the original epiphany largely quoted in the novel, the threat was voiced by Eileen's father, Mr. Vance, while the boy hiding under the table was James Joyce.[6] Joyce can present and Stephen remember the relatively minor incident with Eileen while the deeper love for mother behind it remains submerged. That the incident with Eileen screens something more serious is suggested by its importance in establishing basic patterns for the book. The following scene of football is pervaded by images of inadequacy: "The evening air was pale and chilly. . .the greasy leather orb flew like a heavy bird. . .he kept. . .out of reach of the rude feet. . .felt his body small and weak amid the throng. . .and his eyes were weak and watery" (*P* 8). The chill, inability to rise and sense of smallness and weakness all define a sense of body negation based on genital negation. The "rude feet" show the threat to be masculine by the criteria of Otto Fenichel, who says the boy may be endangered by "a masculine enemy, that is, by a penetrating, pointed tool, or by a feminine enemy, that is by an encompassing instrument, depending upon whether the father or the mother appeared as the more threatening person. . ."[7] As the game goes on, Stephen stays "fearful of the flashing eyes and muddy boots" and has a sense of organ inhibition which seems to express his developing introversion: "He kept his hands in the sidepockets of his belted grey suit" (*P* 9).

His dread of being unmanned or reduced to a female makes him sensitive to suggestions of violence or homosexuality. Such a suggestion propels him to mental flight along paths of association which lead to the main source of his comfort and object of his desire. One of Joyce's key innovations as a writer is to follow these paths by reproducing the movement of the mind beneath its superstructure of logic:

Cantwell had answered [to another boy] :. . .Give Cecil thunder a belt. I'd like to see you. He'd give you a toe in the rump. . .
That was not a nice expression. His mother had told him not to speak with the rough boys in the college. Nice mother!. . .when she had said goodbye she had put up her veil double to her nose to kiss him: and her nose and eyes were red. (*P* 9)

The emotionally charged memory of the parting kiss, with its overtones of moist red exposure, is soon followed by escape into a maternal revery which expands and clarifies a prevailing contrast between paternal threat and maternal haven, using a hearth as womb and varying the hands-in-pocket image of holding oneself as a mode of withdrawal:

It would be nice to lie on the hearthrug before the fire, leaning his head upon his hands, and think on those sentences. He shivered as if he had cold slimy water next his skin. That was mean of Wells to shoulder him into the square ditch because he would not swop his little snuffbox for Wells's seasoned hacking chestnut, the conqueror of forty. How cold and slimy the water had been! A fellow had once seen a big rat jump into the scum. Mother was sitting at the fire. . .her feet on the fender and her jewelly slippers were so hot and they had such a lovely warm smell! (P 10)

The bully embodies the paternal threat visited on Stephen for thoughts of the "hearth" and so is called to his mind by them. Stephen's "little snuffbox" suggests a feminine self-image, while Wells's nut, tied to a string for games, is aggressively male: it resembles the stopper on a chain wielded by father on the next page and seems midway between phallus and whip. Wells founds a series of father figures who emasculate Stephen by knocking him down, striking, degrading or dispossessing him. The most prominent are Father Dolan (Chapter I), Vincent Heron (II), Father Arnall (III), the Jesuit director (IV) and Cranly (V). The fall into the cesspool is not merely an image of virile disgrace: its features of coldness and a rat suggest death (compare P 22 and U 114). Fear of castration often appears as fear of death (Theory, p. 209), and the ditch as grave shows Stephen utterly negated by Wells's masculinity. At this point Stephen is impelled toward comfort and the text returns suddenly to mother and hearth.

Emphasis on mother's feet and "jewelly slippers" is fetishistic in arming her with phallic symbols, for fetishes replace the organ the child imagined his mother to possess until he found otherwise. In a context of sexual anxiety, the discovery that women lack the penis is shocking, according to Freud, because it suggests the possible unmanning of the child himself. If the shock is great, the child may grow up a fetishist, attracted to women wearing male symbols, such as footwear or gloves, or something that serves as genital hair to conceal their gap, such as bloomers or furs. Many standard fetishes recur in Joyce's works and his erotic letters to his wife.[8] In later years Joyce told Frank Budgen he was more interested in bloomers than their contents,[9] and virtually all descriptions of women in Portrait are fetishistic. Thus, mother's feet in the hearth scene are parallel in significance to her nose, which was a salient feature at the farewell kiss.

The contrast between square ditch and hearth also involves temperature. Throughout Chapter I Clongowes and maleness are associated with cold, and Stephen yearns for the warmth of home and mom.[10] But his desires are ambivalent, for he also feels attraction to the cold masculine side. His morbid attitude toward masculinity emerges when he hears

Simon Moonan, who has the same first name as his father, referred to as the prefect's "suck," which means sycophant or pet. "Suck" also has sexual—in this case homosexual—implications, and the text goes on to unfold them:

> Suck was a queer word. . .the sound was ugly. . .in the lavatory. . .his father pulled the stopper up by the chain after and the dirty water went down through the hole in the basin. And. . .the hole in the basin had made a sound like that: suck. Only louder.
>
> To remember that and the white look of the lavatory made him feel cold and then hot. There were two cocks that you turned. . .He felt cold and then a little hot. . .the names printed on the cocks. That was a very queer thing.
>
> And the air in the corridor chilled him too. It was queer and wettish. (P 11)

Stephen's disgust at Moonan's feminine role reminds him of disgust at his mother's genitals, represented quite vividly by the swirling hole. In the da Vinci study Joyce owned, Freud says that before coming "under the dominance of the castration complex" a child feels intense desire to look at the essential mom. The discovery that she does not have a penis generates disgust which can cause impotence, misogyny, homosexuality or fetishism (SE XI, p. 96). The image of father pulling the stopper may be a screen memory for the primal scene, the earliest vision of intercourse between parents. Through the dream technique of distortion by reversal, pulling the plunger may stand for pushing it, but it also represents injury of mother by father. This uneasy memory links sex to violence and castration. The strong association of intercourse and violence in Victorian society, suggested by words like "deflower" and "violate," made it especially difficult for sensitive boys to fit the male role.

Emphasis on alternating cold and hot suggests ambivalence in Stephen's reaction to the scene. Ulysses uses "blow hot and cold" to describe Bloom as bisexual (U 535). Stephen's washbasin scene is given a dense homosexual atmosphere by the lavatory setting and repetition of the words queer, suck and cocks. These are no neologisms, for cock is used in a sexual sense by Shakespeare, while the homosexual senses of queer and suck proceed directly from primary meanings. Joyce managed to slip by his censors a patch of language that would seem more at home in Jean Genet or William Burroughs. In this bathroom vision of anxious mystery Joyce shows consciousness of Stephen's unconscious.

Soon after this the masculine competition at school again drives Stephen into a longing for the womb: "All the boys seemed to him very strange. . .He longed to be at home and lay his head on his mother's lap. But he could not: and so he longed for the play and study and prayers to be over and to be in bed" (*P* 13). His bed remains a cozy maternal haven (*P* 221f.). Now he closes the flaps of his ears to cut himself off from outside, making an aural womb. He believes he does this as an experiment, but as he does it, he calls forth a memory of going through a tunnel in a train (*P* 13). This homeward memory has the shape of sex, and mother is its likeliest object. His tendency to retreat from the world into fantasies and sexualized memories is the basis of later isolation. He moves inward rather than outward and backward rather than forward, though he moves ahead quite nicely on mental tracks.

When Stephen engages the active world of ordinary male competition —and ordinary means giving orders—he becomes sensitive at any image of fatherhood and his body feels rather than pushing as his mind reverts inward. This makes his social situation precarious, for the forward movement of competition that dominates the well-ordered lives of these boys is made up largely of masterful or paternal gestures of push:

Some weeks Jack Lawton got the card for first and some weeks he got the card. . .His white silk badge fluttered. . .as he worked at the next sum and heard Father Arnall's voice. Then all his eagerness passed away and he felt his face quite cool. . .his face must be white because it felt so cool. He could not get the answer for the sum but it did not matter. White roses and red roses: those were beautiful colours to think of. (*P* 12)

Here as elsewhere coolness and light or whiteness, features of the surface or contact with outside, associate with paternal threat. At a key point in the joust of life, Stephen stops paying attention, loses and rationalizes his loss. The signal that triggers this is "Father Arnall's voice" and the Church recognizes Arnall's role in calling him *Father*. Stephen has no idea why his eagerness passes away at this voice, but he gives up the real rose for an imaginary one that he analyzes in esthetic and intellectual terms, an abstract rose. He can't bear to win because to possess the bloom of life would be incestuous. The opposition he reaches at the limit of his ability to extend himself toward his object, the active part of the outside world, is congruent with the role of the father, the one who can't be beaten. This pattern appears when Stephen does, for the first paragraph of *Portrait* ends with baby Tuckoo meeting the moocow and an ellipsis. The fairytale narrative breaks off suddenly as the cow appears and Stephen is confronted with the threatening image of his father reading the story to him. This obliges him to turn inward and make up his own story of imaginary roses. Thus, mother and father appear in the place reserved in epic for invocation of the muse and statement of the main theme of manly accomplishment, of the patriarch who journeyed far, won or was angry. Competition in maleness always implies a female prize, as the *Wake* indicates: whenever Shem and Shaun fight, Issy appears in the background. Because every victory aims at mom, Stephen cannot bear victory, and this is one main reason he gives up the world for art.

He is divided from the other boys by a guilt that gets him threatened by them, a threat currently provided by Wells, who is both patronizing and paternal as he touches the root of Stephen's guilt: "Tell us, Dedalus, do you kiss your mother before you go to bed?" (*P* 14). Whether Stephen answers yes or no, Wells mocks him and the others laugh. His guilt makes him unable to lie or pretend to the male myth of independence: "Stephen blushed under their eyes. . ." Earlier "pull out his eyes" signified emasculation, and at football Stephen feared "flashing eyes" while his own were weak. Throughout the novel both male and female eyes tend to have phallic value, as Wasson observes ("Sight"): they are generally either aggressive and piercing or defeated and downcast. The emotional weight given the kissing of mom suggests it stands for more. Reminded of his guilt, Stephen feels "hot and confused" and perceptually impotent ". . . he did not dare to raise his eyes. . ."

He now punishes himself by going over the square ditch incident in detail, then turns again from unpleasant thoughts to meditate—and cogitate—on motherkiss: "Was it right. . .? What did that mean, to kiss?. . . His mother put her lips on his cheek; her lips were soft and they wetted his cheek; and they made a tiny little noise: kiss. Why did people do that with their two faces?" (*P* 15). Stephen shows a striking distance from physical reality by not knowing what a kiss is for—an alienation from his body caused by guilt. The mysteries behind the many unanswered questions in the novel are usually sexual, though the sex involved is not usually as apparent as here.

When the combination of longing for mother and the male threat it evokes appears next, the hearth-womb is preceded by a half-door as vagina: ". . .he had seen a woman standing at the halfdoor of a cottage with a child in her arms, as the cars had come past . . .It would be lovely to sleep. . .in that cottage before the fire. . .in the warm dark, breathing the smell of the peasants. . .But, O, the road there between the trees was dark! You would be lost. . .It made him afraid. . ." (*P* 18). As with the square ditch, the threat here is more than organ loss; it is reduction to nonentity.

The first fifteen pages of *Portrait* show Stephen morbidly preoccupied with a mental complex in which two opposing forces generate each other: desire for mother and fear of a male threat of castration or destruction, a threat it makes sense to link to father. This basic pattern of *Portrait* varies the usual oedipal configuration of desires to love mom and kill dad by transforming the aggressive side into an attitude of anxiety and passivity. There are two related explanations for this variation, both partly valid. First, that an earlier wish to attack the old man has been transformed by guilt into fear of him; second, that a suppressed homosexual attraction to father has been disguised by guilty censorship as a masochistic tendency to be subject to male threats.

The first is simpler. One sign of Stephen's submerged patricidal wish is his preoccupation with the ghostly marshal supposed to haunt the castle in which his school is housed. He has a vision of a figure in "the white cloak of a marshal" with "his hand pressed to his side" who looks "out of strange eyes at the old servants": "They looked at him and saw their master's face and cloak and knew that he had received his death-wound. But only the dark was where they looked" (*P* 19). Joyce had actually heard of such an apparition (*JJ* 29), but the length and intensity of Stephen's meditation on it suggests it answers his mind. He fears the image, yet is fascinated by it. The marshal's rank and appearance as master to servants indicate a father figure. Stephen's dread is deep, for this vision of wounded mature masculine authority absorbs him primarily through his desire to kill or disarm his father. If Stephen's daydreams of mother showed one aspect of the Oedipus complex, this passage shows the other, patricidal aspect.

Both aspects appear in Stephen's dream of going home for the holidays. Most of the dream consists of railroad travel, for which I have indicated possible sexual association. The object of the train trip is the climax of the dream: "Welcome home, Stephen! Noises of welcome. His mother kissed him. Was that right? His father was a marshal now: higher than a magistrate. Welcome home, Stephen!" (*P* 20). The kiss of arrival is accompanied by guilt: "Was that right?" Stephen seems to confer an honor on his father, but the dream uses this appearance to conceal its latent content. The ghostly vision just before the dream firmly associated a marshal in Stephen's mind with injury and death. By making father a marshal, Stephen kills him, confirming the paternal reference in the earlier vision. Sprinchorn ("Achilles") recognizes this dream as patricidal. The end of the dream indicates both the wish to make love to mother and the wish to kill father.

Fenichel says childhood anxiety about death may be caused by either fear of punishment for death wishes against others or fear of one's own sexual excitement, orgasm being associated with death as it was for the Elizabethans (*Theory*, p. 209). The depth of Stephen's anxiety is indicated by his reaction to the illness building in him as he dreams. This illness may be psychologically induced by guilt, for Stephen feels its cause is emotional, not physical: "But he was not sick there. He thought that he was sick in his heart if you could be sick in that place" (*P* 13). His uneasiness stirs at the school bath: "As he passed the door he remembered with a vague fear the warm turfcoloured bogwater, the warm moist air, the noise of plunges. . ." (*P* 22). This recurring image, like the square ditch, represents a threat of sinking into negation and shows fear of female genitals. Bath and ditch may also associate with male threats as places where young men are seen naked. (Stephen is disturbed by bathers in Chapter IV.)

Committed to the infirmary, Stephen longs for home and writes an imaginary letter addressed only to mother: "Please come and take me home" (*P* 23). Yearning for mom aggravates his guilt and anxiety: ". . . he might die before his mother came." His death will be a revenge on a father figure: "Wells would be there, but no fellow would look at him. . . And Wells would be sorry then for what he had done." He imagines himself buried: "*Ding-dong*! *The castle bell*! / *Farewell, my mother*!" The grave, an extension of square ditch and bath, is the ultimate fantasy punishment of Stephen's guilt. But there is also attraction in his attitude toward death: it is "beautiful and sad" (*P* 24). The grave satisfies desire for the womb as well as guilt, and emasculation would free him from the burden of manhood.

Stephen enjoys the infirmary because it isolates him from the threat of other boys: "It would be nice getting better slowly. You could get a book then. There was a book in the library about Holland. There were lovely foreign names in it and pictures of strangelooking cities and ships. It made you feel so happy" (*P* 26). He already craves escape through literature, and another device protects and insulates him from his own emotions by displacing them onto words: "He wanted to cry quietly but not for himself: for the words, so beautiful and sad, like music. The bell!. . . Farewell!" (*P* 24). Words serve as pretext for exercising feelings whose origins cannot be admitted to consciousness, and the translation of feeling into word is basic to religion. In the infirmary Stephen dreams of a ship bearing Parnell, another image of a dead father. Patricide is in back of his mind as he meditates on his own death. But the altered version of the oedipal complex in which the idea of killing father is transformed into fear of being injured by him is more common in Stephen's experience.

The explanation of Stephen's apprehensiveness as a reaction to father hatred is incomplete because it does not show why all boys who want to kill their fathers—all who have them—are not as apprehensive as he. We must consider Stephen's homosexual side. Freud found that all infants start with ambivalent attitudes toward both parents. Thus, for a boy, in addition to normal love for mother and desire to be rid of father, a secondary or reverse oedipal complex combines love for father with desire to be rid of mother and take her place. Ordinarily, the secondary complex weakens early and is subordinate from infancy. In cases where hetero-sexual development is obstructed, however, the secondary complex may revive (*The Ego and the Id*, *SE* XIX, pp. 33–34).

At Clongowes, of course, Stephen lives in a homosexual (all male) community because his society feels it best for young men to avoid sin. Joyce saw this as a device the authorities used to weaken manhood, to prevent sensitive people from making trouble by enthralling them to shame. Later Stephen is sent to college even though his family is im-poverished. He is, as Joyce was, a favored eldest son, and his relation to his father is close until he rebels. *Portrait* usually presents Simon Dedalus in an affectionate, nostalgic light, though Stephen is exposed to an isolated spot of paternal bile and emasculation when Simon calls him a "lazy bitch" (*P* 175). This suggests a vicious side of Simon that is censored out of *Portrait*, but reflected in Stephen's anxiety with males and a mys-terious, recurring inability to feel the affection he should feel for his father. Eventually, Stephen declares father and son to be inevitable enemies (*U* 207–208).

The first three stories of *Dubliners*, which Joyce called "stories of my childhood" (*Letters, II,* p. 111), may portray the artist as orphan, for the boy in these resembles Joyce, but lives with an uncle. In the part of *Stephen Hero* Joyce allowed to survive, Simon is alcoholic and abusive, though he does not pick on his favorite son (*SH* 109–111). This is close to Stanislaus' 1903 description of "Pappie" as a "domineering. . .quarrelsome . . .abusive. . .lying. . .besotted. . .spiteful. . .drunkard. . .bully," though generous when (rarely) sober.[11] "Counterparts" heavily emphasizes the fatherly option of taking out your failure on the kids. The clearest criti-cism of Simon in *Portrait* is that he is sentimental, "a praiser of his own past" (*P* 241) who projects false heartiness to cover defeat. As senti-mentalist or as bully, and he seems both, Simon is fundamentally weak, and his weakness is crucial to the problem of Stephen's manhood. I will get to the scene that establishes his weakness, the Christmas dinner, after a few theoretical considerations.

Much light may be cast on the developments of both Stephen and Joyce by careful use of an old diagnosis. Since 1917, when H. G. Wells spoke of a "cloacal obsession" in *Portrait* (*JJ* 427) and 1919, when Ezra Pound saw "obsession" in the "Sirens" of *Ulysses* (*Letters, I,* 126), scores of critics, perhaps hundreds, have found this quality in Joyce's writing. The first doctor to call Joyce "obsessive" in print was Dr. Joseph Collins in a friendly review of *Ulysses* in the *New York Times Book Review* of May 28, 1922.[12] Phillip Herring, in his edition of the notesheets for *Ulysses*, remarks his impression that Joyce's accumulative writing method "resulted from an almost psychotic compulsion" (*N* 1). He exaggerates:

Joyce's compulsion, which allowed him family, friends and success, seems well within the bounds of neurosis, unlike some of the severe cases Freud treated, such as the "Wolf Man" and the "Rat Man." A better analogy Joyce had access to is da Vinci: Freud did call Leonardo compulsive, though his analysis of compulsion was sketchy in this case. Even the severe cases include touches that suggest Joyce. The "Rat Man," for example, feared being punished for losing his glasses, dreaded rats, sought uncertainty and acted on omens.[13]

Fenichel says obsessives are obsessed with ideas, while compulsives are compelled to action (*Theory*, pp. 268-269); but the two afflictions resemble each other and the terms are often used interchangeably, as they will be here. Compulsion neurosis tends to occur in people of higher than average intelligence and to appear during latency. The obsessive's anxiety over genital desires causes him to regress to characteristics of the anal stage of development (around ages two to four).[14] Such regression is enforced by the superego, an internalized parental voice, usually father's, that dictates what is forbidden. In obsession, however, interdicted desires are not repressed: in fact, compulsives tend to dwell on sex. This explains why Joyce and Stephen are so well aware of their conflicts. Instead of repression, the obsessive uses defense mechanisms that deny the desires without quite wiping them out of consciousness. Three of the main defenses of obsession are reaction formation, isolation and undoing (*SE* XX, pp. 113ff.; *Theory*, pp. 286-290). Undoing will appear later.

Reaction formation generally denies bad wishes by being very good. A son, for example, who hates his father may react by showing excessive concern for him. In isolation, mental configurations which spur anxiety are broken down into components and the connections between these blocked out to alleviate threat. The most important type is isolation of affect, which separates ideas from the emotions attached to them. Once this analysis is performed, the emotion may be felt in isolation from its source, as when Stephen almost cries over the word *farewell*. The source of the emotion may then be regarded intellectually without feeling, as when Stephen coldly theorizes about parenthood and love.

I have shown that when Stephen thinks with longing of his mother, he feels dread. As a result he comes to associate mother with danger and retreats from her to father. The Christmas dinner shows this situation: in it mother, greatly desired earlier, is anesthetized or entirely isolated from emotion, while Simon is a positive, lovable figure with whom Stephen associates, probably through reaction formation. The center of the Christmas scene is a conflict between Dante Riordan, a supporter of the Church, and John Casey, a Parnellite. But just as Simon Dedalus aligns with Casey, there is reason to believe the pious May Dedalus sympathizes with Dante.

A tie between the two women is first suggested when tension develops over the Church's attack on Parnell. Simon, in his false heartiness, tries to sustain good cheer by serving: "He heaped up the food on Stephen's plate and served uncle Charles and Mr Casey. . . Mrs Dedalus was eating little and Dante sat with her hands on her lap" (*P* 32). Mother couples with Dante again when Simon makes anticlerical remarks: "—Really, Simon, said Mrs Dedalus, you should not speak that way before Stephen. It's not right. / —O, he'll remember all this when he grows up, said Dante hotly. . ." (*P* 33). When Dante gets excited, mother speaks to her "in a low voice," but Dante says loudly, "I will not say nothing. I will defend my church. . ." (*P* 34). She tries to quiet Dante, but May does not seem to disagree with her, and when Dante gets up to leave, she follows her to the door. Despite her neutrality, Mrs. Dedalus is grouped with Dante, and Stephen later resents his mother's devotion to the Church. Fundamental to the pairing of the women is the segregation of the sexes in Victorian society. It must have seemed this segregation could never be eliminated, for men and women had very different values, and women were more pious. Thus, the Christmas episode may be seen as a conflict between races, with Simon, Casey and Parnell on one side and Dante, the old woman of Arklow who insulted Parnell (*P* 36), and May Dedalus on the other.

The scene begins with the men vaunting their masculinity through revolutionary and anticlerical connections. The height of this male assertion is the story Casey tells of spitting on the old woman of Arklow, who shouts, "I'm blinded!" (*P* 37). The castration image of page two here describes male victory in the struggle of sexes, but it is Dante who, using the Church as weapon, finally emasculates the men. The last spit mentioned is hers:

—Blasphemer! Devil! screamed Dante, starting to her feet and almost spitting in his face.

. . . .

—Devil out of hell! We won! We crushed him to death! Fiend!
The door slammed behind her.
Mr Casey, freeing his arms from his holders, suddenly bowed his head on his hands with a sob of pain.
—Poor Parnell! he cried loudly. My dead king!
He sobbed loudly and bitterly.
Stephen, raising his terrorstricken face, saw that his father's eyes were full of tears. (*P* 39)

The scene ends with defeated men. Casey, who has already cramped three fingers "making a birthday present for Queen Victoria" (*P* 28) is collapsed; Parnell is dead, an image of crushed manhood to haunt every Irishman; and Simon weeps in anguish at having his Parnell cut off.

Norman Holland says the image of watching a play often stands for the primal scene.[15] The dinner—a vivid drama Stephen observes building to a traumatic climax—suits this prescription; and its content—a battle of sexes involving parents—also suggests primacy. Of course, mom is isolated, but then so is dad. Simon tries to moderate the fierce Casey and to avoid denouncing the Church: "Nobody is saying a word against them. . .so long as they don't meddle in politics" (*P* 32). The psychologic of remembering a scene with parents distanced from the center of the conflict should be clear. Stephen's genital feelings toward parents are insupportable on this visit, so he is compulsively reverting to seeing them in the anal mode. The violence and atmosphere of powerlessness in the scene suggest this; for aggression develops in the anal (or anal-sadistic) stage before genital distinctions are clear, so anality tends to associate sex with violence and to be bisexual ("The Disposition to Obsessional Neurosis," *SE* XII, pp. 321 ff.). The masochism and homosexuality noticed earlier in Stephen's experience are about to grow more intense.

Father's neutrality, his ladling of gravy on the family rift, may be a muffled indication of a serious fault. His simony consists of selling his own grace for the material comforts of the establishment so that he is not much better than Simon Moonan, "the prefect's suck." Joyce called his father "an Irish suicide" in his Trieste notebook (*Viking Critical Edition*, p. 297). I think he saw the essence of this suicide not in drink or irresponsibility, but in the denial of spirit or manhood which caused them. The defeat of father by matriarchy at the dinner is crucial, and Stephen's recognition of his father's weakness will grow as Simon declines in the world. The scene is traumatic because "terrorstricken" Stephen associates with his father as victim. A boy must follow a strong father to master manhood, and Stephen's image of his father has been broken. But even while this unmanned father is present, another threatening father lurks in Stephen's mind: the godlike father of infancy who is internalized as superego. And every injury to the actual father makes Stephen guilty because he unconsciously wishes it, causing the separate, menacing father to loom more terrifyingly within. Some of the poignancy, the stabbing, that every son feels when he sees his father's weakness derives from the son's secret wish.

This paternal breakage leaves Stephen acutely anxious for the rest of the chapter about being beaten by one of the school's Fathers. On returning to school he is symbolically emasculated almost as a matter of course: ". . .a sprinter had knocked him down. . .He had been thrown by the fellow's machine lightly on the cinderpath and his spectacles had been broken in three pieces and some of the grit. . .had gone into his mouth" (*P* 41). In this state he is confronted by the mystery of a terrible crime committed by some boys. Among conjectures as to the nature of the crime, Stephen is puzzled most by the suggestion of a boy named Athy that it was "smugging" (P 41). Athy was linked to homosexuality when Stephen met him in the infirmary: "You have a queer name, Dedalus, and I have a queer name too, Athy." He then asked a curious riddle about his name, "a thigh," and left Stephen wondering what the other way to ask the riddle was (P 25-26). Neither the alternative thigh riddle nor "smugging" is explained, but both mysteries imply "love that dare not speak its name." Joyce favored this phrase of Wilde's because it suggests not only inversion, but the suppression of sex in general, which Joyce felt to contribute to inversion. Such unanswered questions demonstrate how unhealthy attitudes are promoted by what Blake called making love a mystery. Athy turns the subject with relish from smugging to flogging, and Stephen reacts with intense excitement to cold male aggression:

> It made him shivery: but that was because you always felt like a shiver when you let down your trousers. . .He wondered who had to let them down, the master or the boy himself. O how could they laugh about it that way?
> . . .[Mr. Gleeson's] were terribly long and pointed nails. So long and cruel they were though the white fattish hands were not cruel but gentle. And though he trembled with cold and fright to think of the cruel long nails and of the high whistling sound of the cane and of the chill you felt at the end of your shirt when you undressed yourself yet he felt a feeling of queer quiet pleasure inside him to think of the white fattish hands, clean and strong and gentle. . .Mr Gleeson would not flog Corrigan hard. And Fleming had said. . .it was best of his play not to. But that was not why. (P 45)

The reason Gleeson will not flog hard, another mystery, is also the reason his hands are gentle and Stephen feels "queer quiet pleasure." Gleeson's beating provides within the framework of authority a mode of sexual relation to the father for Stephen. Freud, in "A Child Is Being Beaten," says that masochistic people are deeply impressed by beatings they witness or sustain in youth and later hold these experiences responsible for their affliction. Joyce frequently attacked corporal punishment, and his main intent here is to show how the system breaks people. But Freud says masochism originates earlier as an infantile conception of sexual relation to father. The idea of genital sex with father is blocked by a strong taboo, as Stephen later says (U 207), so the child regresses to the earlier anal-sadistic conception of being beaten, which is also motivated by understandable guilt.[16]

Masochism usually defends against castration, being adopted as a way of enduring pain in order to propitiate paternal power and ward off more serious phallic injury as punishment for sexual excitement. Male masochists construct fantasies or arrange situations of being beaten by women to avoid the idea of homosexually succumbing to father at the root of their perversion. Joyce sees through this in the "Circe" espisode of *Ulysses* when he transforms Bella to Bello. Because the basic premise of masochism is the unrealistic derivation of pleasure from pain, masochists often gratify themselves through fantasy rather than action.[17] A masochist who is highly excited by the idea of beating may only be annoyed by actual blows.[18]

Stephen's actual beating has the effect of turning him away from passivity and spurring his manhood. He experiences it as a terrifyingly direct castration: "A hot. . .tingling blow like the loud crack of a broken stick made his trembling hand crumple together like a leaf in a fire" (p. 50). Actual pain and loss negate pleasurable fantasies and aggravate anxiety rather than placating it. The anticipation of erotic pleasure from Gleeson's white hand is disappointed by the reality of Father Dolan, who offers no erotic possibilities because, like the pervert in "An Encounter," he is frozen into a blind, mechanical sadism. A major cause of Stephen's indignation at his punishment is the fact that the sensuality of the beating is nipped in the bud:

> . . .at first he had thought he was going to shake hands with him be-
> cause the fingers were soft and firm: but then in an instant he had heard
> the swish of the soutane sleeve and the crash. It was cruel and unfair. . .
> because he had steadied the hand first with his firm soft fingers and that
> was to hit it better and louder. (*P* 52)

Stephen's notion that Dolan is going to shake hands is hardly en-
couraged by any show of affability on Dolan's part. It is an erotic,
probably masturbatory, fantasy from Stephen's unconscious. The pandy-
ing resembles the scene in "Circe" where Bloom's masochistic fantasies
are carried to their extreme and then cut short by physical reality so that
he reasserts himself; though Bloom is not actually beaten. Stephen's mind
is not so laden with guilt that he can accept Dolan's perverse world.
Wondering whether he looks like a schemer, he decides "it could not be"
(*P* 53). He is able to derive strength from identification with a father,
though characteristically he can do so only in an indirect way, by identify-
ing with literary fathers, the "great men" of antiquity who protested
injustice in his reading (*P* 53).

Stephen thinks with disgust of Corrigan, who has chosen flogging over
expulsion: ". . .he remembered how big Corrigan looked in the bath.
He had skin the same colour as the turfcoloured bog-water. . .and when
he walked along the side his feet slapped loudly on the wet tiles and at

every step his thighs shook a little because he was fat" (*P* 54). Corrigan is associated with the bath that represents reduction to femininity, and his shaking thighs make him seem female. He represents the repulsive fate Stephen would meet if he submitted. But Stephen is able to assert his identity and masculinity in his mind so far as to reduce Dolan to womanhood: "The great men in history had names like that [Dedalus] and nobody made fun of them. It was his own name he should have made fun of. . . Dolan: it was like the name of a woman that washed clothes" (*P* 55). Stephen's assumption of manhood is accompanied by images of his entering a female: ". . .he would be in the low dark narrow corridor. . .entered . the low dark narrow corridor. . .passed along the narrow dark corridor. . ." (*P* 54-55). After the triple emphasis indicates the special significance of the hall, Stephen passes through a pair of doors to be hailed by the rector as "my little man" (*P* 56).

The first chapter ends on this note of victory—a victory soon to be dissipated when Stephen comes to feel, early in the second chapter, that his Jesuit masters and his father were merely amused by his heroism (*P* 72). Although he has temporarily affirmed his masculinity, his psychological problems are far from solved. The same factor that makes him uniquely able to turn aside from the other boys and protest, his anal tendency to see all relationships as extremes of domination and subordination, also makes him uniquely susceptible to threats. The compulsive seesaw between submission and assertion in his mind will lead him to ever greater temptation, humiliation and pride.

The first chapter establishes a fundamental model for all of *Portrait* and, with modification, for *Ulysses*. The desire for mother is quite clear here and the paternal threat appears in physical action. In later chapters these elements grow more and more sublimated and disguised as the original sources of Stephen's attitudes are denied and isolated from feeling, so that by the end of the book the issues become intellectual, the desires, esthetic, the threat, a principle. And yet a longing for a distant mother and a causally related fear of a threatening father remain as ground plan for all of Stephen's experience.

II

CORK

The assumption of masculinity that ends Chapter I may point to the end of latency and beginning of puberty. Now Stephen grows aware of desire of the body, but he sees flesh only through its opposition to spirit. As his vague brooding focuses on girls, he sees them only in forms shaped by images of his mother. He approaches them first through the distance and protection of words and perceives them as centers of conflict.

The long description of Stephen's absorption in *The Count of Monte Cristo* early in Chapter II is representative of his use of literature, which is intimate, exercising his deepest feelings: ". . .that dark avenger stood forth in his mind for whatever he had heard or divined in childhood of the strange and terrible" (*P* 62). Of course, books serve for escape and defense, and Monte Cristo's cave appeals to Stephen's need for a womb of shelter: "At night he built. . .an image of the wonderful island cave out of transfers and paper flowers and coloured tissue paper and strips of the gold and silver paper in which chocolate is wrapped." This obsessive ritual of accumulation prefigures aspects of the artist. But the most important element in the novel for Stephen is the relation of Monte Cristo to Mercedes. It gives him a chance to examine and solve his most sensitive problem vicariously:

> . . .in his imagination. . .appeared an image of himself, grown older and sadder, standing in a moonlit garden with Mercedes, who had so many years before slighted his love, and with a sadly proud gesture of refusal, saying:
> —Madam, I never eat muscatel grapes. (*P* 63)

Stephen's fantasies are enacted by Monte Cristo, who destroys the usurpers of his rights, including Mercedes' older husband, and gains the power to take her back, but refuses her and turns to another. Romances present deep desires intensely. Monte Cristo's unjust suffering corresponds to childhood restraints; husband and usurpers, to father and authority figures. The obsessed Count's loss of Mercedes appeals to Stephen because it pays tribute to the incest taboo, yet seems voluntary. Freud says the "Rat Man" had fantasies "in which he did the lady some great service without her knowing . . . . his magnanimity . . . was designed to repress his thirst for revenge, after the manner of Dumas's Count of Monte Cristo" (*SE* X, p. 195). Stephen's other heroes, Byron and Parnell, also fit the oedipal pattern of adultery and incest,[1] of taking the forbidden woman from her prior possessor, which has prevailed in European romance since Lancelot and Tristan. Even Satan, whom Stephen later imitates, is described at the retreat as the seducer of our primal mother.

Thoughts of Mercedes generate in Stephen longings which seem preformed without being understood, as if they were forgotten:

. . .as he brooded upon her image, a strange unrest crept into his blood. . .a fever. . . .he was different from others. He did not want to play. He wanted to meet in the real world the unsubstantial image which his soul so constantly beheld. He did not know where to seek it or how; but a *premonition* which led him on told him that this image would, without any overt act of his, encounter him. They would meet quietly *as if they had known each other* and had made their tryst, perhaps at one of the gates or in some more secret place. . .surrounded by darkness and silence: and in that moment of supreme tenderness he would be transfigured. He would fade into something impalpable. . .Weakness and timidity and inexperience would fall from him in that magic moment. (*P* 64–65, my italics)

This passage is reminiscent of "Alastor" by Shelley, a favorite poet of Stephen's. In this early work a young poet dreams in a lonely dell of a veiled maid who enfolds him in her arms. He wakes from rapture to pursue this vision far and wide, but never attains her. The invocation of "Alastor" to "our great Mother" probably refers to Mother Nature, but maternal fixation is easily seen in the poem.

One remarkable thing about Stephen's "strange unrest" is the vagueness of the "unsubstantial image" he seeks without knowing "where to seek it or how." On the next page, after he has moved to Dublin, "a vague dissatisfaction grew up within him. . .he continued to wander up and down day after day as if he really sought something that eluded him." This does not strike us as odd because all adolescents are subject to vague longings and most desires have unknown sources; but it is logically absurd to yearn without knowing what one yearns for. Freud explains such cases by saying that the object of desire has been repressed or concealed. And Stephen provides details that define the unknown he longs for. He associates it with tenderness and security and seeks it in a womblike setting, "one of the gates or in some more secret place" surrounded by oblivion. It seems "as if they had known each other," and later, hearing what Emma's aggressive eyes have to say, he knows "that in some dim past, whether in life or revery, he had heard their tale before" (P 69). Both in his unspecified desire and in his later focus on E. C., he senses familiarity with the object of his emotion from a "dim past." The only possible concrete source for his preformed feelings is mother. But the emotion isolated from her has been transformed to a spiritual ideal associated with transfiguration, misted over by repression, kept at a distance by guilt.

This maternal ideal Stephen pursues in ever-widening circles through the rest of *Portrait*—as whore, queen of heaven and muse. For Jung, the attraction of the *anima* or female spirit is strengthened by a sense of *déjà vu* or correspondence between her and the unconscious. Joyce probably intended this, though he may not yet have made the supernatural assumption which links the "dim past" to mythology. Jung extended Freud's idea of projection by saying that archetypal images make up most of what we perceive in the world,[2] and this is true of Stephen's projection of parental images.

The second chapter continues to present a world constructed on the principles of Stephen's needs. Two themes alternate through the first ten pages of this chapter: the father figure in decline and the quest for the mother ideal. The chapter opens with memories of the aging uncle Charles, who becomes senile (P 60, 66). Then the old trainer Mike Flynn appears and fades after his vague gaze causes Stephen to feel "mistrust" (P 61). From memories of these old men and Simon, the text moves to reveries over Mercedes and wanderings, dwelling on maternally oriented daydreams. Then foreboding returns as "the same foreknowledge which had sickened his heart" as he ran, "the same intuition" of "mistrust at his trainer's flabby stubblecovered face" now "dissipated any vision of the future. In a vague way he understood that his father was in trouble. . ." (P 64). He turns once more to the dreams of an "unsubstantial image" cited; but then reality intrudes again as father is forced by setbacks to move from Blackrock to poorer quarters in Dublin. Mr. Dedalus is now impelled to assert that he has not been unmanned: "There's a crack of the whip left in me yet, Stephen old chap, said Mr Dedalus, poking at the dull fire with fierce energy. We're not dead yet, sonny" (P 66). Following this observation of father's wound, Stephen resumes his wandering after the unknown spiritual female (P 66).

The structural principle of this part of *Portrait* revises the first chapter's alternation of fear of men with matricentric reveries to interweave the decline of father and family with the growth of Stephen's vague presexual longings. As the chapter proceeds, these longings grow increasingly lurid and disturbing. A new duality appears, combining an unclean outside world with an unclean one within:

A dusk like that of the outer world obscured his mind. . .(*P* 64)
. . .angry with himself for being young and the prey of restless foolish impulses, angry also with the change. . .reshaping the world about him into. . .squalor and insincerity. (*P* 67)
It shocked him to find in the outer world a trace of what he had deemed till then a brutish and individual malady of his own mind. (*P* 90)
. . .battling against the squalor of his life and against the riot of his mind. (*P* 91)

Stephen broods on this bond between internal and external disorder and sees it everywhere because he unconsciously blames the fall of the paternal order on his own evil wishes. This line of thought is reinforced by the Church doctrine of Chapter III that the seduction by a patricidally proud son of the female of "our first parents" (*P* 117) brought hardship into the world. Guilt makes him experience poverty as torture, "his sensitive nature . . . smarting under the lashes of", a "squalid way of life" (*P* 78). He isolates himself from experience to contain it and limit its pain by treating as esthetic object what he perceives: "He chronicled with patience what he saw, detaching himself from it and testing its mortifying flavour in secret" (*P* 67). Several epiphanies follow as examples of this detached chronicle. In one of them Stephen's fear of being reduced to female is evoked when he is mistaken for "Josephine" (*P* 68). This mistake may prod Stephen to assert his masculinity, for his interest in Emma first appears immediately afterward.

The scene on the tram emphasizes Stephen's sense of having known Emma before in a "dim past": seeing her temptations, he "knew that he had yielded to them a thousand times" (*P* 69). He wants to "catch hold" of her and believes she wants him to, yet he stands "listlessly in his place, seemingly a tranquil watcher of the scene before him" (*P* 69). His unexplained passivity suggests not only the artist's stance, but the relation of son to mother, and his inhibition probably springs from anxieties about mom; but his attitude toward women is now increasing in complexity. The Christmas dinner presented two views of women: the emasculating virago Dante and an ideal, spiritualized image associated with the lines "Tower of Ivory. . .House of Gold" (*P* 35). This dichotomy of threat and ideal is altered and more pronounced in Stephen's attitude toward Emma.

He thinks she has accompanied him to tempt him (*P* 70) and comes up to his step, lingering in close proximity to provoke him: "He saw her urge her vanities, her fine dress and sash and long black stockings. . ." (*P* 69). Emma's fetishes remind him of Eileen putting her hand in his pocket (*P* 43, 69). Nothing of E. C. is described except her clothing and eyes, the only details Stephen later recalls (*P* 82). Not only do these evoke fetishistic aggressiveness, but by reducing Emma to eyes and apparel, even reducing her name to a shell, Stephen eliminates her body and so spiritualizes her. If he sees her as calculating temptress, his actions show he also sees her as sacrosanct: he cannot touch her and writes a poem to her set between Jesuit mottoes and colored by "the maiden lustre of the moon" (*P* 70). The poem concludes with a kiss, an image associated with mother, and after writing it he gazes at his face in the mirror of his mother's dressing table.

The two aspects of woman as temptress and virgin—a commonplace of Joyce criticism—are presented here. Freud's essay "On the Universal Tendency to Debasement in the Sphere of Love" tells how children cultivate ideal, desexualized visions of their mothers and are unable to connect with these visions the idea of sex, which they come to think of by adolescence as a nasty activity. As men, they separate women into two aspects: one is idealized and loved, but cannot be defiled by sex, while the other is physically approachable, but can never be respected. In such men sex and love are separated and tend to be linked to different partners.[3] Stephen sees both sides in Emma, but the idealizing tendency is clearly dominant, for it dictates action, while the temptress side is expressed only in fantasy.

The poem to Emma links Stephen's interest in art to his erotic life. As Kenner has suggested, the connection between love and art underlies a narrative sequence set on the evening of the school play (*Dublin's Joyce*, p. 124). As Stephen is being threatened for his interest in Emma, his mind flashes to an earlier scene in which he was beaten for his allegiance to Byron. Heron, who strikes Stephen and order him to "admit" in both scenes, carries on the threat of Wells, and the blatant phallic imagery which describes him prefigures the menacing three soldiers of the *Wake* (for example, *FW* 58.25): ". . . a thin hooked nose stood out between closeset prominent eyes. . ." (*P* 76); ". . .as he marched forward between his two attendants, he cleft the air before him with a thin cane. . ." (*P* 79-80).

The narrative equates art with Emma as object of physical anxiety because Stephen's original feeling toward his mother and its companion guilt are now sublimated to a wider area. As I suggested in discussing

Stephen's heroes, not only love, but thought and art are now influenced by oedipal conflicts. The influence of Stephen's complex on his intellectual life is also reflected when he is rebuked for a heresy in his weekly essay. The offending point, that the soul can never approach nearer to God, resembles Stephen's later assertion that fathers are hopelessly sundered from sons (*U* 207). The thought is based on a sense of competition with father and dread of giving in to him. This oedipal theology calls forth a male threat:

> Mr Tate, the English master, pointed his finger at him and said bluntly:
> —This fellow has heresy in his essay.
> . . .Stephen did not look up. . .his eyes were still smarting and weak. He was conscious of failure and of detection, of the squalor of his own mind and home, and felt against his neck the raw edge of his turned and jagged collar. (*P* 79)

The finger and eye images and the pairing of internal and external squalor are typical, while beheading is a common image of castration: later Stephen anxiously sees "headless" coats (*P* 124).

Mother fixation has now consolidated into cultural opposition to the norms of society and the expectations of boy and son. That the artist as young man feels trapped in a false role on a social scrimmage field is not new. What is new is the sense of mental vision that will lead to the artist. Stephen gains power from his opposition to project his conflicts long distances into the outside and inside worlds of society and imagination, but the conflicts retain their parental images:

> While his mind had been pursuing its intangible phantoms. . .he had heard about him. . .his father and . . . masters urging him to be a gentleman. . .a good catholic. . .These voices had now come to be hollowsounding. . .another voice urging him to be strong and manly. . .be true to his country. . .raise up his father's fallen state by his labours. . .all these hollowsounding voices. . .made him halt irresolutely in the pursuit of phantoms. . .but he was happy only. . .beyond their call, alone or in the company of phantasmal comrades. (*P* 83–84)

Defying paternal authority, pursuing his phantoms, Stephen resembles the poet of "Alastor," who "eagerly pursues" a "fleeting shade." Freud said phantoms in dream tended to symbolize mother through their resemblance to women in nightgowns (*SE* V, pp. 403–404). At any rate, the only phantasmal comrade of Stephen's to be identified is May Dedalus, who follows him through *Ulysses*. Long separated from mom, Stephen has separated his image of her from herself and projected it as a distant ideal, while superimposing father on the world that separates them. If the strength of his introjected parent images comes from attachments to mom and dad, his ability to project them depends on separation. Winnicott says that babies use separation from parents to develop a sense of self able to use outside objects.[4] And Stephen uses the outside world as a screen, seeing those parts lit up which fit into parental images.

Stephen has also established within himself the other sides of the images of female ideal and male danger—images of mother as aggressive temptress and father as lover. He strives in vain to escape these disturbing aspects and their ineluctable attraction. The obverse pair often merge as Stephen satisfies desire for a masculine element by making women aggressive. Emma and every other woman to whom Stephen is attracted in *Portrait* always have the upper hand, leaving Stephen no way to assert himself except the sadly proud gesture of refusal.

The masculine role the hollow voices call for is embodied ironically in the school play, where Stephen takes the role of a grown but fatuous man, the "farcical pedagogue" (*P* 73). Emma, whom he has brooded on all day, is the heart of his audience. She comes with Simon (*P* 77) in place of the absent mother; looking into her eyes, Stephen feels capable of maleness: "For one rare moment he seemed to be clothed in the real apparel of boyhood" (*P* 85). But the public role is a ridiculous delusion, and after the play he finds the object of his endeavors gone. So he runs off, "anguished" and maddened with desire, but his superego stops him: "A power, akin to that which had often made anger or resentment fall from him, brought his steps to rest." He has brought himself to a scene of ugly decay: "—That is horse piss and rotted straw, he thought. It is a good odour to breathe. It will calm my heart" (*P* 86). Later, as an ascetic, Stephen will punish himself with the only smell he hates, that of "long-standing urine" (*P* 151); and this, too, is a mortification of flesh. It is clear before he sins or repents that he will tend to punish himself for his desires.

What Stephen finds after the play is mutability, and his division between masculine duty and feminine phantoms of personal desire is also a division between the material, which is mutable, and the spiritual, which is transcendent. Mutability and death are bound up for him with castration. His earliest image of mutability is the decline of his father's fortunes, which is linked in his mind to the growth of his own erotic desires: "For some time he had felt the slight changes in his house; and these changes in what he had deemed unchangeable were so many slight shocks to his boyish conception of the world" (*P* 64). Mutability is the failure of father caused by his desires, a punishment for sexual crime. Preoccupation with control of time is a prime feature of compulsives because control of time is first acquired during toilet training. Excretion is the earliest graphic experience of mutability, for the infant sees his body give off waste and corruption. And concern with defecation, while tied to time, is also tied to castration because anal erotism abdicates genital erotism. The equation mutability-excretion-castration is prominent in the artist's mind.

The second chapter centers on the exposure of Stephen to mutability. Here he finds his mind subject to chaotic "tides within" and "without" (P 98) that sweep toward destruction. His expanding vision anxiously sees decay everywhere: ". . .the filthy cowyard at Stradbrook with its foul green puddles and clots of liquid dung. . .sickened Stephen's heart" (P 63). The main symbol of Stephen's position in life here is cork. Searching for his ideal on the Dublin quays, Stephen finds a "multitude of corks. . . .bobbing on the surface of the water. . ." (P 66). Soon these corks represent Stephen in his subjection to the tides of emotion: "His heart danced upon her movements like a cork upon the tide" (P 69). Cork symbolizes not only the heart subject to passion, but life subject to decay. The trip Stephen and his father make to Cork is primarily an exploration of mutability. This chapter uses soft, cellular cork to present a vision of flesh ridden by lust and mutability.

The male, material, mutable world of Cork is opposed to Stephen's phantoms of desire. On the train there he thinks of the selling of his father's property "and in the manner of his own dispossession he felt the world give the lie rudely to his phantasy" (P 87). As Epstein observes (Ordeal, p. 68), the Latin tag quoted during the visit to Cork might serve as motto for this section: "Tempora mutantur et nos mutamur in illis" (Times change and we change in them; P 94). Most of Simon's Cork friends are gone, and those who remain are old. Here Stephen grows poignantly aware of his position: ". . .a leader afraid of his own authority. . .battling against the squalor of his life and against the riot of his mind" (P 91). Inner and outer threats now heighten, for as Stephen tours this city of the dying, his forbidden desires intensify, aggravated by travel: "His recent monstrous reveries came thronging into his memory" (P 90). Stephen is now attached to unnatural fantasies explainable as distortions of repressed love for parents. He is repulsed from reality by anxiety which makes a strained charade of the male role. He is "sickened" by his father's talk of young manhood: "His very brain was sick and powerless. . .his monstrous way of life. . .seemed. . .beyond the limits of reality. Nothing. . .spoke to him from the real world unless he heard in it an echo of the infuriated cries within him" (P 92). Again he feels reduced to nonentity by guilt: "He had not died but he had faded out like a film in the sun. . .How strange. . .passing out of existence in such a way. . ." (P 93).

A sense of sexual negation over competition with father has extended to an overall feeling of self-negation. Obsessive anxieties may lead to a "feeling of annihilation" (*Theory*, p. 270). The feeling is stirred up by Simon's dwelling on the past, emphasizing that he is growing older and will pass away. This arouses a talionic sensation of passing away in Stephen because he unconsciously desires his father's death. He is forced by this negation to assert his identity with words: "I am Stephen Dedalus. I am walking beside my father. . .Simon Dedalus. . .Our room is in the Victoria Hotel. Victoria and Stephen and Simon. . .Names" (*P* 92). This harks back to the verbal phallus Stephen made to assert himself at Clongowes:

Stephen Dedalus

Class of Elements

Clongowes Wood College

Sallins

County Kildare

Ireland

Europe

The World

The Universe
(*P* 15)

Stephen uses words to understand, contain and compensate for experience. Compulsives withdraw from frightening "emotional impulses into the 'isolated' world of words and conceptions" (*Theory*, p. 156). Cixous says Stephen's "psychic armoury of remedies" is "dependent upon his indirect contact with reality, that is, his way of approaching reality through words. . ." (*Exile*, p. 349). The compulsive attaches great power to words because they are sexually charged for him (*Theory*, pp. 296–299), and Stephen already depends on this potency. When his father says he's a better man than Stephen in singing or running, an old man taps his forehead and says, "But he'll beat you here. . ." (*P* 95).

Seeing decay and futility in the lives of the people of Cork, Stephen raises himself above this negative reality of impotence, this inability to do harm or good (*P* 95), by associating himself with literature: "He repeated to himself the lines of Shelley's fragment. Its. . .vast inhuman cycles of activity chilled him, and he forgot his own human and ineffectual grieving" (*P* 96). Through his power over ideas and words, Stephen now wins prize money for an essay, and he attempts to raise himself and reorder his life with this money. He briefly supplants his father and impresses his mother by playing the role of provider:

> —We had better go to dinner, said Stephen . . .
> —Dinner? said Mr Dedalus. Well, I suppose we had better, what?
> —Some place that's not too dear, said Mrs Dedalus . . .
> —Come along, said Stephen quickly. It doesn't matter about the dearness. (*P* 97)

Stephen also elevates himself by sublimating cloacal obsession into the handling of money: "In his coat pockets he carried . . . chocolate for his guests while his trousers' pockets bulged with masses of silver and copper coins" (*P* 97). Freud's triad of anal personality qualities—orderly, economical and stubborn—is shown by Stephen, as is another feature of anality, ambivalence: the anal system is both masculine and feminine, aggressive and passive, expulsive and retentive.

Stephen's characteristic pattern of control is one in which he tries to retain at first, then yields and takes pleasure in losing: ". . .the money. . . ran through Stephen's fingers" (*P* 97). A compulsive symptom may consist of two phases, an impulse and a defense against it (*Theory*, p. 270); here we have undoing, the third of the main defenses of the obsessional neurotic listed, which first performs and then undoes a dangerous action such as supplanting a father by wealth. The obsessive feels protected by maintaining an order, but his own unconscious anal-sadistic drives combine with events to disturb his system (*Theory*, p. 284). Joyce portrays this syndrome exactly: "He had tried to build a breakwater of order and elegance against the sordid tide of life without him and to dam up, by rules. . .interests. . .and new filial relations, the powerful recurrence of the tides within him. Useless. From without as from within the water flowed over his barriers. . ." (*P* 98). As money runs out, external and internal tides of filth overwhelm him.

Stephen's view of the world and woman remains split between spiritual ideal and physical bestiality: "By night and day he moved among distorted images of the outer world. A figure . . . by day demure and innocent came towards him by night through the winding darkness of sleep, her face transfigured by lecherous cunning, her eyes bright with brutish joy" (*P* 99). Both halves of the night and day duality are distorted because of the split in Stephen's attitude toward mother seen earlier and his essential duality. As he now returns to his wanderings, he alternates between lust and the sacred image of Mercedes. But whereas the spiritual side was earlier strong enough to dictate his actions, now he is overcome by passion and wanders in search of a prostitute.

In obsession "sexual gratification may become so cemented with fearful ideas of castration that finally one becomes inconceivable without the other" (*Theory*, p. 277, *SE*, X, p. 163). Sexual desire is linked in Stephen's mind to dread of being reduced to a female. His esthetic theories isolate consciousness from desire (*P* 206), and uncontrolled emotion, which disturbs his sense of order, seems external to him. Thus, in Chapter III he wonders how sin could have occupied his body (*P* 139-140). And so he experiences his own passion as a sense of being overcome and violated: "he felt some dark presence moving irresistibly upon him. . .Its murmur besieged his ears like the murmur of some multitude in sleep; its subtle streams penetrated his being. His hands clenched convulsively and his teeth set together as he suffered the agony of its penetration" (*P* 100). The violator seems paternal. In the first chapter Stephen escaped an intolerable sense of submission by asserting his manhood in complaint to the rector. Here the anguish of desire forces from him "a cry for an iniquitous abandonment" and he seeks to affirm manhood—and defy authority—with a prostitute. He begins to frequent whores at thirteen or fourteen, as Joyce did (*JJ* 48). Freud says obsessives "invariably" show signs of "premature sexual activity" (*SE* X, pp. 165-166).

Harry Levin says that in Stephen's visit to the prostitute "it is clear that Stephen is still a child and that the woman plays the part of a mother. Joyce's heroes are sons and lovers at the same time; his heroines are always maternal" (*Critical Introduction*, p. 56). Stephen's passive attitude seeks shelter: "His lips would not bend to kiss her. He wanted to be held firmly in her arms, to be caressed slowly, slowly, slowly. In her arms he felt that he had suddenly become strong and fearless and sure of himself" (*P* 101). This passage resembles the earlier one about a transfiguring union with the then "unsubstantial image" of mother.

Rather than assuming a proper male attitude at this point, Stephen has fled from the threatening male side of life to seek relief and shelter in an unreal, aggressive image of woman. "Surrendering himself" to her kiss, he feels "dark pressure" not unlike the earlier "dark presence" of his passion. The peace of sexual satisfaction allays Stephen's anxieties and the "dark" perverse desires influenced by them. But these anxieties and desires influenced by the superego remain present, and they assert themselves in the next chapter to cause Stephen's repentence.

Lacan says Freud's greatest value lies in his sense of dialectic; this is not far from Glover's defense of Freud against Jung on the basis of dynamism. The ability to hold both sides of each issue in view—a prerequisite of dialectic vision—is promoted by the ambivalence of compulsion, which gives up desires without losing touch with them. In Joyce's work, every mental impulse is a reaction against an opposing impulse which continues to exist (Maddox, *Assault*, p. 209). This dialectic resembles such Christian dualities as matter and spirit, God and Satan. Stephen is devoted to the spirit world of imagination not because he has no attachment to the real world—though he is attracted to such an impossibility—but because his deepest attachments to the real world are bound up with their own denial. And it is because heterosexuality is a reaction against homosexuality in our artist that it is held so intensely, that deviations from it in oneself and others are scrutinized with fierce suspicion and shame, that women are regarded with extremes of disgust and exaltation.

III

CIRCLES OF SUPEREROGATION

HELL

Having sinned, Stephen is aware he lives in sin. Knowing "his soul lusted after its own destruction," "A certain pride, a certain awe, withheld him from offering to God even one prayer. . .though he knew it was in God's power to take his life while he slept and hurl his soul hellward. . ." (*P* 104). Stephen cultivates dread of the Father even while "the glories of Mary held his soul captive." "His sin, which had covered him from the sight of God, had led him nearer to the refuge of sinners" (*P* 105). His sinful activity is opposed to father and directed toward mother.

He strives for complete union with her by combining virgin and whore in one devotion: "If ever his soul, . . . after the frenzy of his body's lust . . . was turned towards her whose emblem is the morning star, . . .it was when her names were murmured softly by lips whereon there still lingered foul and shameful words, the savour itself of a lewd kiss" (*P* 105). As he pursues this complicated relation to mother, Stephen is compelled to find "arid pleasure in following up to the end the rigid lines of the doctrines of the church. . .only to hear and feel the more deeply his own condemnation" (*P* 106). He mulls over his guilt in all seven deadly sins. Compulsives protect themselves from dangerous emotions by elaborate systems of rule and ritual which serve penance and atonement as well as disguised self-gratification (*Theory*, pp. 285 ff.), leading Freud to call obsessional neurosis a private religion.[1] The self-condemnation that accompanies Stephen's debauchery from the start makes the later penance inevitable.

The retreat compels repentance because it corresponds to forces operating in the mind. The text suggests that others are not affected as strongly as Stephen by showing Heron "jesting" about the sermons afterward (*P* 125). In fact, Stephen feels that every word of the sermons is directed specifically at him (*P* 115, 125). He is mentally ready for them, and as soon as he hears of the retreat, he feels a sense of collapse: "Stephen's heart began slowly to fold and fade with fear like a withering flower" (*P* 107).

Father Arnall, who delivers the sermons, was established as an apologist for brutality when he led the class in which Father Dolan pandied Stephen. "The figure of his old master . . . brought back to Stephen's mind his life at Clongowes. . .where he had dreamed of being buried. . .His soul. . . became again a child's soul" (*P* 108-109). Soon Arnall brings Stephen back to imagining his burial. Kevin Sullivan believes Joyce altered fact in having the same priest preside at both unmannings,[2] and he may have done so to indicate the regressive nature of the Church's power. Hell expands the earlier square ditch and grave images, and Arnall's comparison of Hell to an ancient punishment for patricide is appropriate to the cause of Stephen's vulnerability.

The Jesuit presents the cause of sin and damnation in a fable about a bad son and a good one. The bad, patricidally proud "son of the morning" (*P* 118), seduces the female of "our first parents" (*P* 114, 117). To atone for this seduction of mother, which exposes "all sons and daughters of Adam" (*P* 113) to want and mutability, the good Son, the only true Son of His Father, submits to emasculation and torture; and the boys are enjoined to imitate Him. In rendering the problems of the boys external by exerting authority over them, the Church renders unconscious or uncreates conscience, exactly the process the artist will set out to reverse.

Arnall's sermons attack Stephen with male images: "The preacher's knife had probed deeply into his diseased conscience. . ." (*P* 115). "The thought slid like a cold shining rapier into his tender flesh: confession" (*P* 126). Emerging shaken, Stephen walks by walls of "overcoats and waterproofs hung like gibbeted malefactors, headless and dripping" (*P* 124), projecting injury. Hell itself, of course, has phallic threats: gnawing and stinging worms (*P* 120, 128), red hot goads and spikes, though filth, stench and corruption are more prominent.

Stephen reacts to this violence by turning to a mother for shelter: "O Mary, refuge of sinners, intercede for him!" (*P* 125). Stephen prays fervently only to the Virgin whose name is his mother's. Halfway through the sermons, Stephen is smitten with shame at the abysmal distance between his romantic ideal of woman and his bestial practices. He escapes this shame into a fantasy of spiritualized love in which the Virgin joins his hand to Emma's and blesses them (*P* 116). Here Emma, who is "near," is used as an intermediary to approach the Blessed Mother, who is "too far from him," "too pure and holy" to be approached directly: Emma is a surrogate. He aggravates his problem through this spiritual solution, increasing the distance between his ideal love and his physical needs.

After the last sermon, Stephen is overcome by fear as he is about to enter his room: "He halted. . .before the door. . .praying silently that death might not touch his brow as he passed over the threshold. . ." (*P* 136). His anxiety focusses on the threshold because he unconsciously feels the sexual significance of entering a chamber. A cozy room appeared at his encounter with the prostitute (*P* 100).

In his room, Stephen dreams of goatish creatures in a field. Though thought of as religious, this dream contains no religious reference and originally appeared as a secular epiphany (*Critical Edition*, p. 269). On one level, it refers to "the leprous company of his sins" (*P* 137), but what it presents directly are scatology and fear of men. The "goatish" creatures are priapic, and while no genitals appear in *Portrait*, their "hard eyes" and "long tails" are prominent. Their visages shine with the "malice of evil" and "cruel malignity" and the dream ends with them "thrusting upwards their terrific faces" and a cry of "Help!" (*P* 137-138). It represents the paternal threat behind the power of the Church over Stephen.

On recovering, he prays to the Virgin and goes out to confess, feeling alienated from those he passes on the street. "One soul was lost. . . : his. It flickered once and went out, forgotten,. . .cold void waste" (*P* 141). Religious perdition repeats his earlier feeling of fading in Cork. A parallel has been observed between the confession episode and Stephen's first visit to a prostitute.[3] Confession is preceded by walking the streets: "The squalid scene composed itself around him: the common accents, the burning gasjets in the shops, odours of fish and spirits. . ., moving men and women" (*P* 141). This walk echoes his earlier one in Nighttown: "He had wandered into a maze of narrow and dirty streets. From the foul laneways he heard bursts of hoarse riot. . .yellow gasflames arose. . . burning as if before an altar. . . .groups were gathered arrayed as for some rite" (*P* 100). The religious imagery that descibes the approach to vice clinches the association between the scenes. Both show Stephen performing an act of submission in a private chamber with a partner who serves others. Both chapters end with Stephen feeling he has found himself in oral reception: the whore's kiss and the eucharist.

Joyce made these episodes parallel because he believed prostitution and the Church inseparable. Stuart Gilbert, in *James Joyce's Ulysses*, gives historical examples of the Church supporting prostitution in order to set immorality apart from the acceptable sphere of life.[4] Joyce supervised the writing of this book (*JJ* 613, 629), and must have approved

Gilbert's remarks on the Church and vice; he may have initiated them, for they seem arbitrary for Gilbert. Joyce links prostitution with religion. The most elaborate such linkage outside the "Circe" episode of *Ulysses* may be the "Nausikaa" episode. Shechner credits me with the idea that the syrupy Gerty MacDowell of this episode may be a girl of ill repute (*Nighttown*, p. 165). Her friends Cissy Caffey, Edy Boardman and Bertha Supple appear as whores in "Circe" (*U* 364, 431, 587ff.); and whether or not Gerty is a pro herself, she acts brazenly in exposing herself to Bloom for masturbation. She is on the side of whoredom, a camp follower follower. Her mind is expressed in narrative interspersed with passages from a litany to the Virgin being sung in a nearby chapel, and Kenner points out that the Virgin and the girl perform the same function here in being exhibited, but not possessed (*Dublin's Joyce*, p. 258).

Shechner says Gerty may be a whore *despite* the saccharine tone of her mind; but Joyce's point is that she thinks in euphemism *because* she is essentially a harlot. This not only indicates that those who are most oppressed will deceive themselves most, but follows Joyce's principle that mental impulses are based on their opposites. Thus, for Stephen, the fact that Ann Shakespeare became religious in late years indicates "an age of exhausted whoredom" (*U* 206). A survey of case histories of prostitutes by Heinz Lichtenstein observes that they often tend toward prudishness.[5]

The Nymph in "Circe" signifies that hallowed virginity is the driving force behind prostitution and perversion. Appearing at the climax of Bloom's kinky fantasies, the Nymph deplores his baseness in prudish, pious terms and tries to castrate him. Bloom denounces her, and as she flees, her surface cracks and a "cloud of stench" escapes (*U* 553). The *Wake* repeatedly shows the Virgin in public relations: "Lord help you, Maria, full of grease. . ." (*FW* 214.18); "the hanging garments of Marylebon" (*FW* 192.32).

Joyce connected prostitution and religion because he realized any attempt to spiritualize love and escape the natural conditions of life must cause a degeneration of the sexual interests denied: to raise the soul above the body must inevitably lower the body. His equating of whoredom and holy virginity springs from his ambivalent attitude toward his mother, but his insight cannot be dismissed as the product of a complex. Civilization can't be understood without standing under neurosis, and the virgin-harlot duality the Church promotes in its iconography has been described by Freud as typical of modern European civilization.[6]

Joyce's mental problems typify his world in that compulsive thinking is an extreme version of key elements of Western culture, both scientific and religious. Compulsives seem "cold, abstract and emotionless," a

criticism levelled at *Portrait*; and compulsive categories represent "a carica-
ture of logical thinking: logical thinking, too, is based on a kind of isolation. But the logical isolation serves the purpose of objectivity, the compulsive isolation that of defense."[7] But "objectivity" and "defense" may
only be different contexts for the same mechanizing device. Freud asked
Einstein in 1932, ". . .does not every science come in the end to a kind
of mythology. . . ?" (*SE*, XXII, p. 211). As for mythology, or religion
seen from outside:

> There is hardly a single compulsion neurosis without religious features:
> for example, obsessive conflicts between faith and impulses to blaspheme,
> which may occur in convinced atheists as well as in consciously pious
> persons. . .
> Since most patriarchal religions also veer between submission to a
> paternal figure and rebellion. . .and every god, like a compulsive superego,
> promises protection on condition of submission, there are many simi-
> larities in. . .compulsive ceremonials and religious rituals, due to the
> similarity of underlying conflicts. (*Theory*, pp. 300ff.)

Obsessives combine tendencies of religion and science: "Their ego
shows a cleavage, one part being logical, another magical"—a fundamental
duality in Joyce's thinking around which this study is arranged. When
Freud wrote that every science, including his, was a mythology, he had
already concluded that if compulsion is private religion, religion is public
compulsion: "the universal obsessional neurosis of humanity" (*The Future
of an Illusion, SE* XXI, p. 43). Science and religion are compulsive insofar
as anxiety leads one to believe through them that some systematic construction produced by the mind is reality rather than myth or hypothesis.
Norman O. Brown's *Life Against Death*, a speculative extension of Freud's
late work, portrays compulsion as the drive behind civilization and man's
efforts to impose order on his world.[8] Joyce, rewriting *Portrait* to see
his mental struggle as central to his age, was first to build an understanding of neurosis as the force of culture.

Recent revelations of how *Ulysses* inspired T. S. Eliot's "Wasteland"
confirm Joyce's holy office as the guts of modern literature. In 1915
Portrait and *The Rainbow* by D. H. Lawrence (another son and lover)
introduced a new level of individuality. No character before Stephen
and Ursula Brangwen had so freed himself from every cultural restraint.
Henceforth, the central conflict in literature is not with outside forces,
but with the self as other. Authority and necessity are no longer in the
sky, in society, in the external world, but must be imposed upon oneself.
Anyone who imposes his own conflict is neurotic; and a neurotic who
invents his own system of authority or personal myth is, I suspect, obsessive. In conveying analytic self-consciousness to the mind of readers

and writers in living form, modernism has made us all responsible for ourselves. In *Love and Will* (New York: Norton, 1969) Rollo May says that whereas most of Freud's patients were hysterical, today "practically all our patients are compulsive–obsessional neurotics" (pp. 26-27).

GRACE

Compulsive symptoms tend to be ceremonial atonements for evil desires at the same time that they are rituals of auto-erotic gratification (Freud, *Anxiety*, p. 116). The sharpest picture of Stephen's absorption in such onanistic rituals is the account of his religious life at the start of Chapter IV. His needs for orderliness, passivity, punishment, mother worship and an economy of retention are served by a tradition that deflects him from free action to a mechanical system of self-satisfaction, something all systems tend toward. The religious period also develops Stephen's reaction formation. The tendency toward violence and reaction against it are constant findings in obsession (*SE* XIV, p. 157), and the primary disappointment of Stephen's religious life is his inability to overcome hostility toward others:

His prayers and fasts availed him little for the suppression of anger at hearing his mother sneeze or at being disturbed . . . It needed an immense effort. . .to master the impulse which urged him to give outlet to such irritation [control what he must expel]. Images of outbursts of trivial anger. . .among his masters. . .recurred to his memory, discouraging him. . . (*P* 151)

Before long, Stephen begins to play with temptation: ". . .surrender had a perilous attraction for his mind now that he felt his soul beset once again by the insistent voices of the flesh which began to murmur to him during his prayers. . ." (*P* 152). Again he is distracted in his pursuit of feminine spiritual phantoms by masculine worldly voices. Now he sees himself approached by a flood of temptation and enjoys the danger and control:

Then, almost at the instant. . .of sinful consent, he found himself standing far way from the flood . . . saved by a sudden act of the will or a sudden ejaculation: and, seeing . . . the flood far away and . . . its slow advance towards his feet, a new thrill of power and satisfaction shook his soul to know that he had not yielded nor undone all. (*P* 152)

The basis of this thrill, sphincter control, is fundamental to much of Stephen's activity. The laxative nature of this laxity must have been obvious to Joyce, if only when he looked back on it from *Ulysses:* ". . .he felt the silent lapse of his soul, as it would be. . .falling, falling but not yet fallen, still unfallen but about to fall" (*P* 162). Compare Bloom in his outhouse: "No great hurry. Keep it a bit" (*U* 68). Stephen compulsively accumulates penances for souls in purgatory and conceives of a spiritual "cash register" (*P* 148). Here, as in his earlier economy with the prize money, retention finally gives way to expulsion: the money flows through Stephen's fingers and he lets himself fall.

As Stephen's sacred deflection from body to spirit goes on, his perverse attitudes, particularly the femininity of his religious feelings, become increasingly apparent, eventually forcing him to affirm his manhood by denying Catholicism. References to his soul (*anima*) as female emphasize the femininity of his faith. She submits to authority to avoid threat, "no longer able to suffer the pain of dread, and sending forth, as she sank, a faint prayer" (*P* 126). But as she poses with "her burden of pieties . . . humiliated and faint before her Creator" (*P* 150), these "dissolving moments of virginal selfsurrender" (*P* 152) become threatening in themselves. Stephen's adoration associates with Mary rather than confronting her.

The interview with the Jesuit director brings Stephen's uncertainties to a head. The looped cord the director dangles before Stephen evokes emasculation by way of hanging. *Les jupes*, the Capuchin skirts mentioned to test Stephen (*P* 155) suggest that the priestly role offered here is female. Although he is initially attracted to priesthood by a vague sense of power, Stephen tends, as he approaches the office, to think of clerical life as a renunciation of manhood. He sees himself as a passive priest:

. . .it had pleased him to fill the second place in those dim scenes of his imagining. He shrank from the dignity of celebrant because it displeased him to imagine . . . that ritual should assign to him so clear and final an office. He longed. . .to stand aloof from the altar, forgotten by the people, . . . holding the paten within its folds, or, when the sacrifice had been accomplished, to stand . . . below the celebrant . . . (*P* 158-159)

He holds the receptacle for the host—and because Stephen sees himself as a female priest, he feels threatened by priesthood. Joyce recognizes here that Stephen's view is biased, but he suggests in *Ulysses* that a priest who believes in priesthood will be a pompous, hollow Father Conmee, just as a lover sure of potency will be a clownish Blazes Boylan.

During the interview with the director, memories swarm through Stephen's mind (*P* 157). His decision to reject priesthood centers on a vivid sensation of Clongowes:

He wondered how he would pass the first night in the novitiate . . .The troubling odour of the long corridors of Clongowes came back to him. . . from every part of his being unrest began to irradiate. . .a din of meaningless words drove his reasoned thoughts hither and thither confusedly. His lungs dilated and sank as if he were inhaling. . .unsustaining air and he smelt again the warm moist air. . .in the bath in Clongowes above the sluggish turfcoloured water. (*P* 160–161)

The mode of association Joyce delineates here and in many other passages reveals a formidable analyst. Here priesthood is linked to the threat of bath, ditch, grave and Hell: negation of sex and being, immersion in feminine submission and nonentity. The vision Stephen has of himself as priest is "eyeless." Some instinct, "waking at these memories," arms Stephen "against acquiescence."

The decision against the Church turns Stephen from the spiritual, feminine side of life to the physical, masculine side. He turns his eyes "coldly" toward "the faded blue shrine of the Blessed Virgin. . .Then bending to the left, he followed the lane. . .to his house. . .He smiled to think that it was this disorder, the misrule and confusion of his father's house and the stagnation of vegetable life, which was to win the day in his soul" (*P* 162). When threatened, Stephen strives for manhood, and now his embarrassment over identification with his mother leads him to turn from her in an effort to identify with his father:

. . .he thought coldly how he had watched the faith which was fading down in his soul aging and strengthening in her eyes. A dim antagonism gathered force within him. . .against her disloyalty: and when it passed. . . he was made aware dimly and without regret of a first noiseless sundering of their lives. (*P* 164–165)

Mary cannot be separated from God. Stephen's sense of betrayal by his mother goes back to the primary betrayal of her love for his father. Freud says the male adolescent often cannot forgive his mother for making love to father, not himself, and "regards it as an act of unfaithfulness" (*SE* XI, p. 171). Though Stephen's attempts to relinquish mother show progress toward independence, contrary forces continue to exist. And he sees little to turn to. Christmas dinner and Cork have shown him paternal injury and decay, and he now sees himself moving toward a father of "stagnation" and "confusion." He has difficulty conceiving of either the masculine role or the physical world except with alienation and dread.

Stephen repeats the established pattern of wandering in search of something without knowing what as he now sets out to discover what he has left the Church for: "The end he had been born to serve yet did not see had led him to escape by an unseen path. . . . He had refused. Why? / He turned seaward. . ." (*P* 165). The sea generally stands for "grey sweet mother" (*U* 5). But a more exact indication of what Stephen is seeking at this time is the great value he places on "a phrase from his treasure" (*P* 166). Money could be taken from him and material things were mutable; grace never belonged to him personally and so could not confirm his identity. But words are exempt from anxiety because one cannot be dispossessed of them. Moreover, they are sublimated and spiritualized, removed from the physical world Stephen finds painful.

As objects of accumulation, words are associated with excrement in the analysis of obsession (*SE* XVII, pp. 126–134) and in Joyce. Stephen will think of words as the inanimate sediment of thought in *Ulysses*, and he already thinks in these terms in *Portrait*: ". . .he walked on in a lane among heaps of dead language" (*P* 179). In the *Wake* Shem writes with ink made from his feces. Words may also represent manhood in compulsion. Father Arnall's dagger words presented a potent image of the phallic force of language. Words are Stephen's major weapon as well as his defense, and he frequently uses the "rapier point of his sensitiveness" (*P* 189) to thrust and parry in the dialogues of the last chapter. J. Mitchell Morse remarks that Joyce "seems to have associated his literary power with his sexuality."[9] Stephen asks himself on the beach what value he finds in words:

Words. Was it their colours? . . .No. . .it was the poise and balance of the period itself. Did he then love the rhythmic rise and fall of words better than their associations of legend and colour? Or was it that, being as weak of sight as he was shy of mind, he drew less pleasure from the reflection of the glowing sensible world through the prism of a language manycoloured and richly storied than from the contemplation of an inner world of individual emotions mirrored perfectly in a lucid supple periodic prose? (*P* 166–167)

He says here that he uses words not so much to describe the outside world as to express his inner feelings, a statement which describes *Portrait's* mode accurately. The statement is made, however, in circuitous, distorted language. The subordination of the vague but important "shy of mind" to the less important "weak of sight," the rhetorical question, the fancy, indistinct adjectives and the general emphasis on sound over sense obscure the meaning of the words. This is typical of the beach scene and the well-known purple prose of *Portrait*, which presents strong ideas and emotions so ornately that what is said is anesthetized by virtuosity and the obscure motive of what is said is masked by elaborate technique. Stanislaus saw this in 1904: "Jim is thought to be very frank about himself, but his style is such that it might be contended that he confesses in a foreign language— an easier confession than in the vulgar tongue" (*Diary*, p. 110).

In this passage the basic use Stephen makes of language is only hinted at indirectly. The terms which describe what Stephen enjoys in words—sensuality, "poise and balance," "rhythmic rise and fall"—only suggest sex through abstract analysis. Even the vaguer, more sublimated statement that he uses language to express emotions is accessible only to careful readers. Because the compulsive "flees from the macrocosm of things to the microcosm of words," language becomes "sexualized" for him and substitutes for real sources of emotion (*Theory*, p. 296). A major limitation of Joyce's method in *Ulysses* and the *Wake* derives from his tendency to assume that mental experience is composed entirely of words, part of his general inclination to promote the aural over the visual. As Erwin Steinberg indicates, most streams of consciousness probably use direct images in greater proportion than Joyce's do.[10]

The words of Joyce and Stephen, then, do express their emotions, but do not "mirror" them "perfectly": expression is limited and distorted by need to prevent certain realizations from emerging. Few artists have expressed their inner lives more completely than Joyce, but it is more than human to express inner life totally. In view of the circuitous way Stephen admits his use of words to express feelings here, it is not surprising that in the following chapter his esthetic theory aims at denying that he uses language to express his emotions. Another sample of defensive vagueness is a nearby passage on Europe "of strange tongues and valleyed and wood-begirt and citadelled":

He heard a confused music within him as of memories and names which he was almost conscious of but could not capture. . .and from each receding trail of nebulous music there fell always one long-drawn calling note, piercing like a star the dusk of silence. Again! Again! . . .a voice from beyond the world was calling. (*P* 167)

The source and meaning, the beginning and end of this strong but isolated magic must be sought by analysis. Described largely in female images, "Europe" is associated with memories of a distant past which seems repressed. It is accompanied by nebulous music like a star of dusk and personified as "a voice from beyond the world." This vision is an extension of earlier images of mother as phantom and Virgin, though it will later be embodied by French prostitutes. Having given up pursuit of the spiritual mother because it involved physical curtailment, Stephen now turns to reproject the idea of mother (distant since Clongowes) into a new distance. Mother herself he now repudiates for ideals, but in Freud's view at least all ideals have a physical basis, and Stephen's are based on an idealized conception of the lady he rejects.

Although Stephen's longings now seem quite distinct from mother, they are followed by anxiety as he is suddenly deflated by some bathing students and their coarse exclamations. As coldness goes with male threat, Stephen is now "chilled to the bone" at the sight of their private parts: "It was . . . a swordlike pain to see the signs of adolescence that made repellent their pitiable nakedness. Perhaps they had taken refuge in number and noise from the secret dread in their souls. But he, apart from them. . . remembered in what dread he stood of the mystery of his own body" (P 168). He overcomes this dread by a defensive "mild proud sovereignty" established through his skill with words.

Regaining his "uplifted" (P 165) state, Stephen has his first vision of Daedalus aflight. He shares this image with da Vinci, who designed Daedalus-like wings; and in the study of Leonardo Joyce owned, Freud says the common dream image of flight represents erection and male sexuality (SE XI, pp. 124–128). Stephen's vision is spiritualized, separated from its physical basis: "His soul was soaring. . . and the body he knew was purified in a breath and delivered of incertitude and made radiant and commingled with the element of spirit" (P 169). The description of flight parallels earlier adolescent longings: "He would fade into something impalpable under her eyes and then in a moment, he would be transfigured. Weakness and timidity and inexperience would fall from him. . ." (P 65). This central passage echoes when Stephen joins the prostitute (P 99, 101) and in religious transfiguration where his soul is raised and "made fair and holy" (P 145). This peaking pattern is based on the original dream of union with mother. Stephen creates images in his mind which then appear in his environment, finding outside what exists as possibility within. As Stephen later applies this pattern to Shakespeare, it has Jungian overtones of making one's own fate, but what we have seen of his feeling for his mother suggests repression behind this magic.

Freud's essay on object choices says some men are driven to pursue one woman after another, finally unsatisfied by each because they really seek an impossible maternal goal. Although he is no ladies' man, Stephen's course is analogous. He has pursued his phantoms through many fields, through childhood and adolescent wanderings, rebellions and daydreams, academic achievement, debauchery, religion and now words. Whenever he settles in an area near some maternal surrogate, senses of dissatisfaction and emasculation arise linked to a father figure in league with established authority. This threat forces him to wander off, expanding his horizons, in search of a new goal. Each chapter ends with a triumphant sense of uplift as he finds his goal, which is generally portrayed with an image of nurture, either maternal or oral. The new goal soon begins to disappoin' and to evoke the paternal threat in the following chapter. Fenichel says of compulsives, "The patients enter an ever growing cycle: remorse, penitence, new transgression, new remorse (*Theory*, p. 294). Here is a diagram of the plot:

CYCLICAL STRUCTURE OF *A PORTRAIT*

	Chapter I	Chapter II	Chapter III	Chapter IV	Chapter V
New world	School	Family homes	Nighttown	Church	College
Maternal goal	Mother (and alma mater)	E. C. as ideal	Prostitutes	Virgin	Irish Muse
Paternal threat	Wells and Dolan	Heron and father's collapse	Arnall's sermon	Director's offer	Cranly (as conventional Ireland)
Wandering	To rector	To whore	To confession	To beach	To Europe
Triumph	Lifted by boys	Kiss	Eucharist	Vocation	Flight
Nursing image	"the brimming bowl" (*P* 59)	Kiss	Taking wafer	"The earth that had borne him ... to her breast" (*P* 172)	"The white arms of roads, their promise of close embraces" (*P* 252)

Parallel form in the chapters of *Portrait* was first pointed out by Kenner ("Portrait in Perspective," p. 169), and others have seen the five chapters as rituals of sacrifice.[11] Such mythic interpretation does match the intentions of Joyce and Stephen, but it must be based on turning from the realistic view of Stephen's development to an overview of his life as a construction aimed at a goal. As he enters each new field of endeavor, Stephen feels he is decisively leaving a state of bondage and nearing maternal perfection: "This was the call of life to his soul not the dull gross voice of the world of duties and despair, not the inhuman voice that called him to the pale service of the altar" (*P* 169). The extent of the anxiety that accompanied earlier stages is revealed as he now rejoices in his sense of release:

What were they now but cerements shaken from the body of death— the fear he had walked in night and day. . .the shame that had abased him within and without. . .

His soul had risen from the grave of boyhood. . .He would create proudly out of the freedom and power of his soul, as the great artificer whose name he bore, a living thing, new and soaring and beautiful, impalpable, imperishable. (*P* 169-170)

Stephen resurrects manhood, leaving a grave of sexless nonentity behind; and the living soaring thing he will make of words is phallic. His pride, ambition and freedom depend upon the continuing existence of the powerful inferiority they react against. At any rate, he escapes the femininity of religion: "Where was the soul that had hung back from her destiny, to brood alone upon the shame of her wounds and in her house of squalor and subterfuge to queen it. . ." (*P* 171). His emphatic assumption of manhood brings an image of passage into woman as his "lust for wandering" now leads him to pick up a pointed stick and "wade slowly up" a rivulet, wondering at the seaweed swaying beneath the current: "The water of the rivulet was dark with endless drift and mirrored the highdrifting clouds. The clouds were drifting above him silently and. . . seatangle was drifting below him" (*P* 170). He feels alone in this envelope of drifting, "happy and near to the wild heart of life" (*P* 171). Now the bathing boys have apparently gone and the absence of male competition is one pleasant thing about the environment in which he now finds himself floating "amid. . .sunlight and gayclad. . .figures, of children and girls."

In this womb of nature, Stephen has his vision of a birdlike girl. His rapport with her stands for a proper mode of heterosexual relationship and of relation to all of life, an acceptance of "mortal beauty" which opposes the need to turn away from reality to an ideal. Stephen calls her "without shame or wantonness" (*P* 171) because he realizes the centrality of the virgin-whore duality to his problem. He also seems to realize that shame and wantonness are inseparable, cannot exist without each other. This prefigures his later idea of a perfect mode of relation in which the subject is neither attracted to nor repulsed from his object. But while he recognizes the need to see beauty without distortion or perversion, the absence of shame or wantonness he posits is more a wish than an actuality.

Description suggests the girl impresses him at least partly because she fulfills neurotic desires. She is not free from shame, for "a faint flame" trembles on her cheek, the telltale Joycean blush. Nor is she free from wantonness, for she holds her skirts up to her hips, showing her drawers, as she returns his gaze. Moreover, the elaborate description of her as a bird makes her phallic, for birds are male symbols in *Portrait;* and the emphasis on her foot stirring the water "hither and thither" is also fetishistic, as well as suggesting vitality. Woman cannot comfort Stephen without the hanging goods of provocation and saintliness.

Stephen's intellectual acceptance of "mortal youth and beauty" (*P* 172) is an advance toward health and release, but his relations to the opposite sex and the world remain subject to neurotic conditions. In withdrawing feeling from genital sex, compulsives withdraw from the world: ". . .regression prohibits the development of mature object relationships" so that they tend to be concerned with "disturbances in their relation to objects" (*Theory*, p. 284), the problem S. L. Goldberg has identified as most crucial to Joyce's fiction. Certainly, the experience on the beach does not constitute an escape from Stephen's mother fixation, though he forcefully repudiates his mother on the conscious level in the last third of the novel. As the beach scene ends, Stephen feels "the earth that had borne him had taken him to her breast" (*P* 172). Mother still holds him. The beach scene shows a young man who is trying to synthesize a revelation of normal youth and beauty in literary and intellectual terms because he is limited by an injured personality.

IV

ART

As Stephen condemns his mother and her representatives, his mind and its productions remain shaped by the template of his contact with her. He continues to see women as virgins or whores and to divide life into unattainable spirit and decaying matter. And the polarization of his mind makes complex identity manifest to him: he sees that the mind is made up of interacting opposites as he denies his mother, yet stays under her spell.

Chapter V opens on Stephen confronted again with the "turfcoloured water of the bath in Clongowes" (*P* 174). His home, family and culture threaten his manhood: "His father's whistle, his mother's mutterings, the screech of an unseen maniac [nun] were to him now so many voices threatening to humble the pride of his youth" (*P* 175-176). Now his mother's voice has joined the "hollowsounding voices" of the second chapter, for he sees her as having gone over to the side of Father and betrayed him. As he walks to the university, Stephen extends the bath image to view all of Dublin, and Ireland, by implication, as a sink of decay and mutability:

. . .choosing his steps amid heaps of wet rubbish. . .stumbling through the mouldering offal. (*P* 175)

. . .he met the consumptive man with the doll's face. . .(*P* 177)

. . .whether he looked around the little class. . .or out of the window. . . an odour assailed him of cheerless cellardamp and decay. (*P* 178)

. . .he walked on. . .among heaps of dead language. (*P* 179)

. . .sloth of the body and of the soul crept over it [statue of Thomas Moore] like unseen vermin. . .(*P* 180)

The soul of the gallant venal city. . .had shrunk with time to a faint mortal odour rising from the earth and he knew that. . .when he entered the sombre college he would be conscious of a corruption. . .(*P* 184)

He now finds beauty and reality in Dublin only by association with the magic world of literature: ". . .he foreknew that as he passed the sloblands of Fairview he would think of the cloistral silverveined prose of Newman, that as he walked along the North Strand Road, glancing idly at the windows of the provision shops, he would recall the dark humour of Guido Cavalcanti and smile. . ." (*P* 176). He will soon find it imperative to leave this land of his morbid vision. The parallel between this and other bog images indicates that Stephen's vision descends from primal anxiety, and this decay reiterates the earlier tides of filth he strove against only to be overwhelmed. Onto Ireland he projects castration, defilement and his attitude toward his mother, which is now repudiation. The story of the peasant woman who offered herself to his friend Davin crystallizes and justifies this new attitude. As the story reverberates in his mind, she stands forth,

reflected in other. . .peasant women whom he had seen standing in the doorways at Clane as the college cars drove by, as a type of her race and his own, a batlike soul waking to the consciousness of itself in darkness and secrecy and loneliness and, through the eyes and voice and gesture of a woman without guile, calling the stranger to her bed. (*P* 183)

The Clane women occurred to Stephen in the first chapter when he missed his mother. Davin's woman fits Stephen's long-standing conception of his mom as a woman who has defiled herself by giving herself to an unworthy other. All boys conceive of their mothers in such terms at a certain stage; but not all dwell on this idea and let it permeate their lives. Stephen sees the woman at the door as a symbol of a motherland who has given herself to domination by England and Rome and elaborates this view of Ireland as unfaithful mother through the last chapter.

The pattern appears at once in a flower girl who takes Stephen's arm and calls herself "your own girl, sir!": "The blue flowers she lifted towards him and her young blue eyes seemed to him. . .images of guilelessness; and he halted till. . .he saw only ragged dress and damp coarse hair and hoydenish face" (*P* 183). She resembles the woman who offered herself to Davin "without guile"; and the linkage of flowers to eyes suggests Stephen thinks of her as selling herself, as merchants tend to. "He left her quickly, fearing that her intimacy might turn to gibing and wishing to be out of the way before she offered her ware to another, a tourist from England or a student of Trinity" (*P* 184). The Trinity man would probably be a wealthy Protestant Anglo-Irishman (*JJ* 58–59). Dwelling on the subjection of his motherland to foreign patronage, he remembers a tawdry tribute to Wolfe Tone and its alien supporters: *Vive l'Irlande!* (*P* 184).

Foreign domination and Irish impotence combine in Father Butt, the dean of studies with whom Stephen now speaks. As Epstein indicates, Butt is ambiguous (*Ordeal*, pp. 110–111). As an English Jesuit, he personifies the two great oppressors; but as "humble follower," he represents the clergyman as eunuch, the role Stephen fled from. The one older man with whom Stephen has a conversation after the Jesuit director, Butt probably reflects in his complexity Stephen's view of his secular father. The phrase from Loyola, "*Similiter atque senis baculus*" (like an old man's staff) is typical of the description of Butt in including both enfeeblement and danger: "to be raised in menace" (*P* 186). Butt is also castrated but aggressive in his lameness: "limping slightly but with a brisk step" (*P* 186). The predominant impression is of emasculation because of the emphasis on his humble submission to the Church and emotional paralysis: "a mortified will no more responsive to the thrill of its obedience than was to the thrill of love or combat his aging body" (*P* 185). Butt's behavior is later "womanish" (*P* 199).

Stephen's conversations with men are duels. Earlier he "parried" the banter of a group of students (*P* 168), and he sends out many a "shaft of thought" (*P* 193) in this episode. He views Butt as a "foe" against whom to turn "a rapier point" of intelligence (*P* 189). But he feels disarmed and defeated by Butt's prior claim, as an Englishman, on the words they use; "—The language in which we are speaking is his before it is mine. . .I cannot speak or write these words without unrest of spirit. . . My soul frets in the shadow of his language" (*P* 189). These feelings reflect not only cultural realities, but the sexual value of language and Stephen's old, thwarting envy of his father's manly possessions. Colonial power is paternal, and Stephen recognizes the political leverage the sons of Ireland lack to be consubstantial with manhood.

The physics class which follows the talk with the dean presents more images of Irish corruption. The first is a crippled male sex organ:

> *On a cloth untrue*
> *With a twisted cue*
> *And elliptical billiard balls.*
>
> (*P* 192)

The words are by Gilbert and Sullivan, who evoke the worst qualities of the Empire, and in this context they portray distorted desire in Dublin. When Moynihan says, "What price ellipsoidal balls! Chase me ladies, I'm in the cavalry!" (*P* 192), balls are established as a motif. Whatever else they may bounce off, the handballs that get slammed around on the field of male competition rebound with masculinity (*P* 196, 198, 200, 204, 218). The physics professor also presents a set of coils, and circling is prominent in Joyce's work from the story of Johnny the horse in "The Dead" to the *Wake*. In *Portrait* circling is tied to perverse neurotic fixation, as in Father Dolan's cycle of sadism: "Tomorrow and tomorrow and tomorrow" (*P* 49). Because Stephen is locked in repetition, he perceives the same dull round everywhere about him: "The droning voice of the professor continued to wind itself slowly round and round the coils it spoke of, doubling, trebling, quadrupling its somnolent energy. . ." (*P* 194).

Stephen sees two fellow students, the crass questioner MacAlister and the cynical mocker Moynihan, as betrayers of Mother Ireland: "Can you say with certitude by whom the soul of your race was bartered and its elect betrayed—by the questioner or by the mocker?" (*P* 193-194). The bartered soul, as female, may be connected to mom, while Stephen doubtless includes himself among the betrayed elect, and this betrayal, like that of his parents, was established before his time. Stephen sees the Irish situation as his family conflict, and he makes his peers conform to neurotic models of paternity.

The distinguishing feature of Stephen's friends is no intellectual trait, though they are fairly willing to listen; it is physical aggressiveness. The three close friends, Davin, Lynch and Cranly, are so diversified as to share little but forcefulness. Davin is an athlete and militant Fenian. Lynch is "muscular" and thrusts out his chest, saying, "Who has anything to say about my girth?" (*P* 201). The righteous Cranly constantly bullies and insults others. He harries Temple and Goggins and mocks Glynn (*P* 229-237). He and Lynch are both noted for ability to swear. The most prominent of the students Stephen does *not* associate with, MacCann and Temple, are characterized as impotent and feminine. MacCann's feminist socialism is rejected as bland and ineffectual: "Do you [MacCann] think you impress me, Stephen asked, when you flourish your wooden sword?" (*P* 197). Temple is shown in the group "glancing from one to the other. . . seeming to try to catch each flying phrase in his open moist mouth" (*P* 196) and "as if he were gulping down the phrase" (*P* 198). This catching of forceful phrases is feminine, as are Temple's talkativeness, his emotion and the weakness that allows others to abuse him.

Stephen chooses friends of force because he needs strong father figures, and his relation to them is neurotic. He confesses to all of them his deepest feelings, secrets and sins[1] —does so even though the coarse Lynch and the naive Davin are hardly suitable sounding boards. Behind these confessions is Stephen's desire to confess his sins to his father, against whom, as strivings for mother, they were committed. Although confession seeks punishing shame, it is also aggressive, flaunting crimes to hurt the father-confessor. Stephen, in fact, reveals things to Davin that make the latter ill (P 202). Because of their filial basis, Stephen's friendships must be relinquished before long: if they grow too close, fear of being unmanned will surface. At college, as in earlier scenes, he will work himself into a position where anxiety becomes unbearable, then feel compelled to wander off in search of a new mutation of mom. The new source of gratification that will lead him through the latest phase of entrapment and escape is art.

The concepts of art in the lectures Stephen delivers to Lynch must be seen as products of his mind to understand their workings. Consider the incidents surrounding the esthetic theories. Before summoning Lynch to his talk, Stephen denounces Ireland to Davin: "—My Ancestors threw off their language and. . .allowed a handful of foreigners to subject them. Do you fancy I am going to pay. . .debts they made?" (P 203). Late in the book Stephen tends to deny the past and look to the future. His sense of betrayal and entrapment originates in mother's giving of herself to father and in his own fixation. Striving to blame his mother and repudiate her, he views Ireland as a degraded and dangerous mom, "the old sow that eats her farrow" (P 203).

Stephen's esthetic attempts to fashion art into a haven from his sense of being sold out by the past and from his crippling bond to his parents. He tries to prove art to be as isolated from intense personal feelings as reason from emotion. To this end he extends Aquinas's statement that art satisfies the mind and not the body into his idea of arrest or stasis. It may be true that art does not satisfy desire or loathing, although, as Lynch suggests, there may be exceptions; but Stephen's explanation of this stasis is false. He claims art operates on a different level than that of the kinetic emotions, that in esthetic emotion, "The mind is arrested and raised above desire and loathing" (P 205). The Neoplatonic "raised above," revives an archaic idea to fit emotional needs. Stephen says that though we are all animals, art exists in a separate "mental world." Desire and loathing are

not more than physical. Our flesh shrinks from what it dreads and responds to. . .what it desires by a purely physical reflex action of the nervous system. . .Beauty expressed by the artist cannot awaken in us an emotion which is kinetic or a sensation which is purely physical. It awakens. . .an esthetic stasis, an ideal pity or an ideal terror, a stasis called forth, prolonged and at last dissolved by what I call the rhythm of beauty. (P 206)

Desire and loathing, however, are not purely physical reflexes: one can feel desire without an object present and rational arguments may contribute to loathing or even desire. Reason and emotion are never independent. Freud explained reason not as a separate entity from emotion, but as a system built through the balancing and negation of emotion that occurs when we adjust our desires to reality ("Negation," *SE*, XIX, pp. 235-240). Stephen is trying to divide the mental mix of reason and feeling into two distinct, mutually exclusive levels. As he does so, however, his ideas are shaped by desires: he is building an intellectual edifice to shelter him from anxiety, an art to fulfill the function of mother. Probably no emotion is nonkinetic, though they may be more or less so. The concept of static emotion parallels the ideal attitude for art presented in *Stephen Hero*, the classical temper that holds to things as they are (*SH* 78-79). But ideal stasis can be unrealistic, unhealthy and even kinetic if it opposes the tendency of things to change. Compulsive systems of defense may cling to the *status quo:* "The fear of any change from the known present condition to a possibly dangerous new state makes patients cling even to their symptoms." Yet "the fear of change may be replaced or accompanied by its opposite, a tendency to change continuously" (*Theory*, p. 298). Stephen's ideal of stasis is based on a retentive desire never to leave the bosom of the family for a new generation, a desire to halt time. Like all of his efforts to retain, this attitude will give way to or alternate with its opposite.

It is not true that art "cannot awaken in us an emotion which is kinetic." Art uses the same drives, conscious or not, that propel life. But these drives are so manipulated by sublimation, indirection and disguise that the participating reader avoids or controls tension and achieves gratification. The peace of stasis is arrived at by balancing opposed psychic forces in a way that is pleasing.[2] If the proper balance is not achieved and drives stick out in such a way as to violate truth, morality or some other function of psychic balance, the work is dismissed as pornographic or didactic, cheap or prohibitive, unhealthy or untrue. *Portrait* exemplifies this process. The force of the novel, psychologically described, is the energy of Stephen's complex. The book appeals to people by enacting the conflicts of youth without offending by making them explicit as it follows the growth of a soul through severance. The stasis *Portrait* achieves is embedded in a balance between desire for mother and fear of father, ideal and reality.

Sprinchorn points out ("Achilles," pp. 38, 44) that Stephen's major solution in *Portrait* relinquishes the reality of mother to construct an artificial mother in the stasis of art. Thus the movement in the novel is one of sublimation, and Freud favored sublimation as a successful defense. But he expressed doubts about its ultimate value as a solution in such late works as *Beyond the Pleasure Principle* and *Civilization and Its Discontents*: "No substitutive or reactive formations and no sublimations will suffice to remove the repressed instincts' persisting tension" (*SE*, XVIII, p. 43). Moreover, the value of sublimation depends on its bringing the subject into contact with others, but Stephen's development in the novel neither resolves his neurosis nor connects him with people. It is a series of sunderings aimed primarily at contact with and control over himself. If Stephen hopes through freedom and understanding to prepare for eventual communion with mankind, it is in his own soul that he wants to reach what is universal. Freud's system makes little provision for such a course. It will be better understood through the ideas of Jung, who believed the symptoms of Freudian neurosis should be taken seriously as guides toward psychic progress.

Tindall says Stephen's esthetic "amounts to a theory of impersonality and autonomy" and demonstrates that neither Stephen nor Joyce is as impersonal or autonomous in art as the theory would make him.[3] As he isolates his art from his feelings, Stephen strives to free himself from social context by flying beyond the existence of various ethnocentric standards of beauty:

> That seems to be a maze. . .we cannot escape. I see however two ways out. One is this hypothesis: that every physical quality admired by men in women is in direct connection with. . .the propagation of the species. It may be so. This world . . . is drearier than even you, Lynch, imagined. For my part I dislike that way out. It leads to eugenics rather than to esthetic. (*P* 208)

Stephen favors the second alternative—that beauty contains relations that coincide with the stages of esthetic apprehension. He denies the first because his repudiation of his mother extends to the idea of childbearing. He renders the connection between childbearing and beauty ludicrous: "MacCann, with one hand on *The Origin of Species* and the other hand on the new testament" (*P* 209).

Stephen is bright enough to recognize that practicality and particular cultural norms affect standards of beauty, but he is trying to separate art from family and tradition, which are linked to his sense of betrayed entrapment. So he turns to his stages of apprehension as the common factor of beauty. By Stephen's definition, *integritas, consonantia* and *claritas* may be found in any object which has unity, is made up of parts and has *quidditas* or identity (*P* 212–213). But these properties are far from explaining the effect of a beautiful object or distinguishing which object is beautiful: Stephen says they may be found in a butcher boy's basket. If Stephen's beauty can be found in any object, it is really a quality of the observer's mind. The "supreme quality of beauty, the clear radiance of the esthetic image," is a "luminous silent stasis of esthetic pleasure, a spiritual state very like to that cardiac condition . . . called the enchantment of the heart." Evidently Stephen has had such "luminous" experiences of ecstasy and the purpose of his theory is to explain something to which he is attracted before he conceptualizes it. By defining his feelings in these formal terms, Stephen constructs a model of his mind as he would like it to be, simplified and free of painful motivation. Neurosis and art serve each other here, for if Stephen did not defend himself by elevating form to eclipse painful motives, he would not be able to explore his mind as thoroughly as he does.

The emphasis on formal esthetics also eliminates restrictions on the content of art. Stephen desires this not simply because he wants to escape the prudish and dogmatic, for he knows his mind is perverted and tends toward obscene and objectionable material. It was, after all, not long ago that Stephen was stricken with guilt because he felt himself engulfed in vile reveries and practices, and he has similar feelings later (*P* 233-234). He is impelled to express in art his obsession with what is shocking for the same reasons that dictate his indiscreet confessions. He is investigating and trying to work out psychosexual areas of his experience which he perceives as crucial.

The final element of Stephen's esthetic is the triad of forms, lyric, epic and dramatic. In the highest, dramatic art, toward which the others tend, the personality of the artist "refines itself out of existence, impersonalises itself" (*P* 215). Stephen adopts this idea from Flaubert[4] because he wants to escape his own personality, to deny neurotic attachment to his parents by becoming "like the God of creation." He will be *causa sui*, his own creator, a common oedipal strategy. Joyce may also have used the term *dramatic* to describe the fundamental ambivalence in his work. "The dramatic form is reached" when the personality of the artist flows into his characters and "fills every person with such vital force that he or she assumes a proper and intangible esthetic life." At this point the author's mind is divided by the conflict in the text and he ceases to express any one point of view. Such a mode of dramatic conflict is manifest in *Ulysses*, where Bloom and Stephen polarize Joyce.

The trinity lyric, epic and dramatic is parallel to wholeness, harmony and radiance. In both progressions the first stage, wholeness or lyric, consists of the simplest, most immediate manifestation. Both second stages, harmony and epic, concern relation of parts, for in epic the image is in mediate relation to the artist and his audience (*P* 214-215). Finally, in both triads the last stage is the most elevated: radiance is the deepest and most intense esthetic perception, dramatic, the greatest art. And the states of mind at the highest stages have much in common: both esthetic stasis and dramatic creation involve realization of the object and escape from self. One is "spiritual" (*P* 213), the other, "purified" (*P* 215); one involves "conception," the other, "creation," and both are "mysterious." In fact, these exalted states are the latest versions of the moment of transfiguration in which Stephen feels weakness fall from him as his mother's arms wrap him round. The fact that Stephen's rationalization of this "enchantment of the heart" does not fit reality is soon demonstrated when Stephen wakes from a dream partly censored out of his memory to feel he has experienced "An enchantment of the heart!. . .ecstasy. . .an instant of enchantment" (*P* 217). He feels this vivid sense of poetic conception without consciously perceiving an object or passing through preliminary stages.

Stephen's theories are hedged in by his striving to relinquish his real mother for a spiritual one. As his lecture was preceded by condemnation of "the old sow," it is followed, as Stephen encounters Emma, with a condemnation of the main human mother surrogate of the novel. The subject all along is Stephen's denial of his external mother in favor of internal controls. He sees Emma as mother betraying him with a Father: "She has no priest to flirt with, he thought with conscious bitterness, remembering how he had seen her last" (*P* 216). But he vacillates, after the maternal pattern, between whore and virgin: "If he had judged her harshly? If her life were a simple rosary of hours. . ." (*P* 216). Mother fixation is explored in the section after the theorizing as we see Stephen's art in action. He is inspired to write a poem by isolated emotions and muffled desires here, not by esthetic apprehension. He attains enchantment in a dream, and the fact that his soul is "all dewy wet" as he awakens ecstatically leads Kenner to conclude, probably rightly, that it is a wet dream (*Dublin's Joyce*, p. 123). The content of the dream is evidently obscured by censorship:

The instant flashed forth like a point of light and now from cloud on cloud of vague circumstance confused form was veiling softly its afterglow. O! In the virgin womb of the imagination the word was made flesh. Gabriel the seraph had come to the virgin's chamber. An afterglow deepened within his spirit, whence the white flame had passed, . . . to a rose and ardent light. That. . .light was her strange wilful heart, strange that no man had known or would know, wilful from before the beginning of the world . . . (*P* 217)

This parallels the veiled, glowing maid the poet dreams of in "Alastor." There is certainly a homoerotic level in Gabriel entering "the virgin womb of the the imagination . . .his spirit" for artistic annunciation. But the main subject of the dream and the villanelle is the roselight of the female heart, and the priority of this heart "from before the beginning of the world" suggests it is maternal. The villanelle presents the virgin-temptress duality that indicates how Stephen's view of Emma is shaped by maternal patterns, and mother may well be seen as the poem's inner subject. Another old pattern reiterates as longing calls forth a male threat in Stephen's mind:

Smoke went up from the whole earth . . .smoke of her praise. The earth was like a swinging. . .censer, a ball of incense, an ellipsoidal ball. The rhythm died out at once; the cry of his heart was broken. His lips. . . went on. . .stammering and baffled; then stopped. (*P* 218)

Joyce is aware of the Freudian lines of association that lead back from the ellipsoid that renders Stephen's inspiration impotent to the ball image of the physics class. Stephen renders himself "broken" and "baffled" by evoking virility. He now seeks to maintain maleness by writing down what he has composed, "fearing to lose all" (*P* 219). The masculine intrusion on Stephen's revery turns his mind to a vision of woman as betrayer and whore. This vision starts with Stephen's jealousy of Father Moran, which was presented earlier (*P* 202). Because he feels Mother Ireland has betrayed her elect by giving herself to England and Rome, he now finds his beloved taken from him by a Catholic Father. It seems difficult to be jealous of a priest, but Stephen manages it through his insight into the sexualized nature of religious confession and shame, insight which is based on neurotic patterns of thought, yet has validity. Joyce's compulsive concentration on instinctual margins of experience gives him phenomenal penetration into these border areas. Stephen refers to Emma "flirting" and "toying" with her "paramour" Father Moran (*P* 221) as

a figure of the womanhood of her country, a batlike soul waking to the consciousness of itself in darkness and secrecy and loneliness, tarrying awhile, loveless and sinless, with her mild lover and leaving him to whisper of innocent transgressions in the. . .ear of a priest. . .she would reveal her soul's shy nakedness, to one who was but schooled in. . .a formal rite rather than to him, a priest of the eternal imagination, . . .(*P* 221)

Emma is presented in the terms used for the peasant woman who offered herself to Davin: as "a figure of the womanhood of her country" she extends betrayal by mother to national distribution. Stephen calls to mind the flower girl who seemed to sell herself, and three other coarse, wanton women who are "distorted reflections of her image" (*P* 220). This is not because all women represent Emma, but because she and the others represent something larger—mother.

Stephen's statement that he has written verses for "her" after ten years recalls the earlier attempt which ended at the mirror of his mother's room. He now has a total recall of the tram scene of a decade earlier, repeating most of the passage (*P* 69). The intensity with which he relives this experience after so long shows how little he has developed, how much he is trapped in the past he strives to leave behind. The enduring power of these few minutes on a tram suggests that they form a screen memory linked to deeper sources. The picture of Emma approaching and receding on the tram stairs (*P* 222) may be influenced by Stephen's separations and reunions with mother during the Clongowes period. This ambivalent pattern is repeated in his memory of Emma dancing toward and away from him at the carnival ball (*P* 219). Thoughts of Emma as betrayer lead to thoughts of male threat: "If he sent her the verses? They would be read out. . .Folly indeed! The brothers would laugh and try to wrest the page from each other with their strong hard fingers. The suave priest, her uncle, . . .would hold the page at arm's length. . ." (*P* 222). Stephen sees the "strong hard" threat as inevitable to Ireland or any country where power dominates love, while Joyce sees it as inevitable to the mind of the artist.

While Stephen sees Emma as whore, he also sees her as virgin: ". . .however he might revile and mock her image, his anger was also a form of homage" (*P* 220). Feeling "he had wronged her," he attempts to combine innocence with defilement: "A sense of her innocence moved him almost to pity her, an innocence he had never understood till he had come to the knowledge of it through sin, an innocence which she too had not understood while she was innocent or before the strange humiliation of her nature had first come upon her" (*P* 222). The learning of innocence in corruption and humiliation, while it follows the myth of the fortunate fall or the need to sin in order to understand virtue, also has neurotic roots. One reason Joyce links innocence to vice here and elsewhere is that he felt release and freedom when he degraded himself, and this gratification by degradation results from the satisfaction of guilt. As piety promotes vice in Joyce's psychology of reaction, so sin promotes virtue. Stephen repeatedly says the soul is born in sin (*P* 203, 222), probably referring to physical erection as well as spiritual being.

Shame and humiliation excite Stephen to an erotic fantasy of return to mom as "a glow of desire" kindles "his soul and body" and he completes the poem: "Conscious of his desire she was waking. . . ,the temptress of his villanelle. Her eyes. . .were opening to his eyes. Her nakedness yielded to him, radiant, warm, odorous and lavishlimbed, enfolded him like a shining cloud, . . .like water with a liquid life. . ." (*P* 223). As fantasies go, this is a lovely one to conclude with. It expresses a living, deep feeling of union with mother, in phrases like "conscious of his desire," which should give Stephen a basis for eventual real love. Before this, he will have to recognize the neurotic snares in his own mind that keep him from getting through to others. He is taking a step toward recognizing them by seeing them objectified in the social institutions he attacks. But analysis of Church, state, family, friendship and romance will not lead to love without first leading away from it any more than his theory will lead to art.

The villanelle scene, beginning with a sexual dream, ending with "desire" for a womb and including interludes of anxiety, bitterness and repulsion, contradicts Stephen's theory that art springs from feelings distinct from desire and loathing. In fact, desire and loathing correspond to whoredom and virginity, those polar attitudes toward women—and all objects—in which the poet of the maternal chant is as firmly ensnared as ever. He will not deal with these polarities creatively until he stops trying to escape them or blame them on others.

Joyce probably saw Stephen's theory as a necessary step forward that was flawed insofar as it attempted to impose a model of purity on the tangle of life. Stephen gives credence to a principle he sees as central to Aristotle: "Aristotle's entire system . .rests upon his book of psychology and that, I think, rests on his statement that the same attribute cannot at the same time and in the same connection belong to and not belong to the same subject" (*P* 208). But the symbolism Joyce moved toward in later works went beyond Aristotelian psychologic: Molly is a same attribute who belongs and does not belong to the subject Bloom. Eventually, Joyce was to define essential reality in terms of mental interaction of opposites like H. C. E. and A. L. P. or Shem and Shaun rather than the discrete, externalized categories of Aristotelian logic. Even within *Portrait* the cyclical structure undercuts Stephen's constant attempts to purify himself, to escape his lower half.

V

FLIGHT

If the villanelle shows fixation, the final section of *Portrait* depicts Stephen's decision to break with mother and Ireland. It begins with his vision of birds as an augury of departure whose soaring will carry Stephen from the castration, stagnation and material grossness of his world. He had similar yearnings for uplift in earlier cyclical stages, but now it is primarily his mother he must escape: "The inhuman clamour soothed his ears in which his mother's sobs and reproaches murmured insistently and the. . . wheeling and fluttering. . .soothed his eyes which still saw the image of his mother's face" (*P* 224). The linked ideas of mother as debased betrayer and nation as stagnant victim now incite Stephen to departure. This section extends the panorama of Irish corruption and emasculation by portrayals of the degenerate "captain," the futile, bleating Temple, the pompous fool Glynn, the suave cynic Dixon, and Goggins, who hails the mention of Stephen's Irish heritage with a fart.

Moreover, Stephen increasingly finds external corruption answered by corruption within. Earlier, "The grey block of Trinity. . .set heavily in the city's ignorance. . .pulled his mind downward. . ." (*P* 180). Now the effect of Dublin on his mind seems to grow more pathological as he writhes entangled in sordid thoughts:

He frowned angrily upon his thought and on the shrivelled mannikin who had called it forth. (*P* 228)

The images he had summoned gave him no pleasure. They were secret and enflaming but her image was not entangled by them. . . Could his mind then not trust itself? Old phrases. . .with a disinterred sweetness. . .
. . .All the images. . .were false. His mind bred vermin. (*P* 233–234)

This mentality, Lepidus would say, is indeed bred out of your mud by the operation of your sun.
And mine? Is it not too? Then into Nilemud with it! (*P* 250)

Disgusted at his perversion, anxious about his manhood, Stephen finds the mental attitudes bred by his situation in Ireland unbearable. Though many internal and external factors combine to make his homeland intolerable and turn his thoughts to flight, the decisive event which makes him go is his discovery or invention of romance between Emma and Cranly. Freud describes "A Special Type of Choice of Object Made by Men" in which common neurotic patterns make certain conditions prerequisites to attraction. Two of these conditions are an injured third party and doubt of the fidelity of the beloved (pp. 168-169), elements already touched on.

These neurotic desires are activated when Emma bows "across Stephen in reply to Cranly's greeting" (*P* 232). The last time they crossed paths, Stephen snubbed Emma (*P* 216): "He had done well not to salute her on the steps of the library" (*P* 220). So it is understandable that she should snub Stephen in the same manner now, and she may bow to Cranly only to pique Stephen and make him jealous. He is irrationally jealous, but not exactly piqued. As he suspects "a slight flush on Cranly's cheek" that explains his "listless silence, his harsh comments," Stephen feels "a trembling joy, lambent as. . .light, played like a fairy host around him. But why?" (*P* 232-233). Stephen answers the mysterious question of why he should be so happy at being passed by with the incredible hypothesis that his joy is caused by the misquoted verse "Darkness falls from the air. . . with its black vowels and its opening sound, rich and lutelike." This typifies his compulsive granting of magic powers to words in order to obscure deep and painful psychological motivations behind formal esthetic considerations. In fact his joy manifests sexual excitement he feels when Emma spurns him for the father figure Cranly. Stephen speaks truly when he says, "I do not fear to be alone or to be spurned for another. . ." (*P* 247), for he enjoys such spurning. The sexual nature of his joy here emerges as his questioning of its cause leads to an erotic revery focussed on seventeenth-century whores and the smell of Emma's body.

Dismissing the subject in disgust, he lingers on the thought of yielding her to another: "Well then, let her go and be damned to her. She could love some clean athlete who. . .had black hair on his chest" (*P* 234). Stephen's relinquishment is also a flight from his own homosexual aspect, suggested by his image of the other man washing. The affair Stephen detects between Emma and Cranly as aggressor expresses sexual feeling Stephen has for his friend. Soon after Emma's bow, his sense of castration by Cranly is dramatized as Cranly seeks a weapon to chase Temple with:

"—Give us that stick here, Cranly said. / He snatched the ashplant roughly from Stephen's hand and sprang down the steps. . ." (*P* 237). As Stephen's ashplant must to some extent compensate for male inadequacy, the representation of his underlying fear could scarcely be more direct.

Observing Cranly's rage at Temple, "Stephen felt that his anger had another cause. . ." He seems to think Cranly is in bad temper because he feels guilty for betraying Stephen with Emma. But on the following page, when Cranly calms, "his voice was no longer angry and Stephen wondered was he thinking of her greeting to him under the porch" (*P* 238). Whether Cranly is angry or not, Stephen takes it as a sign he is preoccupied by Emma. Stephen will seize any behavior of Cranly's as pretext to confirm his feeling of betrayal. This betrayal is also intellectual: in the debate that follows, Cranly, whom Stephen has visualized all along as a priest, advocates acquiescence to the Church, Ireland and mother—forces weighing down Stephen's manhood. Not authoritarian or pernicious in any obvious way, Cranly is a good friend with practical, sensible advice. For Stephen he is thus the most insidious danger, the ultimate temptation.

Cranly asks Stephen to mouth religion to spare his mother from further suffering. Stephen denies his love for mom and cites great men who rejected their mothers: Pascal, Saint Aloysius Gonzaga and Christ (*P* 242). Jesus spurned his mother on a number of occasions, the most notable being the marriage at Cana: "Woman, what have I to do with thee?" (John ii.4; see also *Matt.* x–xii and *Luke* viii.21).[1] Stephen associates with Christ partly because his mother was a virgin, his Father, noncorporeal. He even suggests Jesus was not born of woman at all: "He is more like a son of God than a son of Mary" (*P* 243).

Casting off his parents, Stephen strives to make himself—to be, like Jesus, his own Creator. He tells Cranly that when he was religious, he was not "myself as I am now, as I had to become" (*P* 240). Insisting he has created a new being, Stephen follows religious and Jungian patterns of rebirth and transformation. He gains strength by locating God as a contained parent, a creative principle in his unconscious. But though he says, "I cannot answer for the past" (*P* 243), he is a product of it; and as he asserts to Cranly a desire to express himself in "unfettered freedom," he is in the process of expressing himself in a neurotic fantasy about Cranly and Emma based on parental adhesions. He asserts freedom because he feels trapped.

Cranly asks Stephen whether, in his freedom, he would commit robbery or deflower a virgin. Stephen argues that such aggression is no real breach of social propriety, but "in certain circumstances" a logical concomitant of the practicality of force and materialism Cranly is defending (*P* 246). Stephen aims to achieve true freedom by abstaining from all use of force.

He will not call the law on robbers and will use no arms but silence, exile and cunning. Are we to assume this version of Christ telling his flock to forgive enemies reveals a soul untainted by violence? On the contrary, Stephen's patricidal desires, his violent images of parental relations, the petty angers of his religion and his aggressive conversation show that for him love and all human connection are closely linked to aggression and violence. Aggression is rooted in the stage that underlies compulsion, but sometimes "the anal-sadistic orientation reveals itself in the form of reaction formations only, like. . .an incapacity for aggression" (*Theory*, p. 273). Because Stephen's mind is saturated with violently tending thoughts that arouse great anxiety, our artist is extremely opposed to violence.

Stephen's plans for the future really plan for a past of childhood situations. The primitive nature of his motives flashes forth as he waits for Cranly in front of Maple's hotel, imagining "the sleek lives of the patricians of Ireland" and aiming his pen at them: "How could he hit their conscience or how cast his shadow over the imaginations of their daughters, before their squires begat upon them, that they might breed a race less ignoble than their own?" (*P* 238). He seeks to reform Ireland's mothers; and so he forms an art that is not only designed as a maternal protection from the world, but is actually aimed at the mother he denies. The younger May Joyce was delighted to hear in 1916 that her brother's "novel is being published. . .You have rewritten it since we lived in St. Peter's Terrace when we used to be all put out of the room when you were reading each new chapter for Mother. I used to hide under the sofa to hear it, until you said I might stay" (*Letters, II*, 383). Thus, Joyce read substantial fiction to his mother before she died in 1903—and before the 1904 "A Portrait of the Artist" Ellmann claims to have been written in one day (*JJ* 149). Citing *Portrait* and A. L. P.'s direction of Shem's letter in the *Wake*, Kenner equates Joyce's mother with his muse (*Dublin's Joyce*, pp. 129-130); and Ellmann argues that Joyce's self-assertion was originally meant to impress his mother (*JJ* 302-309).

Stephen addresses to the mothers of Ireland a characteristic desire of the "Special Type of Choice of Object," the desire to save the mother:

> . . .in the unconscious. . .rescuing his mother takes on the significance of giving her a child. . .in the rescue-phantasy he is completely identifying himself with his father. All his instincts, those of tenderness, gratitude, lustfulness, defiance and independence, find satisfaction in the single wish *to be his own father*. (p. 173, Freud's italics)

Stephen binds saving mother to giving her a child by wanting to save both mother and child. The fourth and last characteristic of Freud's type is our artist's addiction to prostitutes, a vice for salvation fantasists.

Near the end of their dialogue Cranly suggests to Stephen the possibility of a simple, direct "real" love, neither idealized nor corrupted. This love is exemplified by the song they hear, "Rosie O'Grady." When Stephen says, "I want to see Rosie first" (*P* 245), he means, in the largest sense, that love is not simple, that it inevitably involves pains because of human psychological limits and deformities, judging by his experience in Catholic Ireland. He is psychologically incisive in regarding "real" love as an unrealistic convention, but he shows a misogynistic tendency to blame women for problems of relationship which originate largely in his own mind (see *The Exile*, pp. 51-87 and elsewhere). Stephen shows why he is not ready to find Rosie by his reaction to Cranly's talk of love, turning his thoughts not to Rosie but to Cranly:

. . .his pale face, framed by the dark, and his large dark eyes. Yes. His face was handsome: and his body was strong and hard. He had spoken of a mother's love. He felt then the sufferings of women, the weaknesses of their bodies and souls: and would shield them with a strong and resolute arm and bow his mind to them.

Away then: it is time to go. A voice spoke softly to Stephen's lonely heart, bidding him go and telling him that his friendship was coming to an end. Yes; he would go. He could not strive against another. He knew his part. (*P* 245)

Stephen sees Cranly and most men as physically strong, but mentally and spiritually weak. Cranly bows his mind to women by supporting existing social conventions, just as he asks Stephen to bow his mind to mother. Stephen's account of Cranly's amorous assets suggests he cannot strive with Cranly because such competition would bring them into too close a proximity. Stephen suggests Cranly is homosexual (P 247, see *JJ* 121) because he is attracted to Cranly and fears this attraction. The sexual competition he imagines probably has no basis in reality. He inevitably sees himself and Cranly as son and father, as he has with all of his friends. "Thrilled by his touch," Stephen says to Cranly, ". . .you made me confess to you." And Cranly replies gaily "Yes, my child" (*P* 247). "My child" refers primarily to priestly confession, but can't help also referring to father and son. Stephen must flee such paternal connections at the point when his mind makes the sense of castration unbearable, as he fled earlier ones. His interview with this normal Irish friend confirms his decisions to leave Ireland and turn from normality.

The diary entries which conclude *Portrait* restate the themes developed in the novel. Stephen continues to deny his mother to Cranly, and it may be that the reason he finds Cranly "still harping on the mother" (*P* 250) is that he is himself preoccupied with her. He still sees life and woman as made up of conflict between physical corruption and spiritual idealism and associates sex with shame: "O life! Dark stream of swirling bogwater on which appletrees have cast down their delicate flowers. Eyes of girls among the leaves. Girls demure and romping. All fair or auburn: no dark ones. They blush better. Houp-la!" (*P* 250).

He also maintains his belief that Cranly and Emma are in love and that he must extricate himself from this parental combination: "21 *March, night:* Free . . . . Let the dead bury the dead. Ay, And let the dead marry the dead" (*P* 248). In this self-conscious paraphrase of Christ (*Luke.* ix.60) and probable source for the title of Joyce's major story, the dead left behind to unite are Cranly and Emma with undertones of Stephen's parents. The oedipal fantasy defines the limits of his freedom. In fact, now that he has given Emma to Cranly in his mind, she fulfills conditions of desirability that renew her attraction: "Yes, I liked her today . . . and it seems a new feeling to me. Then, in that case, all the rest, all that I thought I thought and all that I felt I felt. . .O, give it up, old chap! Sleep it off!" (*P* 252). Though freshly drawn, Stephen cannot reconcile himself to Emma because she remains associated with anxiety. He must escape to his sublimated maternal ideal of freedom. He is eager to proclaim himself free of the past:

. . . she remembers the time of her childhood—and mine if I was ever a child. The past is consumed in the present and the present is living only because it brings forth the future. . .
. . .Michael Robartes . . . presses in his arms the loveliness which has long faded from the world. Not this. . .I desire to press in my arms the loveliness which has not yet come into the world. (*P* 251)

Stephen's desire for the future is as much an escape from present reality as Yeats's memory of forgotten beauty: ". . .as compulsion neurotics think rather than act, they also prepare constantly for the future and never experience the present" (*Theory*, p. 298). As with many *avant-gardistes*, Stephen's vaunted future is really his past. His life is a cycle in which he pursues mother images only to find when he reaches proximity to the latest moocow, from his alma mater to "the old sow," anxiety linked to a father arises to propel him in another direction. When he tries to pray in a forest, "He had lifted up his arms and spoken in ecstasy to the sombre nave of the trees, knowing that he stood on holy ground. . .And when two constabularymen had come into sight round a bend in the gloomy road he had broken off his prayer to whistle. . ." (*P* 232). He now sees Ireland as a place where his aspiration toward the maternal ideal must always be broken off by the paternal policeman. He will attempt to leave progenitors behind by flight, but he cannot escape the parents within, and the vague goals he seeks only project them in a new guise:

16 *April*: Away! Away!
The spell of arms and voices: the white arms of roads, their promise of close embraces and the black arms of tall ships that stand against the moon. . .They are held out to say: We are alone. Come. And the voices say with them: We are your kinsmen. (*P* 252)

This passage occurs in *Epiphanies* (Viking Critical *Portrait*, p. 271) and in *Stephen Hero*, where white arms also appear in a poem of Stephen's: "O, hold me still white arms, encircling arms! / And hide me, heavy hair!" (*SH* 37, 237). These bathetic lines indicate the maternal basis of the white arm image, which also was featured on Stephen's first prostitute (*P 101*).

Fenichel says whatever impulsive running away may mean in particular cases, it generally seeks "a 'helping oral mother,' a 'gratification without guilt' . . ." (*Theory*, p. 369). Moreover, escape from punishment or temptation by running away "will be chosen by persons who in childhood had occasion to apply this measure successfully," and Stephen's divergence to the rector's office inaugurated a pattern of wandering that even extended to peripatetic conversation. Stephen sets out without knowing what he moves toward because it is repressed. "The usual restlessness in wanderers is rooted in the fact that. . .the protection that they seek once more becomes a danger, because the violence of their longing is felt as a dangerous instinct" (*Theory*, p. 370). Stephen will always be a wanderer, as Joyce was. Even Joyce's writing was a compulsively renewed setting forth. He dismissed previous work for each new one: "Ulysses! Who wrote it? I've forgotten it" (*JJ* 603n.). And he changed style and approach not only from work to work, but from section to section within each book of fiction.

If the "white arms of roads" represent mother, "the black arms of tall ships may stand for father. At the end of "Proteus" in *Ulysses*, Stephen is disturbed by the sight of a "crosstrees" on a nearby ship (*U* 51), and this symbol of impending sacrifice seems to prefigure the Christly father figure Bloom. Stephen directed himself toward the secular world of his father in Chapter IV and he invokes the beneficent aspect of father as he leaves Ireland: "Old father, old artificer, stand me now and ever in good stead." He is not addressing Simon, whom he disdained a few pages earlier (*P* 250), but Daedalus, who embodies ideal qualities of fatherhood—stability, craft and contact with reality. But Stephen takes the malevolent side of father with him also, and the father as danger obtrudes heavily upon the penultimate page of the novel when he reports how John Alphonsus Mulrennan met an old man in a cabin in West Ireland. The old man embodies the provincial ignorance of Ireland, and when he reacts to news of astronomy by spitting and saying, "Ah, there must be terrible queer creatures at the latter end of the world," Stephen is impelled to grips with him: "I fear him. I fear his redrimmed horny eyes. It is with him I must struggle all through this night till day come, till he or I lie dead, gripping him by the sinewy throat till. . .Till what? Till he yield to me? No. I mean him no harm" (*P* 252). Stephen says he is engaged in a presumably mental struggle to kill his opponent, but then, appalled by the idea of victory, he denies meaning his old man any harm. Such conflict between desire and guilt rages in his mind throughout his literary life.

In the "Baxter Dawes" chapter of Lawrence's *Sons and Lovers*, Paul Morel drifts into a fight with Dawes, whose wife he has taken. As Morel is about to strangle Dawes, he "suddenly" relaxes and lets the older man win. Life and death struggle between father and son is common in modern literature (if not all literature) and is often salient early in an author's career.[2] John Synge's *Playboy of the Western World* revolves around patricide, making it an Irish archetype. In the second book of Yeats's *Wanderings of Oisin* (1889), the hero battles fiercely with an old man, and the protagonist of Yeats's *Purgatory* kills both his father and his son. And the two major heroes of Conrad's fiction, Lord Jim and Nostromo, are both murdered by obvious father surrogates, Doramin and Giorgio Viola.

Stephen will not leave problems or parents behind; he is not escaping the cycle of compulsion *Portrait* defines—merely beginning another round. His progress toward freedom conforms to the tendency of compulsion to begin with prohibition and shift toward license. Freud's "Rat Man" was devoutly religious up to his fifteenth year, then turned freethinker—but like our artist, he remained superstitious ("Notes upon a Case," p. 169). The "general tendency" of obsessive symptoms is "to give ever greater room to substitutive satisfaction at the expense of frustration" (*Anxiety*, p. 118). Stephen's increasing liberty takes place in a context defined by a primary abdication which can never be reversed.

In the ambivalent compulsive "a ceaseless struggle is being waged against the repressed, in which the repressing forces steadily lose ground . . .the ego and the superego have a specially large share in the formation of symptoms" (*Anxiety*, p. 113). If conscious, social parts of the mind shape symptoms that are substitute satisfactions, we are dealing with sublimation. But here the flower of sublimation shows its physical roots, for in obsession thoughts and words are sexualized and are used for sensual pleasure ("Notes upon a Case," p. 244). Thus, the apparent movement toward awareness and self-satisfaction is a symptom rather than a cure: "The symptom-formation scores a triumph if it succeeds in combining the prohibition with satisfaction so that what was originally a defensive command or prohibition acquires the significance of a satisfaction as well. . ." (*Anxiety*, p. 112). Stephen frees himself by substituting art for life, but he will always be circumscribed by the neurotic antiworld of artifice. "In vague sacrificial or sacramental acts alone his will seemed drawn forth to encounter reality" (*P* 159). And Joyce's need to relate to reality through the order of ritual increases as his art advances.

A more positive view of our artist's progress may be framed from the perspective of Jung, who sees rituals as mechanisms of introversion whose repetition allows the mind to focus on inner resources.[3] Jung says, "The sick man has not to learn how to get rid of his neurosis, but how to bear it" and sees neurosis as an affliction which can lead to a higher state of development.[4] The action of *Portrait* is a definite advance in terms of mythology and analytic psychology. Stephen's separating of himself from family, friends and society accords with Jung's insistence that the self must be defined through conflict: "Differentiation is the essence of consciousness" (*Two Essays*, p. 204). He speaks of the benefit of separation of the individual from the collective mind: "Individuation is a natural tendency inasmuch as its prevention by a levelling down to collective standards is injurious to the vital activity of the individual" (*CW* [Jung], 6, p. 448). This corresponds to the traditional Christian idea that the soul of man is born in sin,[5] expressed by Stephen to Davin: "The soul is born. . .first in those moments I told you of" (*P* 203). If the soul is born in self-division, its existence would seem to be equatable with neurosis, and Jung would accept Stephen's view of his alienation as vocational destiny, a spiritual enlargement.

Sprinchorn, who sees replacement of the real mother by an ideal one as the central action of *Portrait*, argues that the structure of the novel follows the five-stage initiation rites of the ancient Eleusinian Mystery religion ("Achilles," pp. 27–33). Jung defines "the aim of the concretistic primitive initiations up to and including baptism" as "severance from the 'carnal' (or animal) parents and rebirth *in novam infantiam* into a condition of immortality and spiritual childhood" (*Two Essays*, p. 233). Thus, Stephen follows mythological tradition in rejecting actual parents for spiritual ones. In *Totem and Taboo: Some Points of Agreement between the Mental Lives of Savages and Neurotics* (1913, *SE* XIII, pp. 130–160), written just after Jung differentiated himself, Freud argued that religion was based on neurosis. This argument is sound but inadequate: to explain faith as pathology cannot do justice to its universality or value. Without devotion to something higher than reality, to unreal images, no one could accomplish anything more than ordinary.

The victory that ends each chapter of *Portrait* could not occur unless

Stephen was disturbed by his present world into wandering in search of a transcendent goal. And these goals, which progress upward and outward from the rector to Europe, are increasingly unknown to him until he reaches them. Campbell calls this image "The Trackless Way."[6] The hero must leave all known bearings and boundaries behind in order to free the creative potential in his psyche. He becomes a hero by taking a chance, and this passage outside the known will be fruitful because he explores his unconscious by entering the unknown. An obvious example of this configuration is seen in William Faulkner's "The Bear" when Ike McCaslin must leave compass and gun behind and be lost in the woods before he can meet the totem-father bear and get the revelation of his life. The material elicited by such questing, however, need not be moral or progressive, as shown by Kurtz in Conrad's *Heart of Darkness* or by one of Jung's heroes of the thirties, Adolf Hitler.[7]

Joyce meant to show Stephen advancing to spiritual development by his quests: in every case, what he finds is himself. And through self-discovery he will forge in the smithy of his soul the uncreated conscience of his race (*P* 253), forge a consciousness of self or of the reality of life for the Irish and humanity,[8] by realizing his own unconscious. Joyce, however, shared with Jung the traditional belief that whatever promotes spirit denies matter and vice versa (*JJ* 460). He must therefore have realized that Stephen's spiritual victories are physical defeats. For the movement through the triumphant endings of the five chapters—from acceptance by the boys to the prostitute to religion to art to flight—seems to reflect steadily increasing distance from human society and confirmation in a self-absorbed, neurotic perception of reality.

This movement leads to contact with others only insofar as others share the same neuroses. Freud recognized this possibility when he spoke of the "path that leads back from phantasy to reality." The artist, he said, is usually unable to win "honour, power and the love of women" in the real world; so he turns to focus on fantasy. But by sharing his fantasy with others, he may ultimately be able to attain his goals in reality. Freud did not dwell on this beyond pointing it out as a striking paradox.[9] But the path into self that leads to power through creation is taken not only by artists. Freud followed it when he used self-examination to guide his theories, as all thinkers do. And everyone who acts or loves depends in some way for validation on contact with an inner nature which is not realistic, but a repository of dreams. Most people perceive this inner reality as shared culture, but the creative thinker gets back to the original uncreated source of being in himself. This path of desire turned inward is shared by Stephen, Richard Rowan, Leopold Bloom and H. C. E.

PART TWO

DISTANT MUSIC

V I

"THE DEAD"

Before following Stephen into *Ulysses*, I will prepare for reading the later book as Joyce prepared for writing it—through "The Dead" and *Exiles*. These fall between *Portrait* and *Ulysses* in conception, for "The Dead" of 1907 was written after the autobiographical novel was well under way, while *Exiles*, written from 1914 to 1915, was started before Joyce finished *Portrait* and completed after he began *Ulysses* (*JJ* 391–401). These works turn from the youthful concerns of the earlier novel and the dissections of *Dubliners* to the marriage situation and living relationships of the later work, treating problems pertaining to life with Nora Barnacle to focus on forces which threaten an established connection between the sexes. They divide the border on which a person becomes capable of love, which, for Joyce's type, means capable of asking for help. It is striking and touching that while both were written after Joyce and Nora eloped, the first sees marriage as hopeless, while the second shows how Joyce found, around 1909, that marriage could work for him despite the inevitability of the male threat.

The obsessive jealousy Stephen directed at Cranly and the clergy as fellow conspirators extends through these works into *Ulysses*, growing increasingly symbolic of the human condition. In making his compulsion a symbol of human dispossession, Joyce transmuted neurosis into the source and substance of communion. He did so through a series of systems of shared belief—art, literature, love and knowledge—that allowed him to make shared neurosis a basis for understanding.

"The Dead" is Joyce's most ironic, distant study of jealousy, for Gabriel Conroy is a negative example. Though the story of Michael Furey dying for Gretta Conroy is based on that of Sonny Bodkin, who is supposed to have died for Nora, Gabriel is not Joyce, but Joyce arrested by stagnation. Gabriel undergoes an epiphany which reveals his spiritual death to him; but unlike Joyce's later cuckold figures, Richard Rowan of *Exiles* and Bloom, Gabriel does not seem able to regenerate himself as a result of perceiving his deficiency. One reason for this is that Joyce was more ruthless in criticizing mental defects in his earlier works than in his later ones, which move toward an acceptance of human imperfection. A major cause of the shift from the stern "hyperborean" Joyce of *Stephen Hero* and *Dubliners* to the gentle one of *Ulysses* and *Finnegans Wake* was probably Joyce's union, from 1904, with Nora. Love of her gave Joyce the ability to forgive not only because it released his tender feelings, but also because it demonstrated to him progressively that human relations and people were not perfectable. Over the years, his stormy nonmarriage and the infidelities he perpetrated and suspected Nora of (*JJ* 221ff., 288ff., 353ff., 462ff.) made him tolerant. For he came to realize that he was not free from the social and mental diseases which made up the paralysis he had set out to expose in the "nicely polished looking glass" of *Dubliners*.

"The Dead," however, was written only a few years after Joyce's elopement and before most of the major incidents of turmoil and infidelity. Although Joyce could not help finding jealous alienation in marriage, he may not, at this point, have been convinced of its inevitability. So he could distance himself from Gabriel's spiritual cuckoldry and portray it as pathology. "The Dead" is a Gothic story of walking corpses, and its few images of regeneration, such as the cross and thorns in a graveyard on the last page, are ironic and hardly more hopeful than the rebirth of Dracula. Nor is the setting of the story after New Year's much more positive than the holiday of "Ivy Day in the Committee Room." Ivy on the anniversary of Parnell's death should imply rebirth, but Joyce's "Ivy" is a poison plant and "The Dead" is not far from it.

The outstanding quality of the guests at the annual party of the Morkan sisters is their absence. Gabriel, whose head is grooved by the custom of wearing a hat, presides over this affair at which the food has more life than the people. He is free from strain only when speaking the polite language of Dublin hospitality, largely a matter of self-abasement: "kindly forget my existence, ladies and gentlemen, for a few minutes" (*D* 198). A room full of people denying themselves to promote union is an empty room supporting an illusion. When Gabriel makes a polite remark to Lily about his pet illusion, marriage, she shocks him with a harsh view of relations between the sexes. Social discourse depends on reaction, and Gabriel is a reactor: "the girl's bitter. . .retort. . .cast a gloom over him which he tried to dispel by arranging his cuffs and the bows of his tie" (*D* 179). The gloom leads him to a depressed realization of his "ridiculous" role, for playing with his trimmings will not help; when he does not give himself to others, he drifts toward morbidity.

His aunts and wife now rescue him from gloom to sociability, and the old ladies soon have his "happy eyes" wandering over Gretta's form. He seems more at ease with her in their presence than alone. He is addicted to the Irish hospitality he praises in his speech. Joyce blamed the Irish for their close, cheerful social lives because he felt the grace of their sharing was achieved at the expense of individual identity, "that extinction of personality which is death in life" (*E* 123). Gabriel's remaining vestiges of individuality, such as his dreaming of escape into the clean emptiness outside, have no substance. As dreams never to be realized, they merely reinforce his alienation from himself.

After Aunt Julia, who is visibly dying, finishes singing "Arrayed for the Bridal" (more fertility imagery), "loud applause" is "borne in from the invisible supper-table" (*D* 193); after Gabriel finishes his "ludicrous" speech, the acclamation is "taken up beyond the door of the supper room by many of the other guests" (*D* 205). The effect is that of Eliot's "footsteps shuffled on the stair": sound emanating from unseen beings beyond the door suggests the proximity of those who have passed away. Gabriel realizes at the end of the story that the spirits of the dead have been present at the party when he becomes aware that he lives in a world of ghosts: ". . .he saw the form of a young man standing under a dripping tree. Other forms were near. His soul had approached that region where dwell the vast hosts of the dead" (*D* 223).

It is this emanation from the beyond that Gretta is listening to when Gabriel sees her on the staircase in a key scene: "There was grace and mystery in her attitude as if she were a symbol of something. He asked himself what is a woman standing on the stairs in the shadow, listening to distant music, a symbol of" (*D* 210). He thinks he would paint the scene if he were a painter—but he is not. The tableau signifies alienation, for Gretta, listening to Bartell D'Arcy's singing and remembering the dead past, is entranced by another world which draws her from the husband so entranced by her. Soon after being esthetically attracted to "Distant Music," Gabriel is sexually stimulated, for the first time in the story, by the excitement this music has generated in her: "At last she turned towards them and Gabriel saw that there was colour on her cheeks and that her eyes were shining. A sudden tide of joy went leaping out of his heart" (*D* 212). But what attracts Gabriel, his wife or the source of her appeal? It may be that both Gretta and Gabriel are ultimately in love not with each other, but with distant music.

The pattern of Gabriel attracted to Gretta as she is intent upon another recurs through the story: "She was walking before him with Mr Bartell

D'Arcy. . .The blood went bounding along his veins" (*D* 213). He remembers a moment when he felt great affection for her as he watched her watching a man making bottles in a furnace (*D* 213). "Trembling with desire" he follows her following an old man with a candle up the stairs of the hotel. Confronted by his wife alone, Gabriel is embarrassed, overcome by feeling, "fearing that diffidence was about to conquer him." He maintains the absurd social discourse of the party, speaking of the virtues of Freddy Malins even while the subject disgusts him (*D* 217). He waits for her to take the initiative, and then when she does show feeling, he is soon shocked to find her mind is not on him. He is unable to act effectively with her, just as he was ill at ease with Lily and Miss Ivors. He cannot give or take feeling with her directly, but he is readily stimulated by watching her interest in other men. By the end of the story he realizes his entire marriage has reposed on love for a woman who loved another.

Gabriel's inhibition and perversion are parallel to the conformity and fear of assertion of the Morkan gathering. As he is unable to relate to his wife directly, so he is unable to face life directly, but must subject himself to the wishes of others, muffling himself in the defenses of propriety, the standing jokes of a blighted world. Psychologically, his need to be a good boy is an oppressive superego; and since superego is an introjection of the voices of parents who forbade wrongdoing, a person afflicted by superego is a thrall to the ghosts of his parents. Edward Brandabur finds Gabriel unable to unite with Gretta because he acts out his mother's prohibition: "Her 'sullen opposition' to his marriage becomes his own. He must live according to the wishes of the living dead" (*Scrupulous Meanness*, pp. 115-126). There is truth to this, but dealing as it does with conscious material from the recent past, it is too superficial to fully explain Gabriel's impotence.

In fact, Gabriel's need for a third person indicates a complex similar to the one I traced in Stephen, in which another man is required as father. The crucial difference is that unlike Stephen, Richard Rowan, Bloom and other Joycean heroes confronted by the inevitable competitor, Gabriel is defeated. Stephen leaves Cranly and Emma to "marry the dead"; Richard forces Robert Hand to realize that Robert is lifeless, and Bloom maintains his marriage in his mind and Molly's. But Gabriel feels that Michael Furey is the only love Gretta has known and that this fact can't be changed: "So she had had that romance in her life: a man had died for her sake. It hardly pained him now to think how poor a part he, her husband, had played in her life" (*D* 222).

The fact that the case is sealed by time suggests that the competitor who comes from the past and the dead is paternal. Joyce summed up his father as "an Irish suicide" (*Viking Critical Portrait*, p. 297), and the one statement of Michael Furey's to be given (though it is given twice) is "he did not want to live" (D 221). In *Exiles*, as I'll show, Joyce laughs at the sentimental tendency to associate romance with suicide. And in the *Exiles* notes Joyce describes Nora's relationship to Sonny Bodkin, the original of Bertha's to Robert Hand and of Gretta's to Michael: "She weeps over. . .him whom her love has killed, the dark boy whom, as the earth, she embraces in death and disintegration. . .His symbols are music and the sea, liquid formless earth, in which are buried the drowned soul and body. . .weeps remembering the loves she could not return" (E 118). Michael's symbols, distant music and snow, correspond to "music and the sea," and he also stands for "death and disintegration" and love that could not be returned. Gretta could not have stayed fixed on Furey for so long if she had a living marriage: the boy is her equivalent of Gabriel's escapism.

And Gabriel's reaction to Gretta's unhealthy love is itself questionable: "Generous tears filled Gabriel's eyes. He had never felt like that himself towards any woman but he knew that such a feeling must be love" (D 223). In accepting suicide as an ideal Gabriel excludes himself from the possibility of love and continues to reflect the morbid values of a sick society. His final failure to communicate with his wife, "shy of intruding on her grief," is a continuation of the deadness of their marriage, and the abnegation of his "generous tears" is as ridiculous as Gabriel realizes his whole marriage has been.

At the end Gabriel realizes he is a dead member of a dead society, but has no alternative. When he says to himself, "Better pass boldly into that other world, in the full glory of some passion, than fade and wither dismally with age" (D 223), the course he floridly prefers is neither valid for Joyce nor possible for him. The end of "The Dead" is filled with references to earlier lines in the story, and this line harks back to one of Mr. Browne's memories of opera at the dinner: "how one night an Italian tenor had sung five encores to *Let Me Like a Soldier Fall*, introducing a high C every time. . ." (D 199). *Maritana* (1845), the source of this aria, is also referred to in "A Mother" (D 142), and Joyce is probably aware, as he has Gabriel echo the sentiment of "Let Me Like a Soldier Fall," that the song expresses a wish to die by firing squad (military death) rather than hanging (criminal death).[1] This context underlines the absurdity of Gabriel's false desire to pass away "boldly."

At the end of the story when Gabriel has a vision of snow descending on the lifeless world of Ireland like "their last end," it does not seem he will derive any more real benefit from this *memento mori* than the monks at Mount Melleray, who sleep in coffins to remember "their last end" (D 201). The vast image of death descending from the sky completes a series of scenes Gabriel has envisioned with longing through the story and evokes the fatalistic inevitability of power from heaven. The beauty of the ending need not indicate hope, for "A Painful Case" ends on a similar lyrical note of recognition. Gabriel is closer to Duffy than to Bloom. Not only does he lack Bloom's humor and flexibility, but he has no basis on which to rationalize himself to victory.

Such a basis could only be found by connecting his mind to another on a deep level, but Gabriel regards the independent existence of his wife as a threat. Her buried life must be controlled or propitiated; galoshes must be put on her free nature. And Gabriel wants his experience contained by social norms. Like Duffy, he is compelled to control the disorder of life, which includes the irrational aspect of oneself and others. Both intellectuals have the compulsive stiffness of the provincial or member of a minority group who is anxious to be civilized and so follows a system rigidly. And like all the *Dubliners*, both inhabit a naturalistic world where people use each other, where your advantage is gained at the expense of the other, where attention is something that must be paid.

Gabriel wants to be on the well-worn bicycle paths of the Continent, where he plans to spend his vacation brushing up his culture, but he may be moving in another direction: "The time had come for him to set out on his journey westward." There is a faint hint of possible regeneration, but it is heavily subordinated to the idea of death, which is the primary meaning of the Westward journey. Gabriel differs from Duffy in the physical fact of the life of his woman. Insofar as he is devastated by the irruption of the disorder underlying his world, he is brought into contact with Gretta's buried life. To go West is to go into the unknown, and Gabriel may ultimately regain life through the knowledge he is shocked into. But the striking point is that any knowledge of life which could come to Gabriel could come only in the visage of the grave because it would have to be seen from the other side.

The profound realization of death inevitably smuggles in a hint of rebirth, if only as a psychological need, as absence implies presence and bitterness, carried too far, goes through absurdity to humor. The mordant edge of the cold steel pen with which Joyce wrote *Dubliners* is the source of the rich profusion of life-affirming humor in the later works, as the absence of love *Dubliners* revolves around calls forth the presence of life-giving in its followers. Yet Joyce's humor, the source of Beckett's, always maintains the dark tinge which comes of looking at life as an outsider.

Cixous recognizes that Joyce's men are always alienated from the world and from woman by a third person or authority who intervenes (*Exile*, pp. 502-535). She says this prior someone may be either a former lover or God, but the Freudian identification of his basis in father is more explanatory. Cixous says Joyce reached his characteristic stance by a double movement: he first realized he was alienated, then accepted this alienation and made it a basis for relating indirectly (*Exile*, p. 413). The double movement she describes is divided between the subjects of this chapter. "The Dead" discovers the exile Cixous speaks of and curses it; *Exiles* accepts and affirms it. If "The Dead" is the most ironic of Joyce's substantial portayals of conjugation, *Exiles* is the most heroic, the opposite extreme within the confines of the inevitable state of cuckoldry imposed by his neurosis.

In the first years of their union Joyce and Nora considered separating (*JJ* 222), and the process that shifted Joyce's vision of love from the hopelessness of "The Dead" to the affirmation of the *Exiles* notes of 1913 seems to be imprinted on the famous letters Joyce sent to Nora on his visit to Ireland in 1909. Whether or not he left her (as I suspect) in order to write to her, it may well be that only after he had been horrified by the apparition of her infidelity and had poured out his worst doubts and lowest desires did he realize how completely he was bound to her. The 1909 visit was the genesis of *Exiles*, and the play is a symbolic representation of the forces struggling in Joyce's mind as he tested his new love against his established stance of skepticism.

VII

EXILES

LIVING WOUNDING DOUBT

> He toyed also with a theory of dualism which would
> symbolize the twin eternities of spirit and nature in the
> twin eternities of male and female. . . (*SH* 210)

> Each of the play's protagonists is. . .archetypal. . .
> Richard is spirit, Bertha fecundity, Beatrice intellect, and
> Robert body, for instance. (D. J. F. Aitken)[1]

JOYCE'S SCHEMATIC STRUCTURE

The *Exiles* produced by Harold Pinter in London in 1975 and other successful productions of recent years have confirmed what Joyce maintained
in the face of general opposition: that his play is a masterpiece. It is also
a key work because it is his first to explore the possibility that people can
give life to each other, which remains a major theme in both his subsequent novels. *Exiles* develops the idea of the living value of exile or connection through separation. The fifth chapter of *Portrait* suggests this
idea, but Joyce does not portray people who relate to each other successfully until *Exiles*, which establishes a model of interaction for all of his
portrayals of love and union.

The affirmation embodied by the play, however, is limited by ambivalence and circumscribed by an extremely orderly system of symbolism
which prefigures the structural diagram for *Ulysses*. In a section on "Compulsive Systems," Fenichel says, "Everything that is done in a compulsive
way is done . . . according to a prearranged plan, from which the objection-

able impulses are supposed to be excluded" (*Theory*, p. 285). Such systems operate defensively to allow expression of emotion which would
otherwise cause too much anxiety. Richard's love for Bertha can be
affirmed because it is subject to a ritualized system of conditions. But
insofar as Joyce believed in his system, it is more than a defense: it is
an alternate reality, a personal myth. If it is shared, such a myth can
benefit two lovers even if it is neurotic. In fact, Joyce's system comprises
universal truths about love, being no more neurotic than either most
modern treatments of love or the courtly tradition. Therefore, it merits
close attention on its own terms, which will be seen to resemble those of
Jung. This chapter, then, will recreate the consciously deliberated system
by which Joyce defines love in *Exiles*. To clarify this definition, I will refer
to a favorite of Joyce and Stephen who anticipated analytic insights in the
eighteenth·century, William Blake.

Exiles conjugates the complicated conjunction between its four main
characters, each of whom shows both love and hate for each of the others.
Two schematic patterns seem essential, and each of these schemes divides
the characters into two heterosexual couples sharing accentuated qualities.
In an effort to describe Joyce's intentions, I will refer to one of these plans
as the moral scheme of relations and the other as the natural scheme.

The moral scheme opposes Richard and Bertha to Robert and Beatrice.
Richard and Bertha are coupled because they have lived together for nine
years and have a child, Archie; while Robert and Beatrice are linked because they are cousins, they have stayed in Ireland, they were once be-
trothed (*E* 21) and they live in the same house (*E* 94). The main reason
for the moral division, however, is that Richard and Bertha, unlike Gabriel
and Gretta, have fulfilled necessary conditions for freedom and love by
rejecting the bonds of their society: they have avoided marriage and left
Ireland, as Joyce did. Moral ascendancy is defined in *Exiles* by freedom,
which results in creativity, which, in turn, is manifested substantially by
creations; Richard and Bertha, the exiles, are creative because free, although Bertha is free mainly through her connection with Richard. Her
natural tendency is to be conventional, to belong to society as Robert
does. Joyce's morality is opposed to conventional values here: he says of
the most upright character in the play, "Beatrice's mind is an abandoned
cold temple. . ." (*E* 119). He delivered his lecture on Blake (1912, *CW*
[Joyce], 214–222) the year before he wrote his notes for *Exiles*, and he
seems to associate freedom with creativity and restraint with nonexistence
and death in this play as Blake generally did.

Richard is the play's prophet of freedom. Before yielding Bertha to
Robert, he expresses his belief that restraint destroys the possibility of life.
Envisioning the lifeless body of Bertha, he says, ". . . I will reproach myself

then. . .because I accepted from her her loyalty and made her life poorer in love. That is my fear. That I stand between her and any moments of life that should be hers. . ." (*E* 69). Richard is associated with Christ because he attempts to bring about rebirth for himself and Bertha in Jungian terms by following the difficult path of freedom and rejecting the comforts of established order and propriety. Thus, he says, ". . . I tried to give her a new life" (*E* 67); and with regard to himself, he expresses desire "to be forever a shameful creature and to build up my soul again out of the ruins of its shame" (*E* 70). One such rejuvenation took place when Richard and Bertha first went into exile and another takes place in the course of the play. Joyce himself speaks of Richard as "the rearisen Lord" in his notes (*E* 118), but Richard is also freely associated with Satan (*E* 51, 74, 90, 98, 103). Bertha, who says "My God" to him several times (*E* 53, 75), also calls him a devil twice (*E* 51). Satan, as he has come down to us from Milton by way of Blake's antinomianism, is a symbol of freedom and of exile, and it seems that conventional distinctions between heaven and hell do not apply here. Real value lies in the creative potential of the unknown or unconscious, outside the bounds of established moral categories.

Ostensibly the two free characters, Richard and Bertha, are creative, and therefore wealthy, each according to his nature: Richard is wealthy spiritually, Bertha, physically. They are rich in his vision, in her love, and in their possession of each other. The substantial signs of their wealth are his book and her child. In the course of the drama, however, we discover that Richard is attracted to Beatrice and wrote his book for her (*E* 19), and that Bertha is having an affair with Robert. We come to see that Richard and Bertha are separated, exiles from each other. They are separated physically, for Bertha eventually tells Beatrice that Richard "passes the greater part of the night" in his study writing and that "he sleeps there too, on a sofa" (*E* 96). The implication is that Richard spends his nights with his muse, who may be linked to Beatrice. The free pair are also separated mentally, for Bertha says, ". . . I do not understand anything that he writes. . . I cannot help him in any way. . . I don't even understand half of what he says to me sometimes! You [Beatrice] could and you can" (*E* 98).

Moreover, the play suggests that just as Richard's book belongs to Beatrice, so Robert may make some claim on Bertha's son, Archie. Robert's usurpation of Archie completes the symmetry of a criss-cross pattern of dispossession suggested by the similar pattern of adultery in *Exiles*. There are faint hints in the play that Robert may actually be the eight-year-old's father, hints which prefigure Bloom's doubts about his paternity in *Ulysses*. In act one Robert says to Bertha, ". . .nine years ago. We were Bertha—and

Robert—then. Can we not be so now too?" (*E* 33). Richard suspects that Bertha has visited in the past the unsavory cottage which the two men shared at Ranelagh. When Bertha asks where this cottage is, Richard replies, "Do you not know?" (*E* 50); and when she arrives there, he greets her with, "Welcome back to old Ireland!" (*E* 72). There are many undertones of suspicion about Robert's possible earlier intimacy with Bertha in the play.

In the last act, for reasons which we will examine below, Robert is forced to admit to Richard his defeat:

ROBERT: I failed. She is yours as she was nine years ago, when you met her first.
RICHARD: When we met her first, you mean.
ROBERT: Yes. *He looks down for some moments.* (*E* 107)

Actually, Joyce carefully avoids letting us know whether Robert succeeds with Bertha at Ranelagh in the interval between the second and third acts. He also leaves ambiguous the hints he presents about the past. In the same admission Robert declares that Archie is Richard's son, doing so in an odd manner:

ROBERT: Perhaps, there, Richard, is the freedom we seek. . .In him [Archie] and not in us. Perhaps . . .
RICHARD: Perhaps . . .?
ROBERT: I said "perhaps." I would say almost surely if . . .
RICHARD: If what?
ROBERT, *with a faint smile*: If he were mine. (*E* 109–110)

In this scene also Robert goes off with Archie, who asks him to tell a fairy story. "Why not?" Robert replies, "I am your fairy godfather" (*E* 110). Archie, in fact shows a strong attachment to Robert. In the first act the boy runs "all the avenue" to greet him (*E* 27), and Joyce notes, "Problem: Archie, Richard's son, is brought up on Robert's principles" (*E* 117).

Though evidence for Robert's paternity is weak, it could be argued that even if he is not Archie's father, Robert could appropriate the boy by seducing Bertha. Certainly, the boy is closer to his mother than to Richard. She accuses Richard of "forgetting all about" his son in the first act (*E* 52), and we see him forget to ask Bertha to approve Archie's jaunt with the milkman (*E* 46, 56). Bertha also says of Archie to Richard, "I taught him to love you" (*E* 52). Archie is so attached to his mother that Robert, whether we take his insubstantial paternity seriously or not, would presumably possess the boy if he possessed Bertha. Thus, he threatens to despoil Richard of his share in Archie just as Beatrice has usurped Bertha's motherhood of Richard's book.

The moral scheme of the play, then, divides the characters into free and conventional pairs and defines a symmetrical pattern of adultery and dispossession. Joyce evaluates the two pairs in his notes: "It will be difficult to recommend Beatrice to the interest of the audience, every man of which is Robert and would like to be Richard—in any case Bertha's" (*E* 114). It seems that Joyce associates his audience with Robert because they, who are conventional, are absorbing his art, the product of his freedom. Thus, this passage reflects the relative positions of his characters in the moral scheme: Richard and Bertha are rich givers, while Robert and Beatrice, who are poor, are takers.

A passage of *The Marriage of Heaven and Hell* by William Blake coincides remarkably with the moral scheme of *Exiles*. There is no evidence Joyce had this passage in mind when he wrote the play, but he was familiar with the *Marriage*, which he quotes in the 1912 Blake lecture (*CW* [Joyce], 215, 222) and in *Ulysses* (24, 26, 185, 583). Blake describes the conflict between the creative and conventional factions of society in punctuation even more original than Joyce's:

The Giants who formed this world into its sensual existence and now seem to live in it in chains, are in truth. the causes of its life & the sources of all activity, but the chains are, the cunning of weak and tame minds. which. . .resist energy, according to the proverb, the weak in courage is strong in cunning.

Thus one portion of being, is the Prolific. the other, the Devouring: to the devourer it seems as if the producer was in his chains, but it is not so, he only takes portions of existence and fancies that the whole.

But the Prolific would cease to be Prolific unless the Devourer as a sea recieved the excess of his delights.

Some will say, Is not God alone the Prolific? I answer, God only Acts & Is, in existing beings or Men.

These two classes of men are always upon earth, & they should be enemies; whoever tries to reconcile them seeks to destroy existence.[2]

Blake's terms "prolific" and "devouring" give us a clue to the meanings of the characters' names in *Exiles*. Joyce created a special set of four names for this play which do not recur elsewhere, names significant in relation to each other and to the moral scheme. The notes speak of Bertha as "The earth, dark, formless" (*E* 118), and her name suggests not only *earth* but birth, the agency of her wealth. Richard's name suggests not only wealth but power, being derived from OE *ric*—rich, mighty, powerful, strong. As D. J. F. Aitken has indicated, Richard stands in relation to Bertha as a shaping spirit of imagination which inspires and controls her "formless earth" ("Archetypes," p. 44). Thus, Robert says to Richard, "You have made her all that she is" (*E* 67). The parasitic dependence of the devourers upon the prolific pair may be seen by their names having meaning only in relation to Richard and Bertha: Robert is the one who *robs Bert*ha, while Beatrice *eats Rich*ard. Robert is referred to as a thief or robber eight times in the play (*E* 47, 51, 69, 70, 73), and Beatrice's role as a parasite is clear. Bertha says, "You have given that woman very much, Dick," meaning his spiritual devotion, "But I believe you will get very little from her in return" (*E* 55). Blake's passage, then, represents the essential conflict of the play in terms which are relentlessly dialectic. But unlike the Freudian dialectic praised earlier, this one is framed in terms sympathetic to the forces which oppose control, terms we will see echoed in Jung.

The moral arrangement of the characters suggests the relationship of the prolific characters to their devourers, the natural scheme. The moral scheme was a desirable arrangement, but the natural one, based on the natures or appetites of the characters, motivates them to illicit loves which link the prolific to the devouring and represent the fallen state of nature. In the natural scheme, which is largely defined by the play's imagery, the two groups are the spiritual or mental characters, Richard and Beatrice, and the physical ones, Robert and Bertha. The former are mentally and spiritually active, but passive in their physical aspects, while Robert and Bertha are physically strong, but weak in soul and mind.

If the four were arranged on a scale going from the physical below upward to the spiritual (a scale Joyce never forgets), the two groups would be connected by the union of Richard and Bertha. Beatrice and Robert, at either extreme, can scarcely live except by being parasitically attached to the others. Beatrice is so purely spiritual that she is virtually a ghost, as we see in the play's opening scene between her and Richard. Although she has inspired him and his work all during the long period of his exile, he has not been able to unite with her, and this is not only because of her coldness:

RICHARD: Yet that separated me from you. . .Your names were always spoken together, Robert and Beatrice, as long as I can remember. It seemed to me, to everyone. . .
BEATRICE: We are first cousins. It is not strange that we were often together.
RICHARD: He told me of your secret engagement with him . . . . you gave him your garter. Is it allowed to mention that? (*E* 20–21)

Despite what Beatrice says, it is a bit strange for first cousins to be secretly engaged. Strange also to find Beatrice engaged to Robert, who, at the other end of the soul-body scale from her, is entirely and grossly physical. In a manuscript Richard tells Robert he is only concerned with "your body and that function of it which I suppose you call your soul." [3] Among all of the combinations possible to the characters of the play including homosexual ones, Robert and Beatrice are the only couple who manifest no attraction whatever for each other. Their engagement, as Richard describes it, is weird also in form. The incongruities of this passage disappear, however, if we see it for what it is—a description of the land Joyce left behind him in terms of an unnatural, mysterious and impossible union between spiritual sterility and physical perversion, a monstrosity of dissociated sensibility. Nine years after I published this view in *James Joyce Quarterly* (6, i, 35), Ellmann revealed in *The Consciousness* (p. 83) that Joyce was influenced from about 1910 by Bakunin's criticism of modern society for its polarization of idealism and materialism.

Beatrice goes on to say that after Richard left, her interest in Robert evaporated, she grew ill, and the situation brought her "near to death." She is still (after nine years) "convalescent" (*E* 22). Although Richard tries to speak to Beatrice of his love for her and to draw out her feelings, and though he has given her and she has taken his spiritual devotion for almost a decade, the two are like negatively charged particles trying to meet in this scene because he is unable to overcome her physical withdrawal. Nevertheless, their spiritual union is a serious breach of faith on Richard's part, for the spirit is his dominant aspect.

Richard's spirituality is manifested in his reserve, his thoughtfulness and his intense preoccupation with integrity and other abstract concepts. Richard is physically weak and unselfish while strong and selfish in spiritual things. On the physical level, he not only gives his mate to Robert, but shows ascetic tendencies by watching through the night in his study. Joyce specifies that Richard is physically weaker and spiritually stronger than Robert:

ROBERT: . . . You, Richard! You are the incarnation of strength.
RICHARD: *holds out his hands*: Feel those hands.
ROBERT, *taking his hands*: Yes. Mine are stronger. But I meant strength of another kind. (*E* 63)

Richard tends to dominate the minds of the physical characters by the strength of his spirit. He does not, however, dominate Beatrice, who, by virtue of her almost complete separation from physical life, is even more spiritual than he is. Beatrice has most of the surface features of spirituality associated with Richard, but she lacks spiritual insight or vitality.

The natural scheme of *Exiles* appears in the play's imagery. Robert and

Bertha, being physical, are associated with a greater number of material images than Richard and Beatrice. Three things linked to the physical characters are water, sinking and stones. These images represent physical life (water) and materialism and the tendency of physical life to move downward into inanimate matter (stone). Joyce introduces all three images together and suggests the importance of the neoplatonic height imagery early in the play when Archie asks Robert if he can swim:

ROBERT: Splendidly. Like a stone.
ARCHIE, *laughs:* Like a stone! *Pointing down.* Down that way?
ROBERT, *pointing:* Yes, down; straight down. How do you say that over in Italy?
ARCHIE: That? *Giù. Pointing down and up.* That is *giù* and that is *sù. (E* 27–28)

Bertha is drawn to water. She enters the play returning from the beach after a swim with Archie. When she arrives at the cottage in the second act she wears *neither umbrella nor waterproof (E* 72) although it is raining and Richard came earlier with an umbrella. Robert, who owns the cottage at Ranelagh ("rainlake"), also exposes himself to the rain in this scene, although he does so only after hesitation and protected by his coat. After his first exit, he immediately returns and exclaims, "An umbrella." Then he goes out again *(E* 72). The absence of stage direction and Bertha's later concern because he is "drenched" *(E* 78) suggest that he does not take the umbrella. This omission may be an affectation, a ruse to impress Bertha with his soggy misery. But this does not mean that it isn't natural to him: both hydrophilia and falseness are natural to him.

References to water, stones and height abound in the first interview between Robert and Richard *(E* 37–44). Robert, as materialist devourer, seats himself in his "place of honour" in Richard's home, takes one of Richard's cigars, and is served several drinks. Richard himself does not drink and is represented as a hydrophobe. In an earlier version of this scene included in the notes, Joyce actually has Richard say, "Will you add the water yourself?" *(E* 117).

Robert expresses his attitude toward love here, and it is a low one, grossly physical and touching at one point on coprophilia *(E* 41–42). His "cloacal obsession," which prefigures Bloom's, is regarded by Joyce as an attraction toward the movement of life downward into dead matter. Robert also expresses his affection and admiration for a stone in this scene, even kissing it. Richard says of the stone, "Bertha brought it home . . .She too, says it is beautiful" *(E* 42). Robert illustrates the height imagery when he says, "You have fallen from a higher world, Richard, and you are filled with fierce indignation, when you find that life is cowardly and ignoble. . . I have come up from a lower world and I am filled with astonishment when I find that people have any redeeming virtue at all" (E 43–44). These characterizations not only describe Richard's tendency to rise and Robert's to fall, but they appropriately present Richard as filled with fire, Robert with stone. Robert describes two types of statues in an epigram in this scene. Although Richard does not share Robert's interest in statues, he prefers to associate himself with the one that says, "In my time the dunghill was so high" (E 43). This ironic metaphor for the artist's role of recording truth suggests ascent. Robert, by elimination, is evidently associated with the statue that says, "How shall I get down?"

The movement upward into spirit and the movement downward into matter or earth are also represented in the following passage from the notes. Shelley here corresponds to Richard, Bodkin to Robert:

> Moon: Shelley's grave in Rome. He is rising from it. . . He has fought in vain for an ideal and died killed by the world. Yet he rises. Graveyard in Rahoon. . .where Bodkin's grave is. He lies in the grave. . .He is dark, unrisen, killed by love and life, young. The earth holds him. (E 117–118)

The image of Richard's rebirth here seems to be serious.

Shelley is moonlit in this note, while Bodkin is dark. Light is one of the main images associated with Richard, while Robert is associated with darkness. In a passage Aitken cites, Robert, addressing Richard appropriately, says "Good Lord, how warm it is today! The heat pains me here in the eye. The glare." Richard replies that he thinks "the room is rather dark. . ." (E 37). Like Robert, Bertha is associated with darkness. She enters with a hat and sunshade (E 28), which she does not put down until Beatrice leaves (E 31). We see Bertha join Robert in the darkness of the cottage at Ranelagh in act two. When a lamp flickers in this act she asks Robert twice to turn it down (E 83, 88). By the end of the act the room is "quite dark" (E 88).

Beatrice is associated with light mainly through the Dantean reference of her name. She shares with Richard a weakness relating to light imagery: they both wear eyeglasses. This indicates a general sensual weakness in them and places them behind panes of glass, suggesting their souls are cloistered. The most highly developed sense in Richard and Beatrice is hearing, one of the least substantial ones. Early in the play Robert says that he knows "what is in Beatty's ears" and that it is "the buzz of the harmonium in her father's parlour," spiritual and conventional. Beatrice, a music teacher, replies she can hear it (E 30). Richard, referring to his mother in the first act, says to Beatrice, "Can you not hear her mocking me. . ." (E 24). In the last act he describes how he has walked the strand listening to the voices of those who say they love him (*E* 109). When Richard says to Bertha in this act, "It is useless to ask you to listen to me," Bertha says of Beatrice, "She is the person for listening" (*E* 103).

Robert and Bertha, on the other hand, while generally sensual in nature, are especially notable for visual sensuality. In act one Robert tells Bertha that she looked like the moon to him the night before and Bertha tells him how he appeared to her when she first returned to Ireland (*E* 31, 33). Their relationship is depicted in visual images throughout the play. The notes ascribe to Bertha a "persistent and delicate sensuality (visual. . . gustatious. . .tactual. . .)" (*E* 122). With the word delicate removed, this description would fit Robert.

It may seem incongruous that the spiritual figures, who are associated with light, are weak in vision. Apparently, the spiritual characters are creators, possessors and givers of light, but they do not take it in. We have seen that they tend to be ascetic, while the physical characters have strong appetites, and in the case of the men the prolific-devouring polarity coincides with this tendency. In the first act Richard twice lights the cigar he has given Robert (*E* 44). Joyce recognizes the paradox implied here in his notes: "It is an irony of the play that while Robert not Richard is the apostle of beauty, beauty in its visible and invisible being is present under Richard's roof" (*E* 115). Richard explains the means of his possession to Archie: "While you have a thing it can be taken from you. . . But when you give it, you have given it. No robber can take it from you. *He bends his head and presses his son's hand against his cheek.* It is yours then for ever when you have given it. It will be yours always" (*E* 46–47). Here is Richard's basic strategy, which is clearly based on spiritual and Christian principles rather than on empirical ones. Richard holds Archie while he says this as if the boy were one of the things to be won or lost in the game of give and take.

Robert and Bertha show similar responses to Richard's ideas of honesty and freedom in the first two acts: natural reactions of anger, fear and suspicion. They try to use Richard's generosity against him. At one point Robert is, or affects to be, so disturbed at Richard's painful, self-probing honesty that he puts his hand over Richard's mouth to shut him up (*E* 70). Then, when he has managed to assimilate the "ignoble desires" that Richard is revealing into his own inflated image of Richard and when, moreover, he realizes that Richard's proposition may lead to his own possession of Bertha, he manages to grow eloquent on the subjects of honesty and freedom himself:

ROBERT, *with growing excitement:* A battle of both our souls, different as they are, against all that is false in them and in the world. A battle of your soul against the spectre of fidelity, of mine against the spectre of friendship. All life is a conquest, the victory of human passion over the commandments of cowardice. Will you, Richard? Have you the courage? (*E* 70–71)

He goes on for a while in this vein. Although this speech parodies ideas Richard once believed in, it does not represent his present position, as we see when he says, "It is the language of my youth" (*E* 71). Actually, Richard, at this point, has already come out against passion: "I am afraid that that longing to possess a woman is not love" (*E* 63). Robert seems to be calling for some sort of new morality here, but the morality that he presents is really an old one: physical force. There is neither freedom nor honesty in Robert's speech. Whatever truths he may have derived from Richard become false in Robert's mouth. Thus, if Richard were to associate fidelity and friendship with "all that is false in the world" it might reflect his disillusion. When Robert makes this association, however, it is broadly humorous. Robert's very attitude toward freedom is taken from an authority, Richard, whom he evidently needs to be dominated by spiritually. He asks Richard twice in the succeeding passage to give him the freedom to possess Bertha. But this is something he must take, or perhaps give, himself.

The key to Robert's character is thoroughgoing hypocrisy. Thus, after applying to Richard "that fierce indignation which lacerated the heart of Swift" three times (*E* 43, 44, 99), his only action toward Richard on a public level is to stab him in the back with a vicious newspaper article. The source of Robert Hand's last name suggests Joyce's essential conception of this bodkin-wielding manipulator. One of the main negative figures in Blake's *Jerusalem* is Hand, the leader of the twelve fallen sons of Albion. In the following passage from *Jerusalem* there are points that link Blake's Hand to Joyce's:

> Hand sits before his furnace: scorn of others & furious pride!
> Freeze round him to bars of steel & to iron rocks beneath
> His feet: indignant self-righteousness like whirlwinds of the north!
>   [Plate 8]
> Rose up against me thundering from the Brook of Albions River,
> From Ranelagh & Strumbolo, from Cromwells gardens & Chelsea
> The place of wounded Soldiers. but when he saw my Mace
> Whirld round from heaven to earth, trembling he sat: his cold
> Poisons rose up: & his sweet deceits coverd them all over
> With a tender cloud. (*Poetry and Prose*, p. 149)

Blake's Hand is not only described in terms of stone, water and a tendency toward inanimate matter, but he is even associated with the place-name Ranelagh, the name of the site of Robert Hand's cottage. The most important point, however, is that in the last lines Blake's Hand is characterized as a grotesque hypocrite, just as Joyce's Hand is.

The outrageousness of Robert's hypocrisy makes him a comic figure. He is a nominalist in that words and ideas have little meaning for him except as commodities to be employed for his advantages. This is amply illustrated in his scenes with Bertha:

> BERTHA, *closes, her eyes and kisses him quickly:* There ... Why don't you say: thanks?
> ROBERT, *sighs:* My life is finished—over.
> BERTHA: O, don't speak like that now, Robert.
> ROBERT: Over, over. I want to end it and have done with it.
> BERTHA, *concerned but lightly*: You silly fellow!
> ROBERT, *presses her to him:* To end it all—death. To fall from a great high cliff, down, right down into the sea. (*E* 35)

Robert's lines repeat images associated with the physical couple, sinking into a sea death. What he says, however, is falsely sentimental and far from his real intentions. Nor do Robert's romantic overtures have much meaning with regard to Bertha:

> ROBERT: Little Bertha!
> BERTHA, *smiling:* But I am not so little. Why do you call me little?
> ROBERT: Little Bertha! One embrace? (*E* 35)

As these passages suggest, Robert uses language quantitatively: in the second act he calls Bertha "beautiful" seven times in eight lines (*E* 86).

Bertha finds this attractive, and we should not be misled by her protestations to Richard into thinking that she does not share with Robert, her natural mate, a strong tendency toward falsehood and sentimentality. In both Bertha and Robert physical selfishness tends to eclipse integrity. Bertha's attitude toward Richard's freedom reflects her nature, as the notes indicate: "Bertha is fatigued and repelled by the restless curious energy of Richard's mind and her fatigue is soothed by Robert's placid politeness" (*E* 124). Beatrice, on the other hand, is basically independent, like Richard. Thus, when Robert, with his usual condescension toward women, asks her why she didn't notify him in advance of her arrival so that he might have met her, she replies, "I am quite used to getting about alone" (*E* 26).

Bertha's conventional and authoritarian nature is presented extensively. She feels guilty for her choices: "I gave up everything for him, religion, family, my own peace" (*E* 100). Speaking to Beatrice, she shows a tendency she shares with Robert toward self-abasement by such statements as "I am nothing" and "I am only a thing he got entangled with. . ." (*E* 100). Bertha's attitude toward Richard's thought emerges most clearly when, in the first act, she asks Robert whether he doesn't think Richard is mad (*E* 34). Her attraction to Robert is connected with her dislike of freedom from the first sign of their relationship, Bertha's removal of his note from a drawer where she has locked it (*E* 31). Her stage business with the locking of this drawer in the first act (*E* 37) is paralleled in the second by the emphasis upon her wristlet, a symbolic manacle with which she toys as she flirts with Robert (*E* 78, 82). She is attracted to the materialistic world of selfishness, restraint, secrecy and force in which he lives as well as to his tawdry, false romanticism. They are both at home in the cottage at Rane-lagh, which Richard refers to as "old Ireland" (*E* 72). These themes suffuse their dialogue:

ROBERT: Do you command me to?
BERTHA, *laughing:* Yes, I command you. (*E* 78)

ROBERT, *softly*: Still, secrets can be very sweet.
Can they not?
BERTHA, *smiles*: Yes, I know they can. But, you see, I could not keep things secret from Dick. (*E* 80)

Bertha's romantic sentimentality signifies her attraction to a man by expressing the fear that he will commit suicide. This corresponds to the fact that Robert expresses his love for her by saying that he wants to die. There is a grand tradition of courtly love behind the idea of *Liebestod*, but Joyce's irony about this pattern here suggests that he is ironic about Michael in "The Dead." Joyce mocks the repressive aspect, the "refrigerating apparatus" of romance. Bertha fears Robert's suicide twice. When he steps into the next room in act two and says "Love's labour lost," she says, "Come here quickly! Quickly, I say!" (*E* 79). When he returns, she is trembling and says, "I was afraid." In the third act, as Beatrice is telling how Robert came home despondent and Beatrice heard a noise from his room, Bertha bursts out, "My God! What is it? Tell me" (*E* 94). But the last person whose suicide she fears is Richard: "*There is no answer. She beats her hand loudly on the. . .door and calls out in an alarmed voice.* Dick! Answer me!" (*E* 106). That she fears his suicide last is a suggestion of his victory. The "suicide" scenes are only a few among many comic elements in *Exiles* which have been misunderstood.

The natural scheme of *Exiles* divides the characters into two groups with widely differing interests and affinities. It would seem that these groups, the spiritual Richard and Beatrice and the physical Robert and

Bertha, are almost incompatible with each other. Moreover, Robert and Bertha were interested in each other from the first, as were Richard and Beatrice (*E* 20, 85). In the light of these considerations we may wonder how the characters have arranged themselves in the situation in which they have been living for nine years, the moral order of the play. The main factor in this formation has been a conscious decision on Richard's part to unite the physical with the spiritual. This decision has been complemented by a similar decision on Bertha's part that was firm but not conscious. Richard expresses this decision at the end of the play when he speaks of a longing "to be united" with Bertha "in body and soul" (*E* 112). In the notes Joyce says, apparently of himself, ". . .(woman-killer was one of her names for me [thus associating himself with Richard; see p. 103]) I live in soul and body" (*E* 118). On the same page Joyce indicates that Bertha is inevitably drawn to Richard even while she opposes him on another level.

The union of Richard and Bertha is the preferred combination according to both of the schematic patterns. For permanent union between prolific and devouring characters would, in Blake's terms, result in the destruction of existence. The prolific characters would be reconciled with (or devoured by) their mates, creative potential would be thwarted, and they would cease to be exiles and become Dubliners. Richard would become a male version of Beatrice, perhaps resembling Gabriel Conroy or Professor MacHugh of *Ulysses.* As for Bertha, Joyce makes it clear in the notes that she would become a female version of Robert, a dull Dublin matron (*E* 116). In terms of the natural scheme of the play Richard's interest in Beatrice seems to be movement upward into spirit, while Bertha's interest in Robert is a movement downward into matter. Both move away from the fullest life, which Joyce conceives of as a unification of sensibility.

DENOUEMENT: JOYCE'S INTENTION AND NONINTENTION

The first two acts of *Exiles*, largely devoted to revealing the arrangement and relations of the characters I have examined, lead up to the decisive events in the interim between the second act and the last. Although they are shrouded in mystery, these off-stage events constitute the main action of the play. Joyce's notes say, "Perhaps it would be well to make a separate sketch of the doings of each of the four chief persons during the night, including those whose actions are not revealed to the public in the dialogue, namely Beatrice and Richard" (*E* 126). We learn in the third act that all of the characters have been up all night, or, at least, most of the night. Beatrice heard her cousin come in "Long after two" and was alarmed when he began packing his things (*E* 94). Bertha wonders how it happened that she was up that late, and Beatrice explains that she is a "light sleeper," but Bertha remains suspicious. Bertha herself says that she did not sleep at all (*E* 90). Richard says that he stayed up thinking and writing in his study until he went out to walk the beach before dawn (*E* 109). We wonder, however, as we listen to the explanations of the four, exactly what has really occurred.

In the first act Bertha complains to Richard about his interest in Beatrice. She says that he stays up all night writing about Beatrice and that she is shocked at what he writes. Characteristically, she has spied on him and she argues against him from a conventional point of view, saying, "What would anyone say?" (*E* 54). When she bitterly declares that he must be in love with Beatrice, Richard (a poor liar, as Beatrice is) concedes that he cannot argue with her (*E* 53–54). As we have seen, however, Richard's love for Beatrice can only express itself on a spiritual level. If, as we are told in act three, Richard spends the night writing to Beatrice as muse, his spiritual infidelity balances the physical infidelity of which he suspects Bertha. But Joyce goes further to suggest communication between Richard and Beatrice during the night.

In the second act, after Richard leaves Bertha alone with Robert, she keeps imagining that someone else is present. She is worried when the wind blows and the lamp flickers several times, and she imagines she hears noises (*E* 82, 83, 87, 88). Wind, flame and noises are common signs of spirits (compare *U* 503). Thus, in the fourth act of *Julius Caesar* the entrance of Caesar's ghost is signalled by the flickering of Brutus's lamp (IV.iii.275). Richard is associated with Caesar's ghost when he tells Robert that he will meet him "at Philippi" (*E* 45). The sounds that Bertha hears may similarly represent Richard, who, as a spiritual character, is associated with sound. Joyce seems to imply that Richard remains present, at least in spirit.

Still more may be implied. The notes to the play say, "During the second act as Beatrice is not on the stage, her figure must appear before the audience through the thoughts or speech of the others" (*E* 126). This indicates that Beatrice is present in some sense during the act. Virtually the only reference to Beatrice in act two occurs in Richard's dialogue with Bertha just before he leaves. Bertha, at this point, accuses Richard of arranging the meeting between Robert and herself so that he can meet Beatrice (*E* 74). She may be right, in a way, but Beatrice doesn't seem to be conjured up at this point. A more substantial reference to the insubstantial Beatrice may be implied in Richard's full explanation of his ideal of freedom in speeches to Robert and Bertha in this act. He also confesses to Robert that he has long been guilty of infidelity to Bertha (*E* 66). By speaking of these things he may be evoking the spirit of Beatrice, the muse both of his idealism and of his infidelity. Beatrice's presence at Ranelagh may also be suggested by Robert's manifestations of pseudospirituality, which include piano playing. Perhaps the major confirmation of Beatrice's presence in the second act is to be seen in the pink light that Robert burns for Bertha from his bedroom (*E* 78). This pink light probably represents Beatrice, whose namesake is described in the *Purgatorio* in terms of pink light:

Ere now have I seen, at dawn of day, the eastern part all *rosy red*, and the rest of heaven adorned with fair clear sky. . .
. . . . . .
so within a cloud of flowers, which rose from the angelic hands and fell down again within and without,
olive-crowned over a white veil, a lady appeared to me, clad, under a green mantle, with *hue of living flame*.[4]

Thus, the two lamps which Joyce dwells upon in the second act represent the presence of the spiritual characters, possessors and givers of light.

Joyce evidently intends to suggest that a consummation or realization of love involving all four characters is attempted in the cottage at Ranelagh in the interval between the two last acts. Richard and Bertha have been summoned back to Ireland by their attachments to Robert and Beatrice (*E* 95-96). Like Robert and Beatrice, the cottage, referred to as "old Ireland," may be described as the essence of all that they once left behind them—or tried to leave behind. It is a sordid place, filled with the paraphernalia of delusion, sentimentality and lust and the "darkness of belief" which Richard later refers to (*E* 112). Richard and Bertha are summoned there by the same attachments that have brought them back to Ireland to enact a ritual confrontation of their desires.

The complicated emotional assemblage they find there involves various combinations of love and hate among the characters on both heterosexual and homosexual planes. To determine whether love is consummated at Ranelagh and what sort of love it is, let us consider the possibilities. We have seen that union between Richard and the coldly ethereal Beatrice is not feasible. Love between Bertha and Robert, while physically possible, would have to be purely physical. While she might be attracted to it, such a union would not satisfy Bertha; despite her physical nature, she has chosen to join Richard in exile. The notes describe Bertha's feeling for Robert by analogy with Nora's for Sonny Bodkin as "commiseration" for a love "she could not return" (*E* 118). Thus, the question of whether Bertha and Robert make it, however important it may seem in its unanswerableness, is insignificant from the point of view of love, which Joyce is intent on distinguishing from sex here. Love has to combine body and spirit to be alive.

Joyce also sees a homosexual level in the action. In offering Bertha to Robert, Richard is vicariously partaking of Robert's physical energy and so extending his relation to the physical world through Bertha, waking areas of her he could not reach alone. Richard wishes "to possess a bound woman Bertha through the organ of his friend" (*E* 125). This may be why Richard sees her desire to draw Robert and himself together as a wise inclination (*E* 75). There would be a danger, however, if the union of the two men through Bertha is carried too far: "The bodily possession of Bertha by Robert, repeated often, would certainly bring into almost carnal contact the two men. Do they desire this? To be united, that is carnally. . ." (*E* 123). For Richard to become one with the gross Robert would be an undesirable breakdown of the play's moral and natural distinctions. A similar situation to that of the men is shown by the attraction in the last act of Bertha to Beatrice, who represents Richard's spirituality. Joyce shows a new frankness in recognizing and accepting these ties, but he does not regard them as possible bases for love.

With all of these limitations, how can love be realized at Ranelagh and why do Richard and Bertha go there? By exposing Bertha's body to Robert, Richard satisfies his desire to free her; but her freedom is his constraint, "the very immolation of the pleasure of possession on the altar of love" (*E* 114). Richard is spiritually satisfied by his physical sacrifice. Bertha, on the other hand, subjects herself to Richard by submitting to his spiritual relationship with Beatrice. In the last act she repeatedly expresses her sense of being degraded by his attachment to Beatrice and left out of his intellectual life (*E* 98, 103). As her physical nature tends toward spiritual self-abasement, however, she is physically satisfied by her spiritual submission. Thus, there is a pattern of reciprocal fulfillment between Richard and Bertha built into the action. In going to their respective lovers and permitting each other to go, Richard and Bertha satisfy one another and heighten their contact with each other and with the opposite sides of life while at the same time affirming their individual natural identities by following their appetites. They sacrifice themselves to each other; and the strength of each ameliorates the weakness of the other while the weakness of each enhances the other's strength. The only act of love possible among these characters, then, is a fulfillment of the love of Richard and Bertha in which Robert and Beatrice serve merely as intermediary pawns.

Richard seems to indicate the accomplishment of such a phenomenon by his use of the past tense in his powerful final speech, when he says, "To hold you by no bonds, even of love, to be united with you in body and soul in utter nakedness—for this I longed. And now I am tired for a while, Bertha. My wound tires me" (*E* 112). Now he need not long any more for a union of body and soul because it has taken place. It could be said that she is his wound in that Robert the threat is an extension of her, as Beatrice is an extension of Richard for Bertha, and here again the names *Robert* and *Beatrice* fit. But Bertha seems less the agent of the wound than the protectress in charge of it in this scene. I think Joyce realized in *Exiles* that one of the great advantages of marriage is that you can blame your mate for your own weakness, can indulge, say, your softness through her. Before examining the progress toward understanding reflected in the play, I want to justify my claim that Joyce believed such an indirect relationship could constitute love by turning to the definition of love Joyce wrote for *Exiles:*

The soul like the body may have a virginity. For the woman to yield it or for the man to take it is the act of love. Love (understood as the desire of good for another) is in fact so unnatural a phenomenon that it can scarcely repeat itself, the soul being unable to become virgin again. . . (*E* 113)

Joyce distinguishes the virginity of the soul from that of the body. He says that the act of love involves the destruction of the virginity of the soul of the beloved, which is equivalent to the desire of good for her. The term *virginity* is used in a negative sense here: it implies a restriction of the freedom of the individual and is associated with nonexistence and death. This is Blake's view of virginity, as reflected in lines like "the pale Virgin shrouded in snow," from "Ah! Sun-flower," in *Songs of Experience*. Thus, the act of love, a destruction of the virginity of the soul, creates life.

I must return to the second act to show how this definition is followed by Richard and Bertha so that love "scarcely repeats itself" in *Exiles*. Early in the second act Richard, voicing his thoughts to Robert, makes up his mind to give Bertha to him. I have cited a speech of this dialogue in which Richard says he wants to give new life to Bertha by freeing her (*E* 69); let us examine the steps by which he arrives at this plan. Early in the scene Richard says, "I am afraid that the longing to possess a woman is not love" (*E* 63). Robert, who draws out Richard's thoughts without understanding them, asks what else love could be. Richard replies, "To wish her well" (*E* 63). This is one sign that the conception of love on which Richard's action is based fits the Joycean definition cited above. A little further on the following exchange takes place:

RICHARD, *lost in thought:* And I was feeding the flame of her inno-
cence with my guilt. . . I have killed her.
ROBERT: Killed her?
RICHARD: The virginity of her soul.
ROBERT, *impatiently:* Well lost! What would she be without you? (*E* 67)

What Richard means here is that in preserving Bertha's innocence and
the virginity of her soul he has killed her, stifling the possibilities of her
development. Robert misunderstands. Joyce explains what is happening
here in the notes: "Richard having first understood the nature of innocence when it had been lost by him fears to believe that Bertha, to understand the chastity of her nature, must first lose it in adultery" (*E* 119).
Richard says that when he woke Bertha from her sleep to tell her of his
infidelity, he made her know him as he really was (*E* 66). Now he decides
that she must join him completely in his exile. When she arrives, he takes
the virginity of her soul from her by ordering her to stay with Robert and
give herself to him if she wants to or if she can (*E* 75). As he does so, he
says, "I have a wild delight in my soul, Bertha, as I look at you. I see you
as you are yourself."

Richard controls virtually all of the action of *Exiles*, leading Kenner to
compare him to a deity presiding over a mock Eden (*Dublin's Joyce*,
pp. 83–85). His power is the result of his freedom, ". . .the part of Richard
which neither love nor life can do away with; the part for which she loves
him: the part she must try to kill, never be able to kill and rejoice [*sic*] at
her impotence" (*E* 118). Freedom is obviously phallic here. Bertha plays
a role parallel to Richard's in this act by sending him off to Beatrice (*E*
74). Thus, she too possesses the revivifying power of love, although she
apparently does not use it consciously.

Although we cannot determine the nature of the action of *Exiles,* we
can observe the way it is reflected in act three. The results of the indirect
intercourse between Richard and Bertha do not appear immediately, but
seem to make themselves apparent in the course of the act as the characters, through their contact with each other, come to sense what has
happened. The most obvious changes involve Robert and Beatrice and
the attitude of the others toward them. The devouring characters, the
"betrayer" and the "diseased woman" of the earlier acts, seem no longer
to represent a threat to Richard and Bertha. Thus, although she is suspicious at first, Bertha is reconciled to Beatrice and kisses her before they
part (*E* 101). Similarly, Richard and Robert touch hands (*E* 110). Both
Robert and Beatrice are passive and seem vanquished in the last act; perhaps they sense that they have been used as pawns. At any rate, they are
shown in a pitiful light.

Beatrice is made pitiful by emphasis on her poor eyesight (*E* 99, 101,

114). Richard's spectacles, on the other hand, are mentioned only once (*E* 17). This may be because the limitations of Richard's spiritual nature are mitigated by his connection with Bertha. Beatrice, moreover, shows both Richard and Bertha plainly in this act that she doesn't understand Richard's mind at all. She does this by her enthusiasm for her cousin's treacherous newspaper article. "You see, Mr. Rowan," she says, "Your day has dawned at last. Even here. And you see that you have a warm friend in Robert, a friend who understands you" (*E* 100). She seems incredibly stupid here—a reflection of the crushing effect of conventionality on her once-proud intellect. Richard suspected in the first act that Beatrice didn't understand him any better than the others did, but here it becomes obvious.

In the last act Robert is made to admit defeat in humiliating terms to Richard: "She [Bertha] went away. I was left alone—for the second time" (*E* 107). This is evidently Bertha's second rejection of Robert: she left him once before nine years earlier. Thus, the action of the play reasserts the original exile of Richard and Bertha. We cannot be sure if Robert tells the truth about his physical failure with Bertha: he says to her that he had her in a dream. Nevertheless, it is clear that he is defeated, as the notes confirm: ". . .the action of the piece should convince Robert of the existence and reality of Richard's mystical defense of his wife" (*E* 116). Robert is also made to say that Archie is Richard's son here, recognizing Richard's creative power and reflecting his own sterility. At the end of the play Robert goes away, saying that he will visit a cousin named Doggy Justice in Surrey (*E* 105). Surrey is one of the dwelling places assigned to Hand in Blake's *Jerusalem* (Plate 71, *Poetry and Prose*, p. 223). Though Joyce sometimes associates dogs with death, I don't think Robert will become any more dead than he has been. He is probably only temporarily vanquished: he says himself he will return (*E* 110).

Richard says in the last act that he will "never know" whether Bertha made love to Robert no matter what she tells him (*E* 102). This seems to contrast with his earlier statement that he would trust her (*E* 75). Actually, however, it is precisely *by* never knowing that he intends to trust her. To check her truth would diminish the vitality of the confrontation and sacrifice that bind them.

Joyce ends *Exiles*, as he does all of his major works, with a flourish of powerful prose poetry. The lyricism of these closing passages and the slow, deliberate movement of their cadences fix the final dialogue in a stasis, a fine balance of ambivalence which heightens the sense of universal and manifold significance in the situation of the closing tableau. The impression that this scene portrays conversation between archetypal figures is confirmed by the correspondences Kenner has noted between the end of the play and the end of *Finnegans Wake*.

In the speeches that close the play Richard and Bertha are talking to each other and yet not talking to each other:

> BERTHA: I am yours. *In a whisper.* If I died this moment, I am yours.
> RICHARD: *still gazing at her and speaking as if to an absent person:*
> I have wounded my soul for you—a deep wound of doubt which can never be healed. I can never know, never in this world. I do not wish to know or to believe. I do not care. It is not in the darkness of belief that I desire you. But in restless living wounding doubt. To hold you by no bonds, even of love, to be united with you in body and soul in utter nakedness—for this I longed. And now I am tired for a while Bertha. My wound tires me.
> *He stretches himself out wearily along the lounge.* BERTHA *holds his hand still, speaking very softly.*
> BERTHA: Forget me, Dick. Forget me and love me again as you did the first time. I want my lover. To meet him, to go to him, to give myself to him. You, Dick. O, my strange wild lover, come back to me again!
> *She closes her eyes.*

The ideals Richard expresses here may well have originally been inspired in him by Beatrice; she is the absent person he is speaking to. The "strange wild lover" whom Bertha asks to give herself to, speaking as if he were not present, may be associated with Robert, who apes Richard's youth. The notes say, "Robert will go. But her thoughts will they follow him into exile. . .?" (*E* 123). Richard wants to love Bertha—or relate to the world—in "restless living wounding doubt." But Bertha wants to love him in "the darkness of belief," the force which the pressure of the world demands; for she whispers, closes her eyes, and says, "If I died this moment, I am yours," a line typical of the sentimental, authoritarian love of Robert. Richard and Bertha are revealed in the final epiphany as exiles not only from Robert and Beatrice, but from each other. They are divided from each other as the soul is divided from the body, as the ideal is sundered from reality, as subject is withheld from object. They are separated from each other as man is apart from woman, as the artist is alienated from his world, as every person is separated from every other.

LOVE AND OBSESSION

Yet body and soul, woman and man do manage to unite by some mysterious means, making life possible. And Richard and Bertha are more solidly united than ever at the end, as Joyce and Nora probably were after the separation and doubt of 1909. They could not be so united if they were not sundered, for they are bound together by the knowledge of aloneness they share. She is connected to him by his weakness, Robert, and he is tied to her by hers, Beatrice. The reciprocity of their yin and yang relationship of balanced opposites represents a major new development in Joyce's thinking: the idea that two people can support and create each other in a mutual love, which stays at the center of all of Joyce's subsequent work.

Stephen rejected such balance when he told Cranly that he didn't believe in the conventional ideal of "real love,"which is based on balance:

> *And when we are married,*
> *O, how happy we'll be*
> *For I love sweet Rosie O'Grady*
> *And Rosie O'Grady loves me.*
>
> *(P* 244)

He thought that love could only consist of one person taking advantage of another, as in *Dubliners,* that one person's gain would have to be another's loss. In "A Painful Case" James Duffy proves that we cannot love because we cannot get out of ourselves: "Love between man and man is impossible because there must not be sexual intercourse and friendship between man and woman is impossible because there must be sexual intercourse" (*D* 112). Since relations between members of the same sex can only be spiritual and those between opposite sexes can only be physical, love can never combine body and spirit. His arguments are flawless in their logic, but they destroy the illogical substance of life. In order to recognize the value of life and love, it was necessary for Joyce to move from a logic of exclusive categories to one of interacting opposites. This is where he arrived in *Exiles*, a logical goal for an esthetic theory aiming at union.

Some intellectual sources for this theory are suggested in *Portrait* by references to the heretic sixteenth-century philosopher Giordano Bruno (*P* 249) and to Thoth (Hermes, *P* 225). Ellmann says that Joyce, who wrote a review on Bruno in 1903 (*CW* [Joyce], 132–134), learned from the Italian that every entity is made up of coinciding contraries: "Hot is opposite to cold, but they are both aspects of a single principle. . .The deepest night is the beginning of dawn. . .love is hate" (*Liffey*, p. 54). Bruno had close affinities to Hermetism, the science of the god Stephen gives allegiance to,[5] and the physical branch of Hermetism, alchemy, conceived the physical and mental processes of the world on a model of relationship centered on sexual intercourse, as Joyce did. Jung wrote many extensive commentaries on alchemical texts. In *The Psychology of the Transference* (1946) he uses a sixteenth-century description of the union of Sun and Moon to derive insight into the nature of all human relationship. Here he insists that the soul can only live from human relations, that the only way to relate to oneself is to relate to others, and that man generates the mind of woman while woman generates the mind of man (*CW* [Jung], 16, pp. 234, 303).

Joyce shares with esoteric tradition a vital belief in the positive power love gives. Rational energic assumptions that one grows strong at the expense of another are abrogated in love, as in art, where a weakness in an individual can become strength by connection with another. In the Prologue to *Tristan*, written about 1210, Gottfried von Strassburg says that love is the bread and wine of all noble hearts. The myth of love is that lovers give life to each other, and this consubstantiality is a model for refuting the logic of separation. While Joyce criticized the hypocrisies of courtly love, he accepted its basic premise of making union with the opposite sex an alternate religion. Love was second only to art for Joyce, and he realized that the two forms of communion were parallel.

The strength Richard and Bertha derive from each other because each sacrifices himself to confront the unknown in the other is the power behind the victory the play celebrates, what Joyce calls "the existence and reality of Richard's mystical defense of his wife" (*E* 116). For Jung the unknown or unconscious is the great source of strength; and because the major element in a man's unconscious is a female image (*anima*) and the major element in a woman's, a male image (*animus*), and each pursues this image through life, virtually all spiritual power is gained by some form of contact with the opposite sex—including active and passive relations between men.

The dialectic of *Exiles* is so framed as to make the irrational or antimaterial the leading power, an arrangement opposed to Freud's effort to replace id with ego. In *Exiles* Joyce takes the essentially religious step of yielding power to the other, a step embodied by Richard's need for Bertha's help. The Jungian characteristics of the play make it appropriate that Jung expressed approval of what I see as the basic pattern of *Exiles*: "Blake's intuition did not err when he described the two classes of men as 'prolific' and 'devouring.'"[6]

Jung would see Richard's conflict with Robert as conflict between the higher principle of individuation and the lower group manifestation of the collective unconscious. Jung described Europeans as more conscious than members of primitive societies because the Europeans were aware of various forces in their minds, while the primitives, who perceived these forces as external deities, were not. In the play Robert worships Richard and has very little self-knowledge. Jung might well agree with Joyce that "every step advanced by humanity through Richard is a step backwards by the type which Robert stands for" (*E* 119). Simple, materialistic Robert bows down his mind to the mammon of church and state while cultivating the physical side of life, the combination Stephen saw in Cranly. Richard, who attempts to recognize the forces struggling in his mind, is following a program of Jungian heroism by trying to free himself, through increased consciousness, from the bonds of the collective unconscious, which appears as external authority as long as it is unconscious.

Jung, then, defines the spiritual level on which Joyce believed in heroism. But Joyce's heroism is ambiguous and Jung is not as good in explaining why Richard and Bertha, as higher creative types, should need Robert and Beatrice almost as much as the latter pair need them. Mythology describes ideal goals better than the realities of personality. As human beings rather than symbols, Robert and Beatrice are incomplete. Beatrice is the most problematic figure in the play—shadowy, ill-defined and inert. Like the others, she exists mainly in relation to Richard, but her relation to him is not credible. Not only do the two share a love totally immaterial, but she is his inspiration without possessing any spiritual insight or understanding of his mind. Biography does not at first suggest any figure in Joyce's experience who corresponds to Beatrice except the insignificant Margaret Sheehy, a model for Emma. Reflection, however, reveals that Beatrice represents mother, the spiritualized, sublimated, backward-looking relation Richard has to her being a typical pattern between sons and mother figures.

Several things about Beatrice contradict the idea that she is based on Mary Joyce, but the evidence suffices to overcome these difficulties. In a discussion with Richard of his dead mother early in the play, Beatrice generally takes the part of the mother (*E* 22-24). When Richard says, "Do you think I do not pity her cold blighted love for me? I fought against her spirit while she lived to the bitter end. *He presses his hand to his forehead.* It fights me still—in here," Beatrice replies, "O, do not speak like that" (*E* 23). We also learn here that Richard's mother opposed Beatrice and hated her, and this blocks association of the two women. Beatrice, after all, is the muse of Richard's rebellion and art, which led him to break with his parents. Ellmann, however, has shown that Joyce's mother was a major cause of his individuality and early writings even though she didn't understand or approve of his work, an arrangement he repeated with Nora. His desire to be different aimed at standing out from siblings in mom's eyes as well as being a movement of rebellion against paternal authority (*JJ* 302-307).

Beatrice plays the piano, as Mary Joyce did, and she gives the impression of being older than she is because of her frailty, her stiff, restrained manner and her weak eyesight. Bertha says to Richard, "I think you have made her [Beatrice] unhappy as you have made me and as you made your dead mother unhappy and killed her. Woman killer!" (*E* 103). Beatrice, in fact shares with Richard's mother and Joyce's the state of death. A final link between Beatrice and May is revealed by comparison of the characters in *Exiles* with those of *Ulysses*. If Richard corresponds to Stephen, Robert to Bloom, and Bertha to Molly, then Beatrice must correspond to the ghost of Stephen's mother. *Exiles* is more idealistic than *Ulysses* in that it exalts the spiritual character and gives him possession of physical beauty. In *Ulysses* the physical woman is attached to the physical man, while spiritual Stephen has only a ghost.

Robert is a livelier figure, and even resembles Bloom, with none of Bloom's goodness. Yet, like Vincent Cosgrave or "Lynch," one of his models, he is essentially dead. Joyce, in fact, predicted the 1927 suicide of Cosgrave in an epiphany of Lynch's cynicism in *Portrait:* "The eyes . . . were reptilelike in glint and gaze. Yet . . . humbled and alert in their look, they were lit by one tiny human point, the window of a shrivelled soul, poignant and selfembittered" (*P* 206). The notes associate Robert mainly with Sonny Bodkin (*E* 117–118), Nora's dead lover (*JJ* 366). As I have suggested, the link between Robert and Michael Furey of "The Dead," who is also based on Bodkin, raises doubts about Michael's worth in view of Robert's morbid, shallow sentimentality toward suicide. Association with a lover from the past is a paternal pattern, and Robert is fatherly. He is stout and middle aged, and his facetious manner and tawdry sentiment solidly recall John Joyce—as does the Lynch epiphany of materialistic selfishness masking a dead soul.

Cosgrave competed with Joyce for Nora before Joyce and his common-law wife left Ireland in 1904 (*JJ* 166), telling Nora that Joyce was mad, as Robert tells Bertha that Richard is. When Joyce returned in 1909, Cosgrave, abetted by Oliver Gogarty (Buck Mulligan) told Joyce that during the 1904 courtship of Nora the rival Cosgrave succeeded in making love to her. Agonized by this story, uncertain what to believe, Joyce wrote several painful letters to Nora in Trieste, going through deep despair. After several days he was reconciled to Nora by his friend John F. Byrne (Cranly) and by Stanislaus, who assured him Nora had always rejected Cosgrave (*JJ* 288–290). Only after passing through this ordeal of doubt did he write to her the erotic letters that express his passion. It is unlikely, however, that Joyce accepted the assurances absolutely: it may be that in refusing to marry Nora for as long as he did, Joyce was obeying a need to expose her to potential lovers, and the most important of these must certainly have been Cosgrave, his most grievous competitor.

Joyce's hatred of Cosgrave lasted beyond the venomous portrayal of Lynch in *Ulysses,* for in *Finnegans Wake* he writes, "Given now ann linch you take enn all" (*FW* 293). In this play on a brand name for tea (Ann Lynch's), "Ann," as Anna Livia Plurabelle, can be associated with

Nora, while "linch" can't help suggesting Cosgrave. The maxim may reflect Joyce's experience: by giving Nora to Cosgrave, he gained everything. Such a reading indicates how closely Joyce could associate with Richard. Joyce had two children by Nora and lived with her for twenty-three years before his first decision to marry, as recorded by Ellmann:

> He was glad to receive a visit .. from John Francis Byrne, . . . also excited to learn that Cosgrave, the prototype of Lynch, had been found drowned in the Thames, a presumed fulfillment of Stephen Dedalus's prophecy in the Circe episode, "Exit Judas. Et laqueo se suspendit." Byrne, at a hint from Nora, interceded with Joyce to suggest he raise their marriage from common law to civil, and Joyce, who no longer much cared, was surprisingly unresisting. (*JJ* 611)

Read between lines, this passage indicates that because Joyce was exposing Nora to Cosgrave, the death of his rival made it possible for him to marry.

As Cosgrave was present for a quarter of a century at Joyce's love for Nora, so Robert and Beatrice will remain specters present in the love of Richard and Bertha. These presences which haunt the lovers, distracting them from each other, must be seen primarily as father and mother figures. This extends the common observation that one mate will tend to find the other inferior by comparison with father or mother. In 1899 Freud wrote to his friend Wilhelm Fleiss, ". . . I am accustoming myself to regarding every sexual act as an event between four individuals." [7] Freud never clarified what he meant here, and seems to have been referring to underlying bisexuality; but his statement coincides resonantly with *Exiles*, which actually presents a sex act between four individuals. Awareness of a competitor of the same sex tends to indicate bisexual feeling as well as parental fixation.

Here, as elsewhere, Freudian and Jungian interpretations tend to reinforce each other from different sides. In Jung's terms, Beatrice is that part of Richard's major archetype, the *anima*, which is not projected on Bertha, while Robert is that part of Bertha's *animus* which Richard does not satisfy. Jung would grant that the unsatisfied archetypal margin tends to resemble the difference between one's mate and one's parent of opposite sex, for he describes *anima* and *animus* as parental images. Jung, in fact, spoke of every complete marriage as a four-part structure called the "marriage quaternio" (*Aion*, p. 22).

No conflict exists between the roles of Robert and Beatrice as ancestral specters and their functions as examples of the deadening power of conformity, mere *personae* of society who have no individual freedom or identity. The link between parental ghosts and minions of the establishment is the concept of superego—the internalized voice of parental prohibition which enforces social norms of behavior by guilt. People dominated by this force tend to resemble ghosts of their parents. The child who is too good at submitting to and following his parents will imitate their aging and death, never breaking with them to create his own life through freedom as Richard and Stephen do. But even if he breaks away, they may stay with him—they probably will if he has to break—and so Joyce is not only Richard and Stephen, but Robert and Bloom.

Exiles deals with problems of conjugal relation that are essentially universal: the difficulty of desiring what one supposedly already has, of getting outside one's own limits and finding new life in another. Tradition attests to the validity of the play's indication that in order to stay alive, people must confront their opposites and risk death. The four-sided relationship serves as groundplan not only for Joyce's main source, Ibsen's *When We Dead Awaken*, but for such prototypes of romantic love as *Tristan* (Tristan, Isolde, King Mark and Isolde White Hands) and *Wuthering Heights* (Heathcliff, Catherine, Edgar and Isabella Linton). Yet there is a manifestly compulsive quality which alienates audiences from the play's bizarre quadrangle. In deemphasizing plot, Joyce reduced the importance of external determinants to emphasize the responsibilities of his characters and their minds. And the point at which *Exiles* departs from traditional standards into perversion, the acting out of neurotic needs, was a key point of Joyce's thinking which was to remain central in his subsequent work: the acceptance of dispossession. Dispossession in the world is a sound principle in religious thinking, but to give up the attempt to make contact is neurotic in rational terms. The idea of original sin and the oedipal cause of neurosis are equivalent. For centuries man used theology to explain his sense of having been dispossessed before he could remember—his need for authority—while today we explain the same dispossession by psychology.

The dynamic of Joyce's play about oedipal exile from Eden is dictated by neurosis even while it represents real spiritual powers which rational explanations of self-interest can't explain. In love people make contact with each other through their yearnings. As long as they remain defensive, they will stay on the surface; but when they show their needs, their feelings, their weaknesses, they take chances of looking foolish and gain the possibility of deep connection by the mythic path of death and rebirth. The same passivity that makes Richard "unfitted" (*E* 125) for seduction makes him capable of love, capable of the need that holds Bertha. Neurotic needs for threat and order bind them within an enclosure of mutual self-knowledge. Knowing the other's weakness gives the security within which to be free to pursue the shame and danger which are crucial to desire. Andreus Capellanus defined romantic love in the twelfth century as "inborn suffering" caused by "excessive meditation" on the opposite sex.[8] Whether or not such obsession is inseparable from love, it may well be linked to what is most intense and lasting in sexual relations.

Another reflection of obsessive need in *Exiles* is the aching incertitude in human relations which the play virtually advocates. Compulsives, in their ambivalence of prohibition and desire, usually vacillate between two sides, essentially active and passive, and have trouble making decisions. Freud says, "The predilection felt by obsessional neurotics for uncertainty and doubt leads them to turn their thoughts. . .to those subjects. . . which . . .must necessarily remain open and in doubt. The chief subjects of this kind are paternity, length of life, life after death and memory. . ." Compare a suspicion of Cosgrave from one of Joyce's 1909 letters to Nora: "Is Georgie my son? The first night I slept with you in Zurich was October 11th and he was born July 27th. That is nine months and 16 days. I remember that there was very little blood that night. . ." (*Letters, II,* 232). Freud also says, "The creation of uncertainties is one of the methods employed by the neurosis for drawing the patient away from reality and isolating him from the world" (*SE* X, pp. 232–233). He shifts concern from the outside world to his doubts within, like Richard at the end of *Exiles* when he tells Bertha he doesn't care what she says. In fact, Richard can indulge his doubt of Bertha because he holds her by his wound, and withdrawal into self is one of the means by which lovers regenerate themselves through contact with their deepest feelings. As dreams can express the unconscious because there is no risk of action, so in making love one can drop defenses and sink into oneself if the other can be trusted. Closeness to another is closeness to oneself.

Uncertainty increases with the tendency of the compulsive to move, over the years, "ever more closely to satisfaction" (*Anxiety,* p. 115). As Joyce's works grow more positive about the possibility of pleasure, an ever more elaborate network of formal, intellectual and mythic defenses must be engaged, and uncertainty is at the center of this network. Freud says that as compulsives move toward increasing satisfaction, they may be in danger of paralysis of the will because they will see every decision as balanced (*Anxiety,* p. 118). Paralysis of the will was the main subject with which Joyce began writing fiction. He condemned it in *Dubliners,* and tried to free himself from it only to find himself stuck with it in the decade of writing *Portrait.* His works from *Exiles* on both glorify paralysis insofar as it is self-imposed and grieve for it because it really is not.

Inability to decide is a liability in the practical world, but it can keep love alive and it may be a great virtue in the world of art and the spirit, as John Keats observed: ". . .several things dove-tailed in my mind, and at once it struck me what quality went to form a Man of Achievement, especially in literature, and which Shakespeare possessed so enormously— I mean *Negative Capability*, that is, when a man is capable of being in uncertainties, mysteries, doubts, [but he adds] without any irritable reaching after fact and reason."[9]

The ability to remain open-minded is valuable not only to the artist, but to the scientist, who must avoid violating reality by formulating a conclusion too soon. Joyce's obsessive doubt is crucial to his understanding. One of his monumental achievements consisted in piercing through conventional assumptions about human relations and mental experience to reveal new areas of psychological reality. He could never have done this by easy conclusions. He did it so well and so influentially that today virtually every literate person, even if he has not heard of Joyce, who influenced many writers through others, sees reality differently because Joyce saw it differently.

David Shapiro characterizes obsessive-compulsive modes of cognition in *Neurotic Styles* as constantly concentrating attention on a limited area in order to avoid disruption, focussing sharply on details, balancing opposed arguments perfectly, working with great effort and intensity, driven to self-searching, problem solving and analytic thought. In view of the connection between Joyce's doubt and the fidelity of his vision, as well as the neurotic roots of his obsessions with sex, form, time, confession, self-examination and physical detail, it is evident that compulsion neurosis defines quite precisely many of the characteristic features of his work. I do not necessarily mean that genius is caused by neurosis. Joyce might have been a genius if he were not compulsive and could certainly have been compulsive without genius, but his neurosis caused his genius to manifest itself as it did. The *Ulysses* notesheets present the following formulation:

> onanism: Sterne, Swift, Wilde
> pruriency: misanthropy—satire
> prolongation—cloacism—hatred of action

(N 125)

Joyce respected the geniuses of all three of these writers and associated himself with them. He seems to define here a category of obsessive genius in which he would include himself, or an aspect of himself.

PART THREE

THE UNQUIET FATHER

VIII

FROM STEPHEN TO BLOOM

Joyce originally planned to have the action of *Portrait* extend up to June 16, 1904, and manuscript fragments of *Stephen Hero* represent the scene in the Martello tower at the beginning of *Ulysses*.[1] Since *Ulysses* is partly an extension of material that was to have been included in *Portrait*, with the addition of the area of knowledge represented by *Exiles*, it is understandable that there is great thematic continuity between the two novels. They are so continuous that in our examination of Stephen Dedalus's problems and the way in which they are worked out in *Ulysses* we will be obliged to deal with the problems of Leopold Bloom, which actually result from Stephen's.

In the early part of *Ulysses* Buck Mulligan has replaced Cranly as Stephen's friend: "Cranly's arm. His arm" (*U* 7). Mulligan is a male threat to Stephen, as Cranly and most other men were. Stephen's anxiety emerges in no uncertain terms as he imagines Mulligan and friends "ragging" one Clive Kempthorpe: ". . .he hops and hobbles round the table, with trousers down at heels, chased by Ades of Magdalen with the tailor's shears. . . I don't want to be debagged! Don't you play the giddy ox with me!" (*U* 7). At the beginning of the episode Mulligan takes Stephen's handkerchief to wipe his razor (*U* 4); at the end Stephen is preoccupied by the fact that Mulligan wants to take his key away and finally does. Even his students make Stephen anxious at the start of the second episode as he feels powerless before them and imagines them making love aggressively (*U* 24-25).

Stephen's prime defense against the threats he feels emanating from men is his art, and he uses it here: "Parried again. He fears the lancet of my art as I fear that of his. The cold steelpen" (*U* 7). But this defense is not potent: on the following page Mulligan's words leave "gaping wounds" in Stephen's heart. By now it should be apparent that Joyce portrays intercourse as intercourse—that he and Stephen share with Shakespeare a compulsive tendency to see every nuance of give and take in all human contact as genital or aggressive. Critics of analysis call such symbolism reductive, but Freud and Joyce use the technique to make every word and gesture more active with deep feeling and to delineate an immense variety of modes and arrangements of psychic contact more vividly than abstract terms could.

Mulligan pierces Stephen by reminding him that his mother is "beastly dead." The major event of Stephen's life since *Portrait* has been the death of May Dedalus. This loss has exacerbated Stephen's anxieties and weakened his defenses. It haunts him through *Ulysses*. Castration and death being linked in the unconscious, Stephen's mother's death is connected to his personal fears of being unmanned. As a fetishist, he strives to deny his emasculated image of his mother because he identifies with her. Her severance augments in him a profound revulsion from images of female genitals: ". . .he saw the sea hailed as a great sweet mother. . .The ring of bay and skyline held a dull green mass of liquid. A bowl of white china had stood beside her deathbed holding the green sluggish bile which she had torn up from her rotting liver by fits of loud groaning vomiting" (*U* 5). A little later he thinks of "woman's unclean loins. . .the serpent's prey" in death (*U* 14), and throughout the novel he thinks of woman's body with repulsion: "A Shefiend's whiteness under her rancid rags" (*U* 47).

Mulligan castrates Stephen and reenacts the death of Stephen's mother by his repeated references to it. By his brutal scientific reduction of her fate ("I see them pop off every day") Mulligan aligns himself in Stephen's mind with the paternal power that has effected her doom: God. The Buck's opening line is "*Introibo ad altare Dei*," and he carries out an elaborate invocation of God on the first page. On the following ten pages he has these lines:

—God, isn't he dreadful? (*U* 4);—God, . . . isn't the sea what Algy calls it: a grey sweet mother? (*U* 5); God knows. . . (*U* 6); God knows. . .God, Kinch, . . . (*U* 7); What happened in the name of God? (*U* 8);—Do, for Jesus' sake, . . . (*U* 10); Bless us, O Lord, . . .O, Jay, . . .The blessings of God on you . . . *In nomine Patris et Filii et Spiritus Sancti.* (*U* 12)

Later in the episode Mulligan announces a miracle (*U* 15), tells "the God's truth" (*U* 16), passes through one of the stations of the cross ("—Mulligan is stripped of his garments," *U* 16), and finally presents himself as the embodiment of God by singing "The Ballad of Joking

Jesus" (*U* 19). Though Mulligan's references to God are all blasphemies, they reinforce Stephen's view of him as God's agent.

As William Schutte has shown, Stephen is preoccupied throughout *Ulysses* with the idea of God as "*dio boia*, hangman god" (*U* 213), a monster who destroys life through the media of time and circumstance.[2] God has taken Stephen's mother and she, religious woman, has submitted to him. Freud, we recall, says that it is typical of the adolescent boy to feel that his mother has betrayed him by submitting to his father, and Stephen developed the idea that his mother was betraying him late in *Portrait*. Here in *Ulysses* he tells Mulligan that he is concerned not with the offense to his mother involved in her being "beastly dead," but with the offense to himself (*U* 9). Stephen solipsistically sees his mother's death as a final betrayal and emasculation. She has left him to go over to the side of the *dio boia*, the side of the malignant aspect of the father and of Buck Mulligan and his empirical world of medicine. Her death is a final confirmation of her falseness, and the virginal aspect of mother, quite prominent in *Portrait*, virtually never appears in *Ulysses* except as a mockery such as Gerty MacDowell. The major exception appears when Stephen calls on a female spirit to tell him the word known to all men (*U* 49). Initially his female soul or *anima*, this spirit goes through a Jungo-Freudian transformation to become his mother. When he asks her again in "Circe," however, her answer (*U* 581ff.) is a call to repent. This presumably implies that the word known to all is terror, an answer he refuses to accept. The idea of the false mother is a major element in Stephen's association with *Hamlet*, and Stephen emphasizes female betrayal and menace in his Shakespeare theory and throughout the book:

Eve. Naked wheatbellied sin. A snake coils her, fang in's kiss. (*U* 199)

We have shrewridden Shakespeare and henpecked Socrates. Even the allwisest stagyrite was bitted, bridled and mounted by a light of love. (*U* 432)

One of all [little Harry Hughes], the least of all, is the victim predestined. . .It [the Jews's daughter] leads him to a strange habitation, to a secret infidel apartment, and there, implacable, immolates him, consenting. (*U* 692)

In *Ulysses*, as in Chapter V of *Portrait*, the idea of the fallen mother who has gone from Hyperion to a satyr has expanded into a view of politics: Ireland is an old woman who has given herself to foreign masters. This vision of a corrupted mother who has submitted to the power of the usurper is embodied in "Telemachus" by the old milkwoman: "Silk of the kine and poor old woman, names given her [Ireland] in old times.

A wandering crone, lowly form of an immortal serving her conqueror [Haines] and her gay betrayer [Mulligan], their common cuckquean. . ." (*U* 14). A cuckquean is a woman of ill repute, particularly one whose husband is unfaithful to her. If Mulligan and Haines are father figures and the old woman a mother, it is logical that Stephen think of them as married. Mulligan is also a god to the old lady, not only because he subjugates her, but because he will preside over her death, a doctor as priest: "she bows her old head to a voice that speaks to her loudly, her bonesetter, her medicineman; me she slights. To the voice that will shrive and oil for the grave all there is of her. . ." (*U* 14).

Another prominent image of the fallen mother appears in "A Pisgah Sight of Palestine or the Parable of the Plums" (*U* 145-150), Stephen's story for the pressmen. This bitter sketch, which resembles stories in *Dubliners*, shows two sterile Dublin crones laboring to climb Nelson's Pillar, obviously under the phallic domination of the "onehandled adulterer." Molly Bloom also relates to Stephen's mind as a fallen mother. Stephen's mother's castration is his own castration and his motherland's subjugation is his, and so as an Irishman he is continually sensible of the fact that he is dispossessed by usurpers, a servant or "a server of a servant" (*U* 11). He expresses this situation directly in "Oxen of the Sun":

Remember, Erin, thy generations and thy days of old, how thou settedst little by me and by my word and broughtest in a stranger to my gates [image of Stephen violated] to commit fornication in my sight and to wax fat and kick like Jeshurum [Hebrew for "upright one"].[3] Therefore hast thou sinned against the light and hast made me, thy lord, to be the slave of servants. (*U* 393)

"Telemachus," in sum, shows Stephen disturbed by a sense that his mother, who represents woman and Ireland as well as herself, has betrayed him and committed herself and him to corruption and emasculation at the hands of father, God, Mulligan, Rome and England. This formulation describes Stephen's central psychic problem in "Telemachus" and in *Ulysses*.

Other anxieties are present, particularly fear of threats emanating from mother. Stephen's fear of female genitals, seen in fetishism in *Portrait*, has been aggravated by the cutting off of his mother's life. We see this fear again and again in *Ulysses* in his hydrophobia and in female images: "Unwholesome sandflats waited to suck his treading soles, breathing upward sewage breath. He coasted them, walking warily" (*U* 41). At the start of "Proteus," Stephen sees two women carrying a bag and assumes that they are midwives and that the bag contains "a misbirth with a trailing navelcord" (*U* 37-38). We are later told that the bag contains eleven cockles (*U* 242). Freud says that an infant is often used symbolically to represent the penis (*SE*, XVII, pp. 127-133), and one basic meaning of the imagined baby and its severed navelcord is a castration associated with the woman.

If Stephen fears both male and female threats, which fear is the stronger or more basic motivation? If he feared woman's organ more than man's, he would probably be homosexual, though such a hypothesis remains speculative without consideration of further criteria. Stephen does have homosexual tendencies, as most people do, but are they really subordinate or only latent? The trying question of whether Stephen's heterosexual side or his homosexual side is dominant can be resolved through the concept of compulsive ambivalence: the active and passive sides are balanced almost equally.

Fear of the male, however, seems to have primacy in that it is usually behind the female threat: Stephen's horror at mother's injury usually implies the male threat that has dealt that injury. Fenichel says, "As a rule, a better understanding will be attained if it is assumed that the normal Oedipus complex forms the deeper level, whereas the reverse Oedipus complex [i.e., love father, hate mother] is a reaction to the normal one" (*Theory*, p. 336). This suggests that Stephen's fear of his father is more basic than fear of his mother. Epstein's *Ordeal* sees father-son conflict as central to *Portrait* and *Ulysses*. The longest section of *Finnegans Wake*, "The Interrogation of Yawn" (pp. 474-554), resembles a psychoanalysis or interpretation of dreams, for Yawn lies exhausted while the four gospellers dig deeper and deeper into layers of his swooning mind. At the first stage of the inquest, Yawn speaks of brother conflict. At the second, a deeper level of his unconscious speaks in the voice of his mother. And after further examination, the old men finally reach the deepest level, at which the father, H. C. E., appears.

The paternal threat tends to underlie the maternal in *Ulysses*. In the intimate and penetrating "Proteus," the episode on the beach, a major subject of Stephen's brooding is the sexual relation of his parents: "Wombed in sin darkness I was too, made not begotten. By them, the man with my voice and my eyes and a ghostwoman with ashes on her breath. They clasped and sundered, did the coupler's will. From before the ages He willed me. . ." (*U* 38). Note the fusion in the last line of father and God, who are consubstantial in *Ulysses*: God is "Universal Husband" (*U* 420) and "Allfather" (*U* 423). Later in the episode Stephen sees a couple he believes to be gypsy cocklepickers and extends his preoccupation with the observed sex act by imagining them at it. Then he frames the woman in the shape of his mother—oppressed and menaced by God's weapon:

Across the sands of all the world, followed by the sun's flaming sword, to the west, trekking to evening lands. She trudges. . .In sleep the wet sign calls her hour, bids her rise. Bridebed, childbed, bed of death, ghost-candled. *Omnis caro ad te veniet.* He comes, pale vampire, through storm his eyes, his bat sails bloodying the sea, mouth to her mouth's kiss.

Here. Put a pin in that chap, will you? My tablets. Mouth to her kiss. No. Must be two of em. Glue 'em well. Mouth to her mouth's kiss. (*U* 47–48)

The image of "mouth to her mouth," which Stephen fashions into a poem, is a distortion of the primal scene of intercourse between his parents. Stephen has brooded on this scene continually, and he now conceives it as father castrating mother, *dio boia* killing her with a kiss. In fact, Stanislaus and other Joyce children believed that their father had hastened the early death of their mother through hardship and abuse (*Dublin Diary*, pp. 6–10; *JJ* 175). The connections here are clear: the kiss was a symbol of sexual relations in *Portrait* and the association of sex with death, a commonplace of classical and Elizabethan literature, is so fundamental as to need no explanation. The pronoun is changed in the final poem: "He comes, pale vampire,/ Mouth to *my* mouth" (*U* 132, my italics), another indication of Stephen's tendency to associate with his mother as victim.

This image cluster haunts Stephen throughout *Ulysses*—the horrifying vision of the injured mother accompanied by the paternal threat. When the text dips briefly into Stephen's mind during "Wandering Rocks," for example, we find Stephen at first thinking of a female figure with revulsion and then thinking of a nearby dynamo as the threatening *dio boia*:

She dances in a foul gloom where gum burns with garlic [vaginal cave]. A sailorman. . .eyes her. A long and seafed silent rut. She dances, capers, wagging her sowish haunches and her hips, on her gross belly flapping a ruby egg.

. . . . . .

. . .hum of dynamos from the powerhouse urged Stephen to be on. Beingless beings. Stop! Throb always without you and the throb always within. . . I between them. Where? Between two roaring worlds where they swirl, I, Shatter them, one and both. But stun myself too in the blow. Shatter me you who can. Bawd and butcher were the words. I say! Not yet awhile. A look around.

Yes, quite true. Very large and wonderful and keeps famous time. You say right, sir. A Monday morning, 'twas so, indeed. (*U* 241–242)

This passage requires commentary. Stephen is thinking of the *dio boia* in the last two paragraphs: "bawd and butcher" were titles he gave the hangman god earlier (*U* 213). God is seen in the dynamos because he is the power behind the world and the Newtonian universe: "Very large and wonderful and keeps famous time." God runs the temporal mutability machine which has killed May Dedalus. Stephen thinks of shattering the two worlds, outer and inner. But he abruptly halts the tendency of his thoughts toward patricide and blasphemy because he fears the presence of the father, whom indeed, he bears within himself: "Not yet awhile, a look around." Frightened, he retracts his aggression and turns to praising the universe. The key to this is the reference to *Hamlet* in the final lines. Hamlet is mocking Polonius to Rosencrantz and Guildenstern when Polonius himself approaches. The prince suddenly switches discourse when the old man comes within hearing, saying, "You say right sir, o' Monday morning, 'twas so indeed."[4]

When the thought of patricide enters Stephen's head, as it frequently does, the crime must be reacted against and reversed because of the anxiety that it calls forth: "Shoot him to bloody bits with a bang shotgun, bits man spattered walls all brass buttons. Bits all khrrrrklak in place clack back. Not hurt? O, that's all right. Shake hands. See what I meant, see? O, that's all right. Shake a shake" (*U* 42). Stephen repeats such undoing patterns all through *Ulysses,* first striking out at father figures, then turning around and submitting, as at the end of *Portrait* (*P* 252). As Leslie Fiedler pointed out, his Shakespeare theory amounts to the emasculation of a patriarch.[5] As soon as Stephen finishes presenting the theory, he humiliates himself by denying that he believes it (*U* 213-214). Stephen feels constantly hostile to and threatened by his father as he broods over his mother's cutting herself off in betrayal.

Stephen's most intense and terrifying vision of mutilated mother and menacing father occurs, as one might expect, during the climaxes of "Circe," and is triggered by the dance of the hours. Stephen is desperately asserting his manhood in this dance, and the assertion appears as height imagery. Flying, birds and elevation are common symbols of potency with which Stephen has been trying to associate himself since adolescence. Throughout "Proteus," for example, he thinks of himself as trying to fly and being pushed or pulled down: "Get down, bald poll!" (*U* 40). His wish to move upward also seeks to escape matter into spirit. In the dance of the hours he is frantically trying to raise himself and to deny the threat he feels. He cries, "Pas seul!" and is described in these terms: "leaping spurn soil foot and fall again" (*U* 578). In the midst of Stephen's attempt to soar, his father appears and says "Think of your mother's people!" (*U* 579). Then his mother appears, described with intense images of emasculation:

Stephen's mother, emaciated, rises stark through the floor in leper grey with a wreath of faded orange blossoms and a torn bridal veil, her face worn and noseless, green with grave mould. Her hair is scant and lank. She fixes her bluecircled hollow eyesockets on Stephen and opens her toothless mouth uttering a silent word. (U 579)

There are five images of castration here: torn veil, hair, eyes, nose and teeth. Mother is accompanied by Mulligan, who mocks her and calls her "beastly dead." She comes in the service of the *dio boia*, and in his name she threatens her son with phallic attack: "Beware! God's hand!" (*U* 582). The scene ends with Stephen striking the lamp and symbolically destroying the world: "Nothung! (*He lifts his ashplant high. . .and smashes the chandelier. Time's livid final flame leaps and, in the following darkness, ruin of all space, shattered glass and toppling masonry.*)" (*U* 583). The image of shattering the world, which first appears at the beginning of "Nestor" (*U* 24) and recurs many times (*U* 42, 43, 242, 434, 507, 598ff.), represents killing the father or destroying that which the father has erected. But this attempt at patricide doesn't change anything. Stephen inevitably undoes it directly afterward by waving his "green rag" (*U* 592) at the soldiers and inviting them to knock him down. The entire sequence of events late in "Circe"—injured mother, patricide, reversal and male threat—is only an expansion of the combination operating in Stephen's mind all day—a severe version, altered by death, of the complex of maternal haven and paternal threat in *Portrait*. The virgin-whore duality has now become biased toward the whore side, as the setting of the climactic "Circe" indicates.

Stephen's preoccupation with the image of mother as whore is accompanied by an explicit concern with the idea of incest between mother and son. In "Oxen of the Sun" Stephen formulates the theory that if Christ and God were consubstantial and God had intercourse with Mary, then the Virgin "knew" her son (*U* 391). It is probably Stephen, recently returned from France, who says, "Ma mère m'a mariée" (*U* 424) in the confused closing pages of this episode.

In his afflicted state the Stephen of *Ulysses* projects conditions that would satisfy his desires and ease his anxieties. He creates a fictional person structured by his own conflicts who seems to solve his problems: the Shakespeare of "Scylla and Charybdis." The Shakespeare discussion in the library, in which Stephen sets forth his ideas about parenthood and art at some length, is the most extensive statement of theory in *Ulysses*. Critics often sense that this section is the conceptual core of the novel and that it somehow explains the mysterious relationship of Stephen to Bloom. This theoretical centrality may be clarified by analysis.

The Shakespeare of "Scylla and Charybdis" is not free from the problems and pains which burden Stephen, for he would have little validity as a solution or ideal if he were too far removed from Stephen's psychic actuality. Nevertheless, "Shakespeare" is essentially a wish fulfillment, a bard of fetishism. Stephen has shown fetishism since the first chapter of *Portrait*, but it is acute at this point because the cutting off of his mother's life has aggravated his anxiety. Freud says that fetishism is not only a token of protection from emasculation, but it also saves the fetishist from his "aversion from the real female genitals" ". . .by endowing women with the characteristic which makes them tolerable as sexual objects" ("Fetishism," p. 154). The fetishist avoids homosexuality by yoking together arms and the woman.

In "Scylla and Charybdis" Stephen transfers power from the father to the mother so that its threat is felt to originate with her. Making paternal danger maternal alleviates it, for sexual submission to the mother is not as abhorrent as to the father. The masochism Stephen showed in *Portrait* is played down in *Ulysses*, but he continues to think of himself almost incessantly as being attacked or threatened. We recall that Freud found that the common desire of masochists to be beaten by women, when examined in depth, turned out to be based on fantasies of sexual assault by the father, who is disguised as an aggressive woman. Masochism satisfies guilt and limits dread through fantasies of controlled aggression. The disguise of a paternal threat as maternal is a common practice of compulsive masochists such as Leopold von Sacher-Masoch and a preoccupation of obsessive ones like Leopold Bloom. In accordance with this strategy, Stephen reverses the prevailing image of the primal scene in his lecture from father injuring mother to mother injuring father: "You are the dispossessed son: I am the murdered father: your mother is the guilty queen" (*U* 189). The mother referred to here is Ann Hathaway. Shakespeare's wife is described in terms that suggest his mother, and she is associated with Stephen's mother:

—She saw him into and out of the world. She took his first embraces. She bore his children and she laid pennies on his eyes. . .when he lay on his deathbed.
　　Mother's deathbed. Candle. . .Who brought me into this world lies there . . . (*U* 190)

Presumably, Ann saw Shakespeare into the world in the sense that she took his virginity, and by creating his being, making him a man, she became his mother. But before Shakespeare fulfills oedipal desire by marrying mom, he fulfills more individual desires of Stephen's by being raped by her:

—He was chosen, it seems to me. If others have their will Ann hath a way. By cock, she was to blame. She put the comether on him, sweet and twentysix. The greyeyed goddess who bends over the boy Adonis, stooping to conquer. . .is a boldfaced Stratford wench who tumbles in a cornfield a lover younger than herself.

And my turn? When?

Come! (*U* 191)

Stephen assumes Shakespeare married a woman eight years older than he because he was unable to take the lead and transforms that lead into a phallic image. The last two lines, which are not spoken but thought, indicate the gratifying nature of this fantasy for him. The fetishism which stands out in "by cock, she was to blame" swells further in another description of this scene:

—Belief in himself has been untimely killed. He was overborne. . .and he will never be a victor in his own eyes after nor play victoriously the game of laugh and lie down. Assumed dongiovanism will not save him. No later undoing will undo the first undoing. The tusk of the boar has wounded him there where love lies ableeding. If the shrew is worsted yet there remains to her woman's invisible weapon. (*U* 196)

Wish fulfillment is not evident in this passage, for Shakespeare has undergone a painful loss of primary manhood. But given the sense of emasculation or emotional impotence that Stephen has always been susceptible to, it is understandable that he prefers to feel himself emasculated by mother rather than father. The threat remains paternal—as its shape indicates—but it is disguised as female. Fenichel's notion that a phallic threat tends to be paternal no matter in what context it appears fits in nicely with Freud's about masochists putting male threats in drag. By shifting the threat to mother, Stephen avoids the idea that is most painful to him, the idea from which he feels the greatest need to escape, the idea of sexual submission to father:

—Who is the father of any son that any son should love him or he any son?

. . . . . .

—They are sundered by a bodily shame so steadfast that the criminal annals of the world, stained with all other incests and bestialities, hardly record its breach. . .The sun [1934 "son"] unborn mars beauty: born, he brings pain, divides affection, increases care. He is a male: his growth is his father's decline, his youth his father's envy, his friend his father's enemy. (*U* 207–208)

Stephen protests too much against loving father. He is trying to justify patricidal hatred, fear and jealousy which are partly reactions against sexual attraction. One of the main reasons he constantly dreads male aggression is that it includes an element of temptation which must always be denied. The linkage of affection with violence in his mind divides all human relations into absolutes of domination and submission; as a result he sees every son locked in a tragic conflict with the active source of his being. He will have to learn the value of controlled submission embodied by Bloom.

Stephen has Shakespeare solve the problem of sonship brusquely enough by losing John Shakespeare and becoming his own father. The relish with which Stephen carries out this fantasy is reflected in his exultant tone and the emotional casuistry of his argument:

—The corpse of John Shakespeare does not walk the night. From hour to hour it rots and rots. He rests, disarmed of fatherhood [castrated], having devised that mystical estate upon his son. . . .
—Well: if the father who has not a son be not a father can the son who has not a father be a son? When. . .shakespeare. . .wrote *Hamlet* he was not the father of his own son merely but, being no more a son, he was and felt himself the father of all his race, the father of his own grandfather. . .
—Himself his own father, Sonmulligan told himself. (*U* 207–208)

Shakespeare sets out to be his own father, "Hamlet *père* and Hamlet *fils*" (*U* 213): "The boy of act one is the mature man of act five. All in all" (*U* 212). The desire to be one's own father is reflected in Stephen's interest in the Sabellian heresy, which held that the Father and the Son were one (*U* 21, 208). This common extension of the desire for one's mother denies time by denying the generations. Shakespeare, according to Stephen, succeeds in becoming his own father in his works by imaginatively partaking of all ages and phases of life (*U* 212–213). Joyce evidently wishes to do the same in portraying Bloom and Stephen. But in life Shakespeare is incapable of the narcissistic self-sufficiency that he achieves in his work. He has a tragic flaw:

. . .the theme of the false or the usurping or the adulterous brother. . .is . . .always with him. . .it was the original sin that darkened his understanding, weakened his will and left in him a strong inclination to evil. . . an original sin and, like original sin, committed by another in whose sin he too has sinned. (*U* 212)

The original sin is cuckoldry, the giving over to another man or men of his wife, "in whose sin he too has sinned." Freud tells us the man who seeks cuckoldry is recreating in his wife conditions of love in which he originally related to his mother, with the necessary competitor serving as father. Stephen has already shown this tendency with Cranly and others. In this passage the competitor is disguised as a brother, but it is primarily the father and not the brother who threatens Stephen: in the midst of his theorizing he says to himself, "Where is your brother? Apothecaries' hall. My whetstone" (U 211). This is virtually the only reference to Maurice Dedalus (Stanislaus) in *Ulysses*, and it accords with *Stephen Hero* and with biography in representing him as a passive figure.

Stephen's Shakespeare tries to escape and replace his father, but guilt makes it necessary that he be punished by the return of the father and the paternal threat comes back to cuckold him. This "original sin" was hinted at when Stephen spoke of an even more original one, the rape of Shakespeare by Ann Hathaway: "There is, I feel in the words, some goad of the flesh driving him into a new passion [cuckoldry], a darker shadow of the first [rape], darkening even his own understanding of himself" (*U* 196). Cuckoldry is a darker shadow of rape as a reproduction in adult life of the sexual submission of childhood. In both traumatic experiences the threat of the father asserts itself disguised by attribution to mother. In placing the blame for violation and cuckoldry on Ann, Stephen is giving her a more active and aggressive role than women usually play and expressing misogyny. His interpretation of *Hamlet* emphasizes the "guilty queen," and when Shakespeare appears in "Circe," he says, "Weda seca whokilla farst" (*U* 568) or "None wed the second but who killed the first" (*Ham*. III.ii.190), a line which concentrates blame on the woman.[6] But then, it is easier for Stephen to blame mother than father.

In "Scylla and Charybdis" Stephen presents an escape from male danger through fetishism into an environment of feminine authority: "She saw him into and out of the world." By submitting to the female, one supposedly escapes the intolerable possibility of submitting to the male. This process of escape is essential to *Ulysses*, for the ideal which Stephen envisions in Shakespeare is substantially embodied by another henpecked husband, Leopold Bloom. Rudolph Von Abele pointed out that "Stephen's conjecturing. . .yields a Shakespeare surprisingly like Bloom—in all respects but literary aptitude. . ."[7] In *Joyce* and *Shakespeare* (pp. 127-135), Schutte expands on the correspondences between Shakespeare and Bloom, observing that both are "overborne" by women they are forced to marry by "the impending arrival of a girl child." Both lack the self-confidence to win at romance, are ineffective with distant "Dark Ladies," stop mating after the second labors of their wives and lose a son after eleven units of time to be left both fatherless and sonless. Both are cuckolds who do not seek redress though they are preoccupied with the brutes their wives take: they return home despite suffering to achieve contentment. And both are avaricious, incestuous and Jewish, qualities

Stephen links together. Schutte's details add up to indicate that "Shakespeare" is essentially a sketch of Leopold Bloom, though he is created by Stephen and shaped by his desire.

Bloom's love life is congruent with "Shakespeare's" although we are given more naturalistic details in the presentation of Bloom than in Stephen's delineation of the bard. In the key scene of Bloom's courtship, the scene with Molly on Howth Hill in which she "got him to propose" (*U* 782), as she puts it, Molly played the role of nursing mother. Bloom, as his memory indicates, was "ravished," and Molly was larger than life:

> Ravished over her I lay, full lips full open, kissed her mouth. Yum. Softly she gave me in my mouth the seedcake warm and chewed. . . Young life, her lips that gave me pouting. Soft, warm, sticky gumjelly lips. Flowers her eyes were, take me, willing eyes. . .Wildly I lay on her, kissed her; eyes, her lips, her stretched neck, beating, woman's breasts full in her blouse of nun's veiling, fat nipples upright. Hot I tongued her. She kissed me. I was kissed. All yielding she tossed my hair. Kissed, she kissed me. (*U* 176)

The situation of nursing is evoked by the infantile orality of this scene, which is associated in Bloom's mind with an image of woman as a deity who rules the world. Later, in "Siren," when Bloom is titilated by the fetishistic sight of a barmaid's hand on a beer-pull he has the following thoughts: "Beerpull. Her hand that rocks the cradle rules the Ben Howth. That rules the world" (*U* 228). The Molly of Howth Hill now reappears as a phallic mother goddess.

While Stephen tends to view women with loathing throughout *Ulysses*, Bloom tends to adore and deify them. Stephen is absorbed by the thought of his mother's death, but Bloom thinks of his father's. He tends to see women as outlasting the generations of men, as Gertrude and Ann Hathaway do. In "Hades," when he sees an old woman watching a corpse, he thinks, "Glad to see us go we give them such trouble coming" (*U* 87). In "Nausikaa," as Bloom prepares to masturbate while staring at Gerty MacDowell, he is described as "literally worshipping at her shrine" (*U* 361). Although these words are inflated by the sentimental narrator of this section, they have accuracy. In "Circe," when Cissy Caffrey says nothing to defend Stephen, Bloom shakes her and exclaims, "Speak you! Are you struck dumb? You are the link between nations and generations. Speak, woman, sacred lifegiver" (*U* 597). Bloom tries to present Stephen with the image of woman as deity in "Ithaca" when he points out to him the lamp in Molly's window. This phallic symbol standing for a female is described in terms which suggest the Holy Ghost: "How did he elucidate the mystery of an invisible person, his wife Marion. . .denoted by a visible splendid sign, a lamp? / With indirect and direct verbal allusions or affirmations. . ." (*U* 702).

In making a God of woman, Bloom is really putting her in the place of the father. He continually plays a submissive, filial role with Molly, an attitude which emerges most clearly in "Circe." Early in the episode Bloom has a brief vision of his mother which abruptly changes to a vision of Molly:

ELLEN BLOOM

(. . .*appears over the staircase banisters, a slanted candlestick in her hand* [phallic mother] *and cries out in shrill alarm*.). . .Sacred Heart of Mary, where were you at all, at all?
(*Bloom, mumbling, his eyes downcast*, . . .)

A VOICE

(*Sharply*.) Poldy!

BLOOM

Who? (*He ducks and wards off a blow clumsily*.) At your service.

(U 438-439)

Bloom's epistolary affair with Martha Clifford reveals the same urge toward masochistic submission to the armed mother. He has selected Martha correspondent because he likes her letters, one of which appears: ". . . I am awfully angry with you. I do wish I could punish you for that . . .Are you not happy in your home you poor little naughty boy?. . . Please write me. . .if you do not I will punish you. So now you know what I will do to you, you naughty boy. . ." (*U* 77-78). Later, after masturbating in "Nausikaa," Bloom thinks, "Damned glad I didn't do it in the bath this morning over her silly I will punish you letter" (*U* 368). These phrases, then, are sufficiently exciting to Bloom to serve as a focus for masturbation.

In "Calypso" Bloom is attracted to a girl in the butcher's shop partly because he thinks of her "whacking a carpet on the clothesline" (*U* 59). In "Lestrygonians" he thinks of the equestrian women he finds magnetic: "Uneatable fox. . .Fear injects juices make it tender enough for them. Riding astride. Sit her horse like a man. Weight-carrying huntress . . . First to the meet and in at the death. Strong as a brood mare some of those horsey women" (*U* 160). Bloom's masochism arms the woman with male power to punish and unman, and he is also a hard-core fetishist in his obsessive interest in lingerie, footwear, furs and female fashions, which is often present throughout *Ulysses* and particularly obvious in "Circe". Fetishism emerges as Bloom pauses at the window of Brown Thomas, silk mercers: "Gleaming. . .sunwarm silk. Jingling harnesses. All for a woman. . .His brain yielded. Perfume of embraces all him assailed. With hungered flesh obscurely, he mutely craved to adore" (*U* 168). Bloom saves his money to get his wife fancy bloomers and violet garters (*U* 57,

261). In "Nausikaa" he seems more interested in Gerty's transparent stockings and underwear than in Gerty: "A dream wellfilled hose . . . *Lingerie* does it" (*U* 368).

An aspect of Bloom's sexuality which might not seem to relate to the others is his coprophilia, which is allied with a general interest in all sorts of excretions. Bloom's literary life begins with the fact that he likes to eat kidneys, partly because they taste of urine, and ends with him kissing his wife's buttocks. Asked to name his worst crime in a "Circe" fantasy, Bloom recites a series of coprophilic acts ending with "I rererepugnosed in rerererepugnant . . ." (*U* 537-538). The reason Joyce always spelled rear "rere" may lie in a linguistic equation between feces and the multiplicity of matter: the Latin for matter; *res,* becomes *re* in the ablative or causal sense. Fenichel says that coprophilia expresses an unconscious desire to see "something resembling a penis" come out of a woman (*Theory*, pp. 349-350, which also describes another Joycean fetish, urine.) Bloom's smuttiness then, like his masochism and fetishism, has the function of attributing a phallus to mother, or giving the world power over him.

But what of father, from whom this organ must have been taken? As in the case of Shakespeare as wish fulfillment—but not those of Stephen or Joyce—Bloom's father has conveniently passed away. And because Rudolph Bloom has committed suicide, the question of patricide is avoided. But yet, as with Shakespeare, the father returns in Bloom's persistent need to be cuckolded, to be symbolically punished by a male threat. The ugly reality in the mind and its world that occasionally peeps from behind the confectionary figure of the goddess and her magic wand.

Insofar as Stephen creates his Shakespeare of the wounded groin, it may be said that he creates Bloom. But Joyce's biography and letters show that Bloom has a great deal in common with Joyce. The chief documents linking Joyce to Bloom's perverse attitudes are the letters he wrote to Nora in 1909: again and again in these he addresses her as mother and expresses masochism, fetishism and coprophilia directly (*Letters, II*, 232-281 or *Selected Letters*, pp. 171-193), while Ellmann's biography describes Joyce's preoccupation with his wife's apparently unconsummated infidelity.

Stephen and Bloom, then, represent effectively two different stages or aspects of Joyce's life. This suggests that Joyce's life-style of middle age represented a fulfillment of the wishes of his youth: "He found in the world without as actual what was in his world within as possible" (*U* 213). Gratifying as this process seems, it may involve serious problems if the world within is maladjusted, as Stephen, paraphrasing Goethe, points out: "Beware of what you wish for in youth because you will get it in middle life" (*U* 196).

IX

JOYCE'S SYSTEM
AND JUNG'S TYPES

> . . .we even behold the disintegration of his [Joyce's]
> personality into Bloom, *l'homme moyen sensuel,* and the
> almost gaseous Stephen Dedalus, who is mere speculation
> and mere mind. C. G. Jung.[1]

STEPHEN

Most of the psychosexual patterns in his work were evident to Joyce, but
he had his own ways of understanding their significance. Fenichel says
the egos of compulsives show "a cleavage, one part being logical, another
magical" (*Theory*, p. 300). In *Ulysses*, as in *Exiles*, astonishing psychological insight and candor combine with an implacable compulsion for the
defensive order of a personal mythology. Joyce is able to explore his
psychological problems so relentlessly just because he is all the while
elaborating a supernatural or magic defense against the threats they entail.

The mythology of *Ulysses* is not as narrow, abstract or mechanical as
that of *Exiles*. Yet the systematic arrangement of the imagery of the
novel retains many of the obsessive characteristics seen in *Exiles* and
develops certain compulsive elements even further than the play, particularly an obsession with time so extreme that it served as the basis for
Wyndham Lewis's condemnation of *Ulysses* as a "time book."[2] As Joyce
moves through his career the mythic side of his work grows in complexity,
scope and importance, moving toward the total myth of *Finnegans Wake*.
Mythology encompasses about half of the reality of *Ulysses*, competing
with naturalism for domination of the novel; and because this Joycean
system is so meaningful, I must understand it in its own terms rather than

simply explaining it causally in Freud's. My effort to reconstruct Joyce's mythic system in *Ulysses* will reveal extensive links between Joyce's thinking and Jung's, and this is no coincidence: both Joyce and Jung built their systems on traditional religious categories and patterns. One of the most basic of these is the distinction between spirit and matter, and this division separates Stephen from Bloom.

An indication of how carefully the body-spirit duality is designed into the book appears in Joyce's structural diagram, which assigns an organ for every episode except the first three. These three episodes, the "Telemachia," deal with Stephen, and the only other episode which Stephen clearly dominates is "Scylla and Charybdis," the organ of which is the brain. Bloom's episodes, however, focus on many organs and organ systems.[3] Joyce may be suggesting by this arrangement that Bloom has most of his organs except for a brain, while Stephen is a disembodied mind.

A similar indication is the fact that Stephen, after rejecting room and board at the Martello tower in the first episode, does not eat in *Ulysses*, while considerable emphasis is placed on eating and other bodily functions in Bloom's case. I must add that although Stephen doesn't eat after "Telemachus," he does drink a good deal. He seems to be limited to the liquid level, either because it is thought of as a necessary minimum or because liquid is considered as close to spirit as to matter. "Oxen of the Sun" opines that ". . .only the plasmic substance can be said to be immortal" (419). In "Eumaeus," Bloom, after emphasizing that he is "a stickler for solid food," asks Stephen, who must be famished, to eat something solid. Stephen replies, "Liquids I can eat," but asks Bloom to take away the knife, which reminds him of Roman history (*U* 635). In "Oxen of the Sun" Stephen rejects the bread of the Eucharist and accepts only the wine as "his soul's bodiment" (*U* 391). In "Ithaca," when Stephen and Bloom share all that they have in common, they meet on the liquid level, drinking and urinating together.

The matter-spirit polarity relates to the attitudes the two protagonists have toward sex. The previous chapter demonstrated that Stephen loathes and denigrates women while Bloom adores and deifies them. For Joyce, their attitudes toward the opposite sex are analogous to their attitudes toward the world. This analogy is founded upon a major convention of European literature, one popularized by Petrarch, which equates man's relation to woman with his relation to the world. Jung's theory of the *anima* coincides with this convention, holding that the major component of a man's unconscious will be a female archetype which he will project to make up his environment. The idea that a man's tie to woman is his tie to the world is a commonplace, and as such it is expressed by Bloom. In his youth he writes to Molly, *"Dearer far than song or wine / You are mine.*

The world is mine" (*U* 678). Unfortunately, Molly and the world no longer belong directly to Bloom at the time of the novel's action.

The world of *Ulysses* is one of mutability, and both of its protagonists are continually preoccupied by thoughts of the transience of the material world and of the inconstancy of human love. The spiritual Stephen, however, is concerned with the abstract concept of mutability and with a ghost while Bloom is disturbed by the concrete physical problem of his wife's infidelity. Stephen views the world as a nightmare in which a paternal monster god uses time to devour the corrupted corpse of mother and all dying flesh. In "Oxen," when the medical students are debating why infants die, Stephen offers the theory "that an omnivorous being which can masticate, deglute, digest and apparently pass through the ordinary channel . . . such multifarious aliments as cancrenous females emaciated by parturition [such as May Dedalus], . . .and chlorotic nuns, might possibly find gastric relief in an innocent collation of staggering bob [young calf] " (*U* 420). In other words, God must get tired of eating old people and enjoy a tender infant now and then.

Bloom's god is identified in the same episode after he calmly explains thunder to Stephen as "a natural phenomenon" and Phenomenon is personified as the deity who commands death and copulation (*U* 395). Bloom invokes natural phenomenan many times to alleviate anxieties (*U* 529, 549, 694, *et al.*). In "Cyclops," for example confronted by a violent phallic image (a hanged man's erection), he says, "That can be explained by science. . .its only a natural phenomenon, don't you see." Here the sarcastic narrator remarks, "Phenomenon! That fat heap he married is a nice old phenomenon with a back on her like a ballalley" (*U* 305). In marrying Molly, Bloom has married Phenomenon, the material world, which is for him both benevolent god and mother. As a Latinist, Joyce must have been aware that mother and matter are the same word (*mater = materia*). On his notesheets, he wrote, "MB = spinning Earth" (*N* 515) and "nat phen = phys. chem. change" (*N* 451). At the end of "Ithaca," even though Bloom knows that Molly's mutability is symbolic of his own death, the earth passing from one possessor to another, he can feel equanimity about her transgression partly because it is ". . .as natural as any and every natural act. . .executed in natured nature by natural creatures in accordance with his, her and their natured natures. . ." (*U* 733).

The shift from paternal to maternal threat described above in motivational terms fits well with Stephen's vision of God as a threatening "Allfather" (*U* 423) and Bloom's of Him as a Great Mother or Mother Nature. But their differing views of the world of inconstancy they share also point to a paramount descriptive distinction: Bloom's fundamental attitude toward the material world as well as time and woman is one of attachment and involvement, while Stephen's is predominantly an attitude of withdrawal and aloofness. As S. L. Goldberg puts it, "Where Stephen . . .rejects, Bloom accepts" (*Temper,* p. 178). Another formulation of the distinction is that Bloom is oriented toward the outer world, while Stephen is oriented toward the inner.

This opposition between outer and inner, related to the spirit-matter conflict, is central to the thinking of Jung, who wrote, ". . .the tragic counter-play between inside and outside. . .represents, at bottom, the energetics of the life process, the polar tension that is necessary for self-regulation" (*Two Essays,* p. 196). At the heart of *Ulysses* is the distinction Jung was developing in his *Psychological Types* (1921) while the novel was being completed:

> The introvert's attitude is an abstracting one; at bottom he [Stephen] is always intent on withdrawing libido from the object, as though he had to prevent the object from gaining power over him. The extravert [Bloom], on the contrary, has a positive relation to the object. He affirms its importance to such an extent that his subjective attitude is constantly related to and oriented by the object.[4]

Campbell points out that Stephen is introverted and Bloom extraverted in *Creative Mythology* (p 460); but the alchemical interpretation of *Ulysses* in this book does not develop this particular point beyond a parenthetical observation. Joyce did not refer to the terms himself until he used "extravert" in the *Wake* (*FW* 412.5). Yet Jung's distinction fits snugly to reveal sinews and muscles of *Ulysses*.

Bloom's identity is his relation to the physical world. His mind, usually engaged in sensuous apprehension of the world of matter, is composed largely of concrete physical and sensual impressions and of feelings linked to other people and objects. His thinking on more abstact levels is limited and nonsubjective, being composed mainly of inert clichés and spiritless banalities. When Jung's extravert has ideas, they do not come from internal sources; rather they are "derived from tradition or borrowed from the intellectual atmosphere of the time," and so "fall into the category of objective data" (*PT* 343). Thus, Bloom's ideas are often compared to physical phenomena in the novel. For example, the technique of "Lestrygonians," which Joyce describes as "peristaltic" on his structural diagram, expresses Bloom's thoughts in prose which rhythmically imitates the expansion and contraction of digestion (*U* 169-176). Similarly, Bloom's thoughts go through "incubism" in "Hades" and "detumescence" in "Nausikaa." At the end of "Eumaeus," after Bloom has given one of his longest and most inspired speeches, a banal adjuration to Stephen to advance himself in the world, the text immediately turns to a nearby horse: "The horse . . . halted, and, rearing high a proud feathering tail, added his quota by letting fall on the floor . . . three smoking globes of turds" (*U* 665).

Except for his reactions to his body, which abound, Bloom has very little sense of self. Cixous calls him "deprived by the world around him of any existence in the first-person" (*Exile*, p. 590). His personality tends to be composed of the matrix of his social and ethnic positions, his possessions, his background, his home, his relations to those around him, his job, his scientism (which strives for objectivity) and so forth. Indeed, it is difficult to identify Bloom's personality except in terms of his positive relation to his physical environment: most of the terms which characterize him, such as open, warm, sensual, practical, resourceful, adaptable and thrifty, describe this relationship. "Everyman or Noman" (*U* 727), Bloom exists in relation to everything, for he accepts all, but, ironically, he doesn't exist at all, for his position is one of self-negation.

Stephen, on the other hand, is virtually never positively engaged in the sensuous apprehension of matter in *Ulysses*. In fact, his introversion was apparent in the subordinate role played by the external world in *Portrait*. Jung says that "the introvert interposes a subjective view" between himself and the object he perceives (*PT* 373). All of Stephen's observation of the material world is colored by bitterness and repulsion. He sees the great crime of father violating mother, empire killing spirit, in every objective manifestation. Stephen rejects the imperfection and mutability of the world and turns inward or introverts to concentrate his attention upon his own selfhood and the abstractions of his mind. "You suspect," he says to Bloom, "I may be important because I belong to. . .Ireland. . .But I suspect. . .Ireland must be important because it belongs to me" (*U* 645). Stephen apparently has scarcely any possessions except for his hat and staff. He gives up his job and his home, and his personality lies outside his ties to family and society.

Stephen possesses creative power or potentiality because he has individuated himself, cultivated the freedom of his personality. But the inner identity that he possesses cannot express itself and is in danger of self-destruction or perversion because of its opposition to all sensible phenomena. Jung says that introverted thinking has trouble bridging the gap between its inner concerns and the outer world: "This kind of thinking easily gets lost in the immense truth of the subjective factor. . .visions of numerous possibilities appear on the scene, but none of them ever becomes a reality until finally images are produced which no longer express anything externally real, being mere symbols of the ineffable and unknowable" (*PT* 382). Stephen has been attracted to the ineffable concerns of Symbolism, and throughout *Ulysses* he is concerned with the Aristotelian problem of possibilities which do not become actual. At one point, for example, he berates himself for creating in youth a hypothetical series of works with letters for titles (*U* 40).

The possibilities that Stephen is worried about are cut off by time as his freedom is limited by God. Mutability dominates the objective world of *Ulysses*, the characters operating within a structured system of traditional patterns in which time is central. Jung says that the introvert perceives the world "*sub specie aeternitatis*" because he sees it as reflected in inner primordial images: "The bare sense impression develops in depth, reaching into the past and future, while extraverted sensation seizes on the momentary existence of things open to the light of day" (*PT* 395). Stephen hates time because he sees it from the perspective of eternity, sees it in its opposition to the spirit, while Bloom is avidly absorbed in its stream. Stephen's role and Bloom's are well defined in two early episodes: "Proteus" and "Calypso."

The transformations of "Proteus" take place along a Christian or Neoplatonic scale of being such as we saw in *Exiles*. Spirit, which is not subject to time, is at the top of this scale, mutable matter and corruption at the bottom. Life is poised between the two extremes (as present is poised between future and past), partaking of both and tending toward both. Stephen's reluctant passage through the "ineluctable modality of the visible," his conscious life itself, is represented as a process in which his mind continually strives to move upward into spirit while his body and senses constantly move downward into matter. Downward movement is represented concretely by excretion when Stephen urinates and picks his nose (*U* 49-50). Joyce makes the link between snot and mutability explicit in "Cyclops," when he speaks of a handkerchief as covered "by the rich incrustations of time" (*U* 332), and Stephen's dirty handkerchief was salient in "Telemachus." Stephen also worries about his rotting teeth in "Proteus," but these are not the only instances of movement toward death.

It might seem that Stephen's tendency toward spirit is represented by the stream of his consciousness, his constant creation of thought. But Stephen is aware that language itself, because it has physical qualities, can stand for material things, and can solidify into cliché, can constitute a sort of inanimate matter, as Bloom's often does. Stephen says, "These heavy sands are language tide and wind have silted here" (*U* 44) and describes his own language as "Monkwords, marybeads [which] jabber on their girdles" (*U* 47). He also describes the sound of his micturition as "a fourworded wavespeech" (*U* 49) and later, in "Scylla and Charybdis," he sums up his intellectual discourse by the Latin for urination, "*Mingo, minxi, mictum, mingere*" (*U* 205) and conceives of the library as "Coffined thoughts. . .in mummycases, embalmed in spice of words. . .They are still. Once quick in the brains of men" (*U* 193). In the light of this association between words and matter it may be seen that the poem Stephen writes in "Proteus" and many passages of ornate prose virtuosity in this episode are regarded as excretion.

In *Finnegans Wake* Shem the Penman writes his work in ink made of his own excrement (*FW* 185). In this case Stephen writes the poem by stilling the stream of his consciousness with a pin and setting his vital thoughts down on the same rock upon which he later deposits his snot: "Here. Put a pin in that chap, will you? My tablets. Mouth to her kiss" (*U* 48). "My tablets" refers to Hamlet's, "My tables—meet it is I set it down" (*Ham*. I.v.107). The poem Stephen sets down into dead matter is about the transformation from life to death: "He comes pale vampire . . .mouth to her mouth's kiss." Stephen constantly imagines God kissing his mother with death as Bloom imagines Blazes kissing Molly with infidelity. The two situations are parallel as versions of the same complex. In traditional Christian terms, infidelity and death are versions of the state of man. I indicated in Chapter 3 that the idea of the fall is built on an oedipal framework. For Stephen the union of the "Universal Husband" (*U* 42) with his mother is always going on everywhere that matter exists in its perpetual state of being destroyed by time and God—including his own mind.

Stephen is aware of the spiritual emptiness of his words as he goes through such verbal gymnastics as the elaborate prose poem on his urination. He ironically indulges the excretions of his mind, just as he indulges those of his body, both being inevitable; but part of him is detached from all this, as if his spirit were observing it from a distance. Jung, speaking of the intuitive introvert, Stephen's type, describes "an extraordinary aloofness . . . from tangible reality" (*PT* 401).

Stephen's world, then, is a system of continual transformation in which even thoughts tend toward lifeless matter. He opposes it bitterly and the desire is always implicit in his thinking to soar above the limitation and transience of all sensible realities, including even those of language. He speaks of a language of gestures (*U* 432). He resents the attempt of the revolutionary movement to "yoke" him to political realities (*U* 43) and thinks of himself as Satan forced downward: "Allbright he falls, proud lightning of the intellect" (*U* 50). The impact of the power of time manifested in mother's death forces Stephen to see the world and woman as fields of corruption waiting "to suck his treading soles" and drag him down into a swamp of mutability: "God becomes man becomes fish becomes barnacle goose becomes featherbed mountain.

Dead breaths I living breathe, tread dead dust, devour a urinous offal from all dead" (*U* 50). Bloom, in "Calypso," also devours urinous offal, but he enjoys it (*U* 55), as he enjoys the formed language, the sediment of thought, he receives from other men.

The first page of "Proteus" sums up Stephen's position. Bitterly pre-occupied by the idea of the succession of sensory impressions in dura-tion, the *nacheinander*, which is Bloom's chief delight, Stephen attempts to make the sensory world disappear by closing his eyes: "Open your eyes now. I will. One moment. Has all vanished since? . . .See now. There all the time without you: and ever shall be, world without end" (*U* 37). This last idea is close to a thought from which Bloom derives strong consolation: that there is a regularity and continuousness in the incon-stancy of the world, even though situations and individuals change. This is no consolation for Stephen, for whom self is all. For him, as for Hamlet, the world without end is a great falsified, decaying prison, history, a nightmare from which he strives to awake (*U* 35). At the start of "Proteus" Stephen speaks of "signatures of all things I am here to read," but he is ironical. He later says, "I never could read His handwriting except His criminal thumbprint on the haddock [a fish with a dark spot]" (*U* 562), and here in "Proteus" the only signatures he sees are those of decay: "seaspawn and seawrack, the nearing tide, that rusty boot. Snot-green, bluesilver, rust: coloured signs" (*U* 37).

The detachment of Stephen's mind from his body is reflected in his attitude toward sex. Theoretically, he recognizes the value of sex in "Oxen of the Sun" and elsewhere, just as he theoretically sees the value of contact with "the now, the here" at the start of "Scylla and Charybdis" (*U* 186); and we will later see the value of these theories. Stephen's accept-ance of the world, however, is purely theoretical, just as Bloom's attempts at higher ideas turn out to be no more than physical. And although Stephen inveighs against continence in the name of the "Godpossibled souls that we nightly impossibilize" (*U* 389), he has no positive feeling for love. We have already seen that he generally thinks of "woman's unclean loins" in traditional terms as a sink of decay.

Stephen engages in rebellious libertinism, but his attitude of oppo-sition makes sex a painful experience. One of the novel's few references to his erotic activity occurs in "Scylla and Charybdis" when he thinks of the pound he borrowed from AE: "You spent most of it in Georgina Johnson's bed, clergyman's daughter. Agenbite of inwit" (*U* 189). Stephen, bless his art, has selected a clergyman's daughter as whore. His relation to her, like a lot of modernist sex, involves not only guilt, but patricide; for if daddy could see her then, he'd have an art attack. A de-structive element is also prominent in Stephen's description of things that attracted him in Paris: "perfectly shocking terrific of religion's things mockery. . .vampire man debauch nun very fresh young. . ." (*U* 570). In his libertinism of defiance, Stephen needs to attack his object as much as Bloom needs to be attacked by his. And because Stephen's rejection of all corruption is a rejection of life, his sex life is bleak.

Stephen's addiction to prostitutes is a mode of sex without love which ultimately contrasts to Bloom's love without sex. In Joyce the sex act defines the being of a character. Just as Stephen is unable to love creatively because his rejection keeps him from sensitive contact with any object, so he is unable to carry out his mental, artistic or moral life effectively because he is out of touch with the world. Though he hurts others through his selfishness, he hurts himself most. So his attitude finally resembles Bloom's masochism even though the two start from opposing premises. Though Joyce probably suspected that Stephen and Bloom have to end up in the same essential position because they share the same complex, he seems to have regarded it as a major irony of *Ulysses* that Bloom's and Stephen's relations to the world are both self-destructive even though Bloom accepts the world Stephen rejects. His argument on this level is that both excessive materialism and excessive spirituality are destructive positions. "Extremes meet" (*U* 504).

Contrast between Stephen's attitude toward sex and life and Bloom's is built diagrammatically into "Scylla and Charybdis" in a pattern which typifies Joyce's polar thinking. He presents the following correspondences for "Scylla and Charybdis" on his structural scheme:

The Rock—Aristotle, Dogma, Stratford:
The Whirlpool—Plato, Mysticism, London:
Ulysses—Socrates, Jesus, Shakespeare.

These correspondences do not indicate that either Stephen or Bloom manages to pass between the rock of materialism and the whirlpool of mysticism because they are themselves the embodiment (and the spirit) of the two extremes, though they can combine to form Shakespeare. But the terms of these correspondences may be extended. Stephen says, "Elizabethan London lay as far from Stratford as corrupt Paris lies from virgin Dublin" (*U* 189). London and Paris are associated with prostitution, Stratford and Dublin with conjugal chastity: "Twenty years he [Shakespeare] dallied there [London] between conjugal love and its chaste delights [Ann in Stratford] and scortatory love and its foul pleasures" [London whores] (*U* 201). Thus, Bloom, Dublin, conjugal love and Stratford are associated with Aristotle and dogmatic materialism, while Stephen's Paris, scortatory love and London are linked to Plato and mysticism. Prostitution is an appropriate mode of sex for those who reject the world and devalue their bodies. This is why Joyce's brothel scenes are drenched in religious imagery, why he links the church with whoredom, why his prostitutes speak of visiting clergymen. Joyce may seem kinder to marriage, but remember that his "conjugal bliss" means cuckoldry. We have shown why this is so in analytic terms; in the terms of this chapter, marriage is cuckoldry because the man who desires to possess matter or the world can never really do so; they will be taken from him by time or God.

The epigraph of Jung's *Psychological Types* is a quote from Heine which begins, "Plato and Aristotle! These are not merely two systems, they are types of two distinct human natures, which from time immemorial, under every sort of disguise, stand more or less inimically opposed" (*PT* 2). Heine goes on to contrast the "visionary mystical" Platonic nature to the "practical orderly" Aristotelian. Jung then spends hundreds of pages tracing various polarities through history which prefigures his two great types, including, of course, idealism and materialism. Here again the parallel between Joyce and Jung, both readers of medieval Latin, illustrates their use of traditional insight.

Further articulation of Jung's theory will refine our understanding of the protagonists and their intertwined roles. Jung states that a person's unconscious is characterized by the attitude which opposes the one which dominates his consciousness. Thus, a conscious extravert will have unconscious introverted drives, an introvert will have unconscious extraverted drives. This is because leadership of the psyche by one attitude subverts the other; and the side which is turned away from consciousness tends to regress to a primitive and archaic state. As a result, the extravert has crude, undeveloped selfish feelings in his unconscious, while the introvert has a primitive attachment to objects in his. As in Freud, the more the unconscious elements are denied, the more they will assert themselves. For Jung, however, the unconscious serves a positive purpose in compensating the limits of the conscious attitude as long as it is not too far alienated from consciousness (*PT* 340). Bloom's undeveloped assertion may appear in his occasional indulgence in aggressive phrases toward women he will never meet: "Possess her once take the starch out of her" (*U* 73).

The introvert's subordinate extraversion may be manifested in a desire to cling to the objects of the outside world: "Anything strange and new arouses fear and mistrust, as though concealing unknown perils; heirlooms and suchlike are attached to his soul as by invisible threads; any change is upsetting, if not positively dangerous, as it seems to denote a magical animation of the objects [as in "Circe"]. His ideal is a lonely island where nothing moves except what is permitted to move" (*PT* 379-380). This may explain Stephen's obsession with mutability, the fact that he can't bear to see change even though he can't bear things as they are. Bloom, as extravert, is attached to matter with none of Stephen's horror of change: this side of his personality is not regressive.

Jung's conception may explain the doubt which haunts Stephen and opposes his drive toward separation from the world with moments of longing for contact: "I am lonely here. O touch me soon, now. What is that word known to all men?" (*U* 49). Stephen addresses this plea to his unconscious. The complementary thrust of the unconsciousness may also be seen behind Stephen's quest for a theory to relate his art to the objective world, an effort that has succeeded only in theory. There are contradictions in the idea of someone whose theories represent his unconscious while he is consciously turned inward; and Jung's descriptions suggest that *dominant* and *subordinate* might be more accurate terms for what he often calls conscious and unconscious attitudes.

In addition to the two basic attitudes, Jung's theory of types presents four functions: thinking, feeling, sensation and intuition. Readers may recognize a correspondence to Blake's four Zoas. In addition to his attitude, each person has a leading function and a secondary function, while his remaining two functions are repressed. This diagram is a mandala, a four-sided figure such as those Jung ultimately came to believe in as therapeutic subjects for meditation. Stephen is an introverted intuitive type whose secondary function is thinking, while Bloom is an extraverted sensation and feeling type. This extends the complementary natures of their roles, dividing the functions along the dotted line.

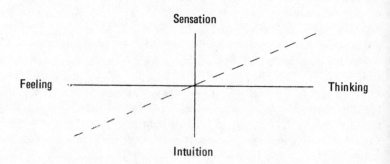

"Intuition tries to apprehend the widest range of possibilities" (*PT* 367), as Stephen does. The intuitive type seizes each new possibility with great intensity, as if it were the turning point of life, but then each situation becomes a prison and the intuitive seeks a new release (*PT* 367–370). He considers himself superior and exempt "from the restrictions of reason only to fall victim to neurotic compulsions." Because he is open to every possibility, "what happens to him is not accidental—here he is the master—instead, the accidents that befall him take the form of rational judgments and rational intentions. . ." (*PT* 371-372). Compare Stephen: "A man of genius makes no mistakes. His errors are volitional and are the portals of discovery" (*U* 190).

The "normal representative" of the introverted intuitive type, the type most turned inward, is the artist; and a more extreme form is the prophet or visionary. Moral problems tend to appear as esthetic problems to the artist. If his thinking is well developed, he may question himself about the relationship of his identity to his vision. As a result, he may see himself as "involved in his vision" and this may lead him to make himself and his life symbolic. Denial of the external world may cause compulsion neurosis. Often nothing of his personality may be "outwardly visible but reserve, secretiveness, lack of sympathy, uncertainty and an apparently groundless embarrassment" so that he may be "a complete enigma to his immediate circle" (*PT* 401-405). And yet he belongs to a valuable segment of humanity because he represents areas of life that are usually overlooked. He struggles to express the eternal forms of things which lie buried within (archetypes). Compare Stephen's desire "to express, to press out again, from the gross earth. . .from sound and shape and colour which are the prison gates of our soul, an image of the beauty we have come to understand. . ." (*P* 207) and his quest for archetypes of beauty.

The extraverted sensory type is described as supremely realistic because of his devotion to tangible reality, and students of Bloom should bear his attachment to matter in mind. Because Bloom is highly moral and unselfish, some readers have suggested that he is an idealist. But examination of passages which express his morality will show that they are grounded in his physical feelings of life and his empathy with the feelings of others: "He bore no hate. / Hate. Love. Those are names. Rudy. Soon I am old" (*U* 285).

Like most extraverts, the sensory type tends to conform to prevailing values, to react to environmental stimuli, to lose himself in absorption in the object. In pronounced cases, "The bondage to the object is carried to the extreme limit. In consequence, the unconscious is forced out of its compensatory role into open opposition. Above all the repressed intuitions begin to reassert themselves in the form of projections. The wildest suspicions arise; if the object is a sexual one, jealous fantasies and anxiety stages gain the upper hand. More acute cases develop every sort of phobia, and, in particular, compulsion symptoms" (*PT* 364-365). Bloom composes in "Ithaca" a list of twenty-five suitors whom he evidently believes to have seduced Molly (*U* 731); but Molly's thoughts in "Penelope" suggest that she only flirted or dallied with most of them.

The most notable point about feeling, Bloom's second function, is that extraverted feeling types are "almost without exception women." This type tends to shift from one state of feeling to another in response to external stimuli so readily that, at the extreme, she "dissolves into a succession of contradictory feeling states, the identity of the ego is lost and the subject lapses into the unconscious" (*PT* 358-359).

The "self-disunity" and "lack of credibility" of this type are central problems for Bloom: his identity is not consistent. Whereas Stephen is disturbed, especially in "Proteus," to feel himself shifting roles constantly, Bloom moves from one feeling to another with such facility that he may be said to enjoy it; it is his equivalent of Odysseus's adaptability. Thus, Bloom, who has been a Catholic, a Protestant, a Mason and Jewish, and who admires Buddhism (*U* 80) and the mystic East, bears resemblances to the "Protean Man" whom Robert Jay Lifton sees as typifying our contemporary scene.[5] He loves Molly, yet in the course of one day he devotes himself in various ways to a girl he sees in Dlugacz's butcher shop, to a lady who boards a carriage impressively (*U* 74), to Gerty MacDowell, to Josie Breen (*U* 442-446), to Zoe Higgins and to Bella Cohen, not to mention the barmaids at the Ormond, Mrs. Yelverton Barry, Mrs. Bellingham, The Honourable Mrs. Mervyn Talboys (*U* 465-468), Blazes and Stephen.

Joyce's success in portraying both of Jung's types and all four of his functions raises questions about the absoluteness or depth of Jung's distinctions, particularly when we recall that many characteristics of Stephen and Bloom are Joyce's. The divisions between the two protagonists of *Ulysses* are not so pronounced from a Freudian point of view. Perhaps Jung's distinctions operate on a more conscious level, a level closer to the surface than Freud's, and therefore may be overstepped more easily by intelligence. After all, the kinds of distinctions Jung makes have been explicit for thousands of years, as Jung demonstrates; whereas Freud's discoveries, though implicit in Sophocles, Shakespeare and others, were shockingly new.

BLOOM

Bloom is as preoccupied with mutability in "Calypso" as Stephen is in "Proteus"; and because Bloom is more strongly attached to matter and to time than Stephen is, his physical nature is far more substantial and extensive in its manifestations. There seem to be three primary branches to Bloom's desires as Joyce conceives them. His devotion to temporal and material phenomena is represented as an interest in the movement downward into inanimate matter, a sexual attraction to excretions and other inanimate objects, such as fetishes, photographs and private property. Secondly, Bloom's acceptance of the inconstancy of the world is shown by his position as a cuckold who, despite occasional misgivings, is contented and in fact titillated by his lot.[6] Lastly, the self-negation of Bloom's involvement in the external world and the self-destruction inherent in his acceptance of time are ironically portrayed as masochism.

All of these themes are indicated in "Calypso," though most references to time in this episode are not as noticeable as those in "Proteus" because they are not discordant. Trivial phrases such as "another time" show Bloom's harmonious involvement in time and his desire to make use of it. While Stephen is hardly ever shown anticipating anything favorably, Bloom is often seen in this stance. On the first page of "Calypso" he waits for his tea, thinking, "cup of tea soon" (U 55). A bit below he reflects that Thursday is not a good day for mutton kidney at Buckley's. Going out, he tells Molly that he will be back in a minute and thinks of her father, who was smart enough to make a "corner" in stamps: "Now that was farseeing" (U 56). The art of this episode is economics, and Bloom's attitude toward time and matter is economical. We see how economies of time and matter go together as he tries to calculate the sum of money made by a pub owner in a given period.

Like the busy bee, Bloom constantly studies to "improve the shining hour" (U 647). His mind is filled with plans for counteracting the effects of the passage of time and making the most efficient use of it. These plans range from such relatively noble preoccupations as the desire for a son and a vague conception of the cyclical repetition of history (U 377 ff.) through a profusion of various vacation, money-making and civic improvement schemes to such appropriate interests as metempsychosis and scientism, which give hope for the future, and mnemotechnique and Sandow's exercises, attempts to save the past; and finally they include such nonsense as recording the voices of those who are to die (U 114) and the industrial use of human excrement (U 718). Ironically, Bloom's compulsive planning, while it is an effort to oppose the effects of time, actually increases his dependence on time, placing his goals in the future and making him more open to the injury and loss that time can inflict. Moreover, he wastes his time by daydreaming.

The first of these plans occurs to Bloom not long after the beginning of "Calypso": ". . .set off at dawn, travel round in front of the sun, steal a day's march on him. Keep it up for ever never grow a day older technically" (U 57). All of Bloom's plans, even such seemingly profound thoughts as his cyclical conception of history, are essentially cut from the same cloth. Based on physical perceptions, they serve to represent

Bloom as a figure who strives to make the best of the passage of time and all are useless to him in the physical terms in which they are defined (won't work), although they are profitable insofar as Bloom contents his mind by thinking of them.

On the next page we get our first glimpse of Bloom's characteristic sexual tendencies as he enters the shop of the butcher Dlugacz. These tendencies are unveiled in a setting of dead meat and the smell of blood, and Bloom is sexually attracted by the tendency of life toward inanimate matter. This attraction is presented explicitly by Robert Hand in *Exiles*. Fondling a stone, symbol of inanimate matter, Robert says that he is attracted to woman by "how quickly she changes by digestion what she eats into—what shall be nameless" (*E* 42). Bloom shows masochism by taking an interest in the girl next to him partially because he visualizes her "whacking" a carpet with vigor. In addition, she is attractive to him as meat. He refers to her as "new blood," "sound meat," "moving hams," and "prime sausage."

The girl also makes Bloom think of the cattle market where he used to work. As he believes that his cattle market boss, Joe Cuffe (*U* 97, 315) has seduced Molly (*U* 731), his sexual stimulation here may be associated with cuckoldry. The passage on the cattle market, moreover, suggests masochism and coprophilia: ". . .the beasts lowing in their pens, branded sheep, flop and fall of dung, the breeders in hobnail boots. . .slapping a palm on a ripemeated hindquarter, there's a prime one, unpeeled switches. . . [back to the girl] the crooked skirt swinging whack by whack by whack" (*U* 59). When the girl leaves, Bloom is mildly excited by the fantasy of yielding her to another: "The sting of disregard glowed to weak pleasure within his breast. For another: a constable off duty cuddled her in Eccles Lane" (*U* 59-60). An early indication of the sexual pleasure Bloom derives from being cuckolded.

Joyce regards Bloom's need for loss as subjection not only to time and matter, but to their human controllers, Church and State. Of course, Bloom doesn't believe in the Church or the State in any idealistic way, but he admires their effectiveness. Of the Church, he says, "Wonderful organization certainly, goes like clockwork" (*U* 82-83). The meat market that Bloom associates with masochism relates to Stephen's image of God (and Shakespeare's father) as a butcher. When Bloom thinks, "She does whack it, by George" (*U* 59), Joyce intends a reference to English royalty to be linked to sadism. And the image of the girl going to a policeman represents Bloom's subordination to temporal authority.

Bloom weaves another plan for combatting time in the butcher's when he dreams of "quiet long days" in Agendath Netaim, where things are "always the same, year after year" (*U* 60). At this point a cloud passes over the face of the sun and Bloom envisions Jerusalem as a grey waste-land. Like most of Bloom's thinking, this passage proceeds from external stimuli. After the cloud has turned his thoughts grey, an old woman passes, giving him the principle image of "the grey sunken cunt of the world." Throughout the day Bloom has several such realizations of the terror of mutability; his reactions to them are always similar and always different from Stephen's brooding rebelliousness. He changes the subject, transferring his thoughts to practical considerations. We see this in "Hades," where he is glad to turn away in the graveyard from images of death back to the "real" world or to some plan for improving burial: "Enough of this place" (*U* 114). In "Lestrygonians," after another cloud covers the sun, he has a depressing vision of human mutability and of everyone preying on everyone else: "No one is anything"; then he explains this vision by telling himself that it is "the very worst hour of the day" (*U* 164), consolidating his involvement in time. This flight from muta-bility into busyness is the same pattern that he follows when unpleasant thoughts of Blazes occur.

In "Calypso" he dismisses the disturbing subject in the next para-graph by blaming his thoughts on his physical condition and turning to one of his supposedly practical plans for counteracting the effects of time: "Well, I am here now. Morning mouth bad images. Got up wrong side of the bed. Must begin again those Sandow's exercises. On the hands down" (*U* 61). Joyce ironically represents this particular plan as a form of obeisance that Bloom makes to the *dio boia*. For in "Circe" Bello repeats to Bloom the direction for this exercise, "On the hands down!" (*U* 531), with sharper emphasis.

Bloom now arrives home and has breakfast. The morning meal con-sists of a kidney, one of his favorite delicacies because of its "tang" of urine (*U* 55), and bread, which he eats in the form of "dies" (*U* 65), the word *die* suggesting day, death and chance. In addition to eating his daily bread, Bloom also serves "our daily press" (*U* 647). During break-fast he reads Milly's letter, which brings up the temporal inevitabilities of her growth, separation and fall. We learn elsewhere that Milly has been seduced by Alec Bannon (*U* 21, 397, 427). Bloom does not know this, but he is suspicious. His typical reaction: "Destiny. Ripening now. . . . Will happen, yes. Prevent. Useless: can't move. . .the flowing qualm spread over him. Useless to move now" (*U* 66–67).

Now Bloom goes to the outhouse, where he shows the same economy which he practices with all matter and time: "No great hurry. Keep it a bit" (*U* 68). Joyce has insight close enough to the Freudian to realize that this anal control represents a key pattern of Bloom's relation to his world. For example, Bloom thinks of easing Martha Clifford into using obscene language in her letters: "Go further next time. . .A bit at a time" (*U* 78). And notesheets for "Circe" juxtapose "Dreck" and "gold" (*N* 314).

Bloom often consults his watch, while Stephen evidently has none. Nosey Flynn later says of the older man, "If you ask him to have a drink first thing he does he outs with the watch to see what he ought to imbibe" (*U* 178). Joyce originally conceived Bloomsday as a story for *Dubliners* to be called "Mr Hunter" (*JJ* 238-239). This early narrative about a Jew looking for a son would probably have been more negatively ironic than *Ulysses* in keeping with the outlook of *Dubliners*. Now hunter was a well known type of watch and "a fat gold hunter watch" is mentioned in *Ulysses* (253). It may well be that Joyce conceived of Bloom as a human timepiece.

Bloom's watch stops at the nadir of his day, at the end of "Sirens," as Blazes and Molly are making love; and while it is stopped, Bloom visits Paddy Dignam's bereaved family. While Bloom's watch is not working, from the end of "Sirens" to the middle of "Nausikaa" (*U* 291-361)—or from about 4:30 to about 8:30—we do not enter his stream of consciousness. Joyce uses the narrators of "Cyclops" and "Nausikaa" instead of Bloom's point of view. It seems as if the highly physical and temporal mechanism of Bloom's mind were being compared to a clock. Gerty MacDowell sees Bloom winding his watch shortly before we reenter his mind in "Nausikaa."

In "Ithaca" we learn that Bloom has instructed his daughter in "the principle of the pendulum, exemplified in bob, wheelgear and regulator, the translation in terms of human or social regulation of the various positions clockwise of movable indicators on an unmoving dial" (*U* 694). On the final page of "Calypso" Bloom recalls timing his wife as she dressed. He then thinks of Boylan, who is to be equated with time, of the dance of the hours, which pleases him, and of Dignam's imminent funeral (*U* 69-70), three elements linked to time. Finally, the bells toll the hour, Bloom characteristically hearing them as "Heigho! Heigho!"

"Calypso" has suggested ways in which Bloom's sexual attitudes parallel his ties to matter and time, and these parallels extend through the novel, hedging Bloom about with irony. Jung says that the extravert who carries his attachment to matter too far and loses contact with his introverted unconscious side will cause a reaction of introverted symptoms, "one of the most typical being a morbid intensification of fantasy activity" (*PT* 337).

Bloom's incessant daydreaming defines him as a man so strongly driven by desire that he is unable to effect real contact with the object of his desires. Lost in fantasies, he is always planning, but never achieving. His characteristic sexual activity is ejaculation without entrance. Thus, if Stephen leads a life of intercourse without love, Bloom leads one of love without intercourse. The complementary natures of the two characters and their need for each other are obvious. Bloom needs Stephen's detachment, while Stephen needs his contact with matter. As Jung says, extraversion and introversion benefit from contact with each other "since in themselves both orientations are one-sided and of limited validity, so that each needs the influence of the other" (*PT* 345). Thus, the two men may help each other by their relationship, developing themselves toward the Jungian goal of wholeness.

We have seen that Bloom has three fundamental drives: his masochism, his cuckoldry and an attraction to inanimate matter and the tendency toward inanimate matter in life. The showing forth of Gerty MacDowell in "Nausikaa," the major staging of Bloom's mode of love without intercourse, elaborates his interest in matter and excretions. Earlier Stephen deposited his snot and his poem on a rock on the beach, and now Gerty is seated on one; and although we cannot tell if the two rocks are identical, it is clear that both represent lifelessness. As I suggested earlier, Bloom is as much excited by Gerty's underwear here as he is by her body: "*Lingerie* does it" (*U* 368); "O sweety all your little girlwhite up I saw dirty bracegirdle made me do love sticky . . ." (*U* 382).

Significantly, Gerty is menstruating while Bloom observes her, as Molly is in "Penelope." The sentimental narrator points this out: ". . . he was looking all the time that he was winding the watch or whatever he was doing to it and then he put it back and put his hands back into his pockets . . .that thing must be coming on because the last time too was when she clipped her hair on account of the moon. His dark eyes fixed themselves on her. . .literally worshipping at her shrine" (*U* 361). Bloom is soon aware of Gerty's menstruation, evidently because of her complexion (*U* 368-369, 442); and his perception here indicates his acute physiological sensitivity.

Sexual intercourse, for Joyce, should be a movement upward into spirit because it can call a soul out of eternity into time and matter, an important point to which I will return. But if intercourse can rise into spirit, masturbation, or the spillage of seed, is an excretion, a sinking into dead matter. Thus, masturbation and menstruation go together well to constitute an anti-coition, or apotheosis of sterility. Menstruation represents time not only as a passage of life downward into matter, but also as a periodic phenomenon. In "Nausikaa" the close linkage between Bloom's winding of his watch and his masturbation shows his sexual excitement as involvement in time, worship at the shrine of matter as well as *mater*. (Gerty shares with Molly the Virgin Mary's birthday, September 8, and her color, blue.) Bloom's thoughts on the stopping of his watch while Molly and Blazes were fornicating are worth examining:

Very strange about my watch. . .Wonder is there any magnetic influence between the person because that was about the time he. Yes, I suppose at once. Cat's away the mice will play. . .Also that now is magnetism. Back of everything magnetism. Earth for instance pulling this and being pulled. That causes movement. And time? Well that's the time the movement takes. Magnetic needle tells you what's going on in the sun, the stars. Little piece of steel iron. When you hold out the fork. Come. Come. Tip. Woman and man that is. Fork and steel. Molly, he. Dress up and look and suggest and let you see and see more and defy you if you're a man to see that and, like a sneeze coming. . .Have to let fly. (*U* 373-374)

Here is a central statement of the Bloomian metaphysic: an attempt to provide a naturalistic explanation which really expresses religious devotion to the power of feminine attraction. The force behind the universe is the natural phenomenon of magnetism or desire. This view resembles that of Jung, who accepted extrasensory phenomena and occultism because he believed the physical universe to be controlled at least partly by unconscious archetypal mental forces, as we will see.

Joyce puts a scatological pun into Bloom's statement that time is "the time the movement takes." Waste matter and desire are indissolubly linked in his well-developed excremental vision. Bloom's logos of lust, by causing movement and change, causes time; and therefore time, as a function of matter, is a function of desire. This is why the state of Bloom's watch is so intimately related to his emotional life. The idea that time is caused by desire is a standard concept in occultism, mysticism and Eastern thought, where it usually supports the idea that he who can overcome desire can transcend time. Bloom, however, is absorbed in the field of matter and time, driven by desire and anxious to keep his watch wound. He has another insight related to occult or Eastern thought in this scene when he perceives time as cyclical: "The year returns. History repeats itself" (*U* 377). But here again, instead of desiring to escape the cycles, he draws comfort from them. Jungians such as Joseph Campbell also derive satisfaction from the idea that patterns repeat in history.

In "Ithaca," after a long budget which takes account of the expenditure of his substance in shillings during the day, Bloom trims an aching toenail before retiring. This excretion is another personal expense:

[He] raised the part lacerated to his nostrils and inhaled the odour of the quick, then with satisfaction threw away the lacerated unguical fragment.
Why with satisfaction?
Because the odour inhaled corresponded to. . .odours. . .of other unguical fragments, picked. . .by Master Bloom, pupil of. . .juvenile school . . .each night in the act of brief genuflection and nocturnal prayer and ambitious meditation. (*U* 712)

The three religious acts which Bloom performed in school, brief genu-flection, nocturnal prayer and ambitious meditation, are dutifully per-formed on June 17, 1904, the last being Bloom's long fantasy of an estate in Flowerville. These are the evening services of the middle class and are addressed to Natural Phenomenon, a god who is, in Ellmann's phrase, "substantially" present as excretion. Here Bloom follows a typical pattern of finding soothing consistency and order within change, even in the steady passage of his body into lifelessness.

Another component in Bloom's religion of the physical is "The Wonder-worker, the world's greatest remedy for rectal complaints . . ." (*U* 721). "It heals and soothes while you sleep. . ." as Bloom's fantasies do and "assists nature in the most formidable way" as Bloom does by introducing Blazes to Molly (*U* 732). It brings about regeneration, as a religious instrument should, "making a new man of you" (*U* 722). And it represents the need for authority as a need to be screwed.

Bloom says in "Circe," "I have paid homage on that living altar where the back changes name" (*U* 551). He earlier examined the mesial grooves of statues of Greek goddesses. His devotion to matter and excrement must be seen as a religion to be appreciated. Norman O. Brown, in *Life Against Death*, traced the line of medieval Christian thinking which associated the material goods of the world with excrement because the world belonged to the devil (pp. 207-226). This idea, held intensely by Martin Luther, is held ambivalently by Joyce. It allows his Stephen side to laugh at his Bloom side, as one side of him laughs at the other through most of the book. The theological tie between the world, the devil and love reduced to excrement is at the heart of "Circe," Joyce's definitive presentation of the modern world of industrialism and capitalism. This is why the episode presents a Black Mass as one of its climaxes. Joyce's vision of the modern world as whorehouse is echoed in Norman Mailer's *Deer Park*, a key novel of the American fifties, which are back.

In "Ithaca" Bloom reacts to Boylan's seduction of Molly with "envy, jealousy, abnegation, equanimity" (*U* 732). We have seen the import of his accepting cuckoldry with equanimity as a natural phenomenon. The ex-planation of his jealousy also touches on his most basic values: rather than describing his resentment, this passage goes far to explain why he has allowed or arranged the meeting of Blazes and Molly, as the paragraph following this one indicates:

Because a nature full and volatile in its free state, was alternately the agent and reagent of attraction. Because action between agents and re-agents at all instants varied, with inverse proportion of increase and decrease, with incessant circular extension and radial reentrance. Because the controlled contemplation of the fluctuation of attraction produced, if desired, a fluctuation of pleasure. (*U* 732)

Bloom realizes that Molly is subject to constantly changing desires. Unable to fulfill her desires, largely because his own are misdirected, he gives Molly up to Blazes because he wants to satisfy her and to preserve her "nature full and volatile in its free state." Bloom enjoys watching the variations of Molly's desire, and his "controlled contemplation of the fluctuation of attraction" is a key to his character. The passive pleasure he takes in observing change is diffused throughout his part of the novel and all along he finds consolation for the disorder of mutability in the regularity and permanence of nature. In "Ithaca" we see his fondness for "neverchanging everchanging water" and for the moon, which resembles woman in "her constancy under all her phases, rising, and setting by her appointed times, waxing and waning. . ." (*U* 702). We are also told that "in middle youth he had often sat observing through. . .a multicoloured pane the spectacle offered with continual changes of the thoroughfare without. . ." (*U* 681).

After Bloom completes his evening meditations and daydreams Joyce sums up all of his involvement with matter and time as an attraction to excretion:

> In what final satisfaction did these antagonistic sentiments and reflections, reduced to their simplest forms, converge?
> Satisfaction at the ubiquity in eastern and western terrestrial hemispheres. . .of adipose posterior female hemispheres, redolent of milk and honey and of excretory sanguine and seminal warmth. . .insusceptible of moods of impression or of contrarieties of expression, expressive of mute immutable mature animality. (*U* 734)

The parallel references to hemispheres indicate association between woman and the world, both magnets to Bloom. He now becomes excited and kisses Molly's behind, fulfilling Bello Cohen's epithet, "adorer of the adulterous rump!" (*U* 530). I will give Molly the last word on Bloom's sexual interest in matter. In "Penelope" she recalls one of Bloom's higher flights of spirituality during their courtship: ". . .his mad crazy letters my Precious one everything connected with your glorious Body everything underlined that comes from it is a thing of beauty and of joy for ever something he got out of some nonsensical book" (*U* 771).

The second aspect of Bloom's sexuality, his cuckoldry, is a function of time because Molly's inconstancy is the inconstancy of the earth and Bloom is devoted to both. Therefore, the action of his cuckolding is linked extensively to mutability. This association emerges most strongly in key passages of "Ithaca" which explain why Bloom accepts his horns:

If he had smiled why would he have smiled?

To reflect that each one who enters imagines himself to be the first to enter. . .whereas he is neither first nor last nor only nor alone in a series originating in and repeated to infinity. (*U* 731)

This passage implies, as "Penelope" does, that the men who come and go in Molly's life are like generations on the abiding earth (Gilbert, *Ulysses*, p. 382). Here is another example, at a critical juncture in the novel of Bloom's deification of the earth mother. On his notesheets for "Ithaca" Joyce wrote, "God a woman" (*N* 421).

The comparison of mortality to cuckoldry, incidentally, fits traditional patterns, as this passage from a fifteenth-century lyric indicates:

I see this worldes joye lasteth but a sesoun:
Wolde to God I hadde remembred me biforn!
I seye namore but be war of an horn.
This feble world, so fals and so unstable,
Promoteth his lovers for a litel while;
But atte laste he yeveth hem a bable,
Whan his peynted trouthe is turned into gile.[7]

Whether or not the word "horn" in the third line refers to cuckoldry as well as the trumpet of judgment, the comparison of the world to a fickle lover is evident and appears to be a convention.

Connection between Bloom's cuckoldry and mutability is suggested in "Hades" when Bloom and others in a carriage pass Boylan. Joyce delineates a subtle sequence of responses: Bloom first appears to spot Blazes subliminally. Then he turns to distract himself with trivial physical details, and when others see Blazes, he decides that his thoughts of Blazes were coincidental:

He's coming in the afternoon. Her songs.

Plasto's. Sir Philip Crampton's memorial fountain bust. Who was he?

—How do you do? Martin Cunningham said, raising his palm to his brow in salute.

. . . . . .
—Blazes Boylan, Mr Power said. . .

Just that moment I was thinking.

. . . . . .
Mr Bloom reviewed the nails of his left hand, then those of his right hand. The nails, yes. Is there anything more in him that they she sees? Fascination. Worst man in Dublin. . . I am just looking at them: well pared. And after [she has made love to him] : thinking alone. Body getting a bit softy. . .But the shape is there. . .Shoulders. Hips. Plump. Night of the dance dressing. Shift stuck between the cheeks behind.

He clasped his hands between his knees and satisfied, sent his vacant glance over their faces. (*U* 92)

In attempting to distract himself from thoughts of Blazes by gazing at his nails, Bloom only compounds his mortification, for these "excrescences" represent his passage into death. Thoughts of Blazes lead Bloom to think of his wife's mutability as well as his own and he invokes one of his favorite formulas for consolation, the idea that there is a constancy within change—in this case, the constancy of Molly's figure even though she is getting older. Bloom is now "satisfied," and whether it is because of the vicarious thrill that he got from the thought of Blazes or from the contemplation of his nails, his rational victory over mutability or his wife's buttocks, it is all one, for they are all aspects of his acceptance of time and matter.

A similar pattern may be observed in "Lestrygonians" when thoughts of astronomy and clocks lead Bloom's mind to a vision of entropy or cosmic mutability. The idea of entropy, seen as a descent from spirit into matter, is succeeded immediately by the painful image of Blazes and Molly holding hands, and Bloom escapes from these images by focussing his attention on his environment:

> Gas, then solid, then world, then cold, then dead shell drifting around, frozen rock. . .The moon. . .
> . . .She was humming: The young May moon she's beaming, love. He other side of her. Elbow, arm. . .
> Stop. Stop. . .
> . . . . . .
> With a keep quiet relief, his eyes took note: this is street here middle of the day Bob Doran's bottle shoulders. (*U* 167)

Both Stephen and Bloom are constantly haunted by the primal scene, which both see in terms of father time forcing himself on mother matter. Bloom's flight from Blazes to material distractions is a flight from father to mother, from agent to patient, as well as being a flight from phallic sexuality to anality, the movement typical of compulsion neurosis if not of modern civilization. Bloom has another encounter with Boylan which leads him to intensify his engagement in time at the end of "Lestrygonians." When he sees Blazes, he rushes ahead into the museum, thinking, "Quick. Cold statues: quiet there. Safe in a minute. / No, didn't see me. After two" (*U* 183).

Blazes Boylan and Molly's adultery are associated with time in Bloom's mind because he knows the hour, four o'clock, at which their illicit meeting is supposed to take place. This is illustrated most forcefully when Nosey Flynn, after inquiring about Molly's projected singing tour, asks, "Isn't Blazes Boylan mixed up in it?" (*U* 172). Bloom reacts as follows: "A warm shock of air heat of mustard hauched on Mr Bloom's heart. He raised his eyes and met the stare of a bilious clock. Two. Pub clock five minutes fast. Time going on. Hands moving. Two. Not yet." In "Sirens," when Bloom encounters Boylan again, thoughts of adultery are again accompanied by thoughts of "clockhands turning" (*U* 260, 263-264). And Blazes symbolically rings the hour when he plays *sonnez la cloche* with Lydia Douce. When Bloom realizes that it is four o'clock he knows that Boylan is on his way to Molly. Thus, the action is so framed as to suggest that Bloom is actually being cuckolded by time itself. Bloom's cuckoldry is also linked to time by prominent references to cuckoo clocks (*U* 382, 469).

The connection between Bloom's masochism and the pleasure he derives from cuckoldry should be clear. In the two major scenes of masochism in "Circe," the trial scene (*U* 455-472) and the scene with Bella-Bello (*U* 527–544), Bloom imagines himself taunted for his perversions and derided for his cuckoldry during the fantasies in which he is physically abused. Downward motion into matter is suggested both times as Bloom bends down for punishment. His masochism enacts the self-abasement inherent in all aspects of his position. He is victimized in these fantasies either by members of the ruling classes of society or by persons who are physically aggressive and embody the principle of force. All of these oppressors are agents of the *dio boia* or Natural Phenomenon and associate with time as fellow contributors to the force of circumstance. They include the aristocracy, seen in mesdames Bellingham, Barry and Talboys, the clergy, three of whom present Bloom with a marble cuckoo clock (*U* 469), and Bella Cohen, who represents the middle class *nouveaux riches* who have risen through administrative skill (hardness) and social grace (falseness) and who boast of acquaintance with upper-class gentlemen. Joyce refers to her by the unfriendly Irish word for a police officer in his notes: "flattey BC" (*N* 350).

Stephen's two masters, Rome and England (*U* 20) rule Joyce's Dublin, enforcing the power of time which ensnares and destroys the Dubliners. Sultan shows that this is why "Wandering Rocks," a portrayal of a subjugated and lifeless city, begins with Father Conmee's tour and ends with the English Viceregal procession (*Argument*, pp. 206-213). Bloom's particular bondage to matter, time and fantasy is also a bondage to Rome and England. His subjection to Rome is suggested in "Nausikaa" when he performs a parody of mariolotry with Gerty, a parody of the Virgin, to the tune of liturgical chanting from the nearby chapel where men are adoring Saint Mary, all by the light of a candle fittingly Roman.

Not only do priests humiliate Bloom in "Circe" but the final temptation is presented by a nun, The Nymph, whose pure surface covers putrescence within. I have cited the line in "Lotus Eaters" where Bloom admires the Church even though it drugs its followers: "Wonderful organisation certainly, goes like clockwork" (*U* 82-83). And his dream house in Flower-ville will feature "ormolu mantel chronometer clock, guaranteed time-keeper with cathedral chime" (*U* 713). A list of the contents of Bloom's drawers that follows this suburban fantasy includes many items showing his subjection to England:

> 2 fading photographs of Queen Alexandra of England and of Maud Branscombe, actress and professional beauty. . .a press cutting from an English weekly periodical *Modern Society*, subject corporal chastisement in girls' schools: . . .two partly uncoiled rubber preservatives with reserve pockets, purchased by post from. . .Charing Cross, London, W. C.: 2 erotic photocards. . .purchased by post from. . .Charing Cross, London, W.C. . . . prospectus of the Wonderworker. . .direct from. . .London. . .(*U* 721)

"London, W. C.," has been providing Bloom with fantasies upon which he wastes himself: his attachment to the world puts him in thrall to the powers of the world.

I have shown that even though Stephen and Bloom are opposites, their positions finally are ironically parallel. Self-destructive and sterile, both are locked in faulty modes of relation to life and time. Bloom is excessively attached to time, matter and woman, while Stephen is unhealthily re-pulsed from them. Joyce suggests a further paradox in "Circe" when Stephen speaks of the distance between "the fundamental and the domi-nant" (*U* 504), or between the rectal and the theological, Bloom and himself. At this point Lynch mocks an idea of Bruno's he's heard from Stephen: "Jewgreek is greekjew. Extremes meet. Death is the highest form of life. Bah!" This parallels Jung's idea that if a person develops one func-tion too far, he will end up ruled by the opposite function. And Joyce knew that just because Bloom is totally materialistic, he ends up a spiritual being, while Stephen's complete opposition to physical life lands him in the materialistic position of libertinism. For Bloom, unable to conceive of anything except in physical terms, can never stop wanting what he can never possess, so he lives in a perpetual spiritual state of exclusion. And Stephen feels the material world with extraordinary intensity because he hates it so.

The ideal relation to life would seem to be midway between the two extremes, a position of unified sensibility which would be vital both materially and spiritually. Such a position would be in tune with time and matter because it would balance the involvement of Bloom with the distance, irony and intellectual understanding of Stephen, the unselfish-ness of the former with the self-assertion of the latter. This middle posi-tion corresponds to what Goldberg, adopting a term from *Stephen Hero*, calls "the classical temper."

Neither character attains such a position in *Ulysses*, however, nor do they even appear to progress toward it. *Ulysses* presents both sides of its thematic dualities in a state of dramatic contrast. The *Portrait's* definition of the dramatic mode elucidates this situation: Stephen says that in this mode the author, like God, disappears "within or behind or beyond" his characters, who assume a life of their own (*P* 215). Thus, Stephen and Bloom project isolated aspects of Joyce's personality: neither represents his whole soul. Perhaps his soul is to be found in the conflict between them. In this case, Stephen's definition of the dramatic artist implies serious self-alienation and inner conflict, an implication borne out by his portrayal of Shakespeare.

Jung recognizes the difficulty of harmonizing Stephen's side and Bloom's when he says that extraversion and introversion cannot be balanced in an individual because the two attitudes oppose one another and clash until one takes the upper hand (*PT* 405 ff.). Joyce saw a similar reciprocity in the conflict between the material and the spiritual which permeates his work. Professor MacHugh, in the "Aeolus" episode, says, "Success. . .is the death of the intellect and of the imagination" (*U* 133), reminding us of Joyce's remark of the *Ulysses* period, "Material victory is the death of spiritual preeminence" (*JJ* 460). And harking back also to *Exiles* and the prolific-devouring duality. The world of *Ulysses* is ruled by brutish material power, symbolized nationally in MacHugh's discourse by the conquerors Egypt, Rome and Britain; but the spiritual realm of creativity belongs to the victimized aspect of humanity, seen in Israel, Greece and Ireland. Skeptical insight into the corrupt nature of life here derives from a spiritual perspective and makes its holder see the value of the world of spirit, a world in which passivity is morally superior to action.

Joyce creates Stephen and Bloom, juxtaposes them, and defines their positions as widely and rigorously separated in order to dramatize a conflict within himself and within humanity which he is unable to reconcile. We will see that he suggests the possibility of such a reconciliation, but it must remain only a possibility. There is no tangible evidence of reconciliation or improvement in the characters themselves. Indeed, we are given a sharp contrast between their two positions as they part and walk away from each other in "Ithaca":

What sound accompanied the. . .disunion of their (respectively) centrifugal [Stephen] and centripetal [Bloom] hands?
The sound of the peal of the hour. . .in the church of Saint George [time imposed by Church and England].
What echoes of that sound were by both and each heard?
By Stephen:

Liliata rutilantium. Turma circumdet. Iubilantium te virginum.
Chorus excipiat.
   By Bloom:
      Heigho, heigho.
      Heigho, heigho. (*U* 704)

Both continue to apprehend time as they did at the start of *Ulysses*
the sound of time is cheerful to Bloom, but Stephen hears it as a bitter
reminder of his mother's death (compare *U* 10, 70). Time separates
Stephen and Bloom not only because it is late at night, because their
meeting is temporary and accidental, and because one is almost a generation older than the other, but also because time is the factor which prevents reconciliation of their ontological positions. Time itself constitutes
the essential difference between spirit and matter and therefore holds
apart the internal and the external and prevents the ideal relationship
between subject and object. Therefore, reconciliation between Stephen
and Bloom would constitute a triumph over time, while their separation,
which is what objectively occurs, represents the fallen, temporal state
of man.

In the pages which precede the exit and separation of Stephen and
Bloom, the text asks what factors render problematic for Bloom the
realization of his proposals to see Stephen again. The answers, which are
illustrated at length, are, "the irreparability of the past. . .the imprevidibility of the future. . ." (*U* 696). After this the text asks, with Bloom's
mind, whether human life could be "infinitely perfectible" (*U* 697). This
last question is essentially the same as the previous one, for the union of
Stephen and Bloom would presumably produce the ideal state of life
represented by a balanced compromise between their two attitudes; and
the answer given is similar to the previous answer. A list of natural conditions which prevent the perfection of life is presented, describing the
fallen state of existence in terms of the temporal and the accidental. The
same list also mentions the distance between individual human beings,
thus furthering the association between the separation shown in "Ithaca"
and the principle of time: ". . .the painful character of the ultimate functions of separate existence, the agonies of birth and death: the monoto-
nous menstruation of. . .females. . .painful maladies. . .catastrophic
cataclysms. . .the fact of vital growth, through convulsions of metamor-
phosis from infancy through maturity to decay" (*U* 697). Thus, Joyce
indicates that time is responsible for the failure of communication between Stephen and Bloom. Time has enslaved Bloom and driven Stephen
to revolt, and neither is capable of the attitude of harmonious equanimity
necessary for a proper and fruitful relation to time and the world.

Joyce's conscious framing of the problems of his characters in these metaphysical terms is in itself an imposition of compulsive magic formulas on life's reality. The primary defensive aim seems to be to render threats abstract and impersonal. The problem of time may not be solvable on an individual level, but neither does it attack one as an individual.

X

LOVE AS CREATION IN *ULYSSES*

The bard of the wounded groin whom Stephen creates in his lecture is significant not only as a view of Shakespeare, Stephen, Bloom or Joyce, but as a view of the world. The most creative person is psychologically castrated for the same reason bards like Homer were blind, because the making of new realities must be carried out by those who are unable to find satisfaction in existing ones, who find the bed of actuality "second best." As Stephen is dispossessed by Buck and Bloom, by Blazes, the spiritual people in Joyce's world virtually always appear in physical fact under the control of brutal, insensitive materialists. Jews, Greeks and Irish are inevitably conquered by Egyptians, English and Romans of Empire or Church. Mulligan the doctor, Boylan the organizer and Bella Cohen the administrator are the kinds of people who run the world. In "Circe" Stephen and Bloom have to be rescued by Corny Kelleher, a police informer. In the Grail myth the wound which the virtuous King Anfortas bears symbolizes the fallen nature of the wasteland.

But the wound Shakespeare feels whenever he thinks of the "dull-brained yokel" on whom the world's favor has declined (*U* 202), a satyr to his Hyperion, is a bitterness for which Stephen knows of a cure:

. . .the shadow lifts. What softens the heart of a man, Shipwrecked in storms dire, Tried, like another Ulysses, Pericles, prince of Tyre?

. . . . . .

—A child, a girl placed in his arms, Marina. (*U* 195)

Though sensitivity seems on the face of things a disadvantage, it may prove stronger than force in the long run because it is capable of creating life. Marilyn French observes that Bloom "allows other people to be."[1] What is passive receives, recognizes and generates beyond itself. Perhaps this is why the surviving children Marina, Perdita, Miranda and Milly are female, extensions of the passive aspects of their fathers. Passivity separates itself from the life it perceives by giving up an active role, and destruction controls the seemingly meaningless world that Stephen calls "the hell of time" (*U* 195), but creation points to a world beyond time and to possibilities of meaning and order. Reconciliation to the world through transcendence of it may be seen in the images of rebirth so prominent in Shakespeare's late tragicomedies.

Jung is the psychologist of transcendence, and his late work increasingly expresses belief in an eternal world which he perceives through his archetypes. The metaphysical implications of this eternal world are worked out in the essay on synchronicity published during the early fifties.[2] Synchronicity is meaningful coincidence, and is manifested in such forms as foreknowledge and extrasensory perception. Jung adds synchronicity to the conventional scientific trio of space, time and causality to form another of his mandala-like foursomes. Citing personal experiences and statistics from E.S.P. experiments, he says meaningful coincidence operates in cases where chance and physical causality break down. Subjection of physical events to the mind accords with Jung's lifelong tendency to view the external world as at least partly a projection of an inner one. The unconscious forms of the archetypes generate the meaning which causes synchronicity. Acausal acts are "creative" because they are "the continuous creation of a pattern that exists from all eternity, repeats itself sporadically, and is [like God] not derived from any known antecedents." These acts reach outside time to relate to eternity.

Jung says the idea that the universe is pervaded and controlled by a principle of meaning is widespread in Eastern thinking and was accepted in the West until recently: "Causality occupies this paramount position with us, but it acquired its importance only in the course of the last few centuries."[3] The force of meaning in determining events was accepted as long as religion ruled. Jung does not treat literature in this essay, but as late as the great novelists of the nineteenth century, synchronicity was freely employed. Writers such as Dickens, Dostoevsky, the Brontes, Hardy and even George Eliot are crowded with examples of meaningful coincidence, prophetic dream and even extrasensory perception, as when Jane hears Rochester's voice at the end of *Jane Eyre*. Realism began as a reaction against myth, as *Don Quixote* shows, and it has always retained that attitude. To this day the novelist is confronted with the task of making a meaningful world (myth), though he may do his best to reject or avoid that task.

Ulysses is built on meaningful coincidences, though finished over with irony; and these coincidences suggest a fateful order beyond causality, the eternal world for which Northrop Frye uses the term *romance*. This is apparent in the heroic mythic correspondences in the book, which point to a permanent world of spiritual forms. However ironic Joyce may be in making Bloom a version of his favorite hero Odysseus, making Stephen Hamlet or filling the book with literary and theological references, he uses archetypal thinking to see his characters in contexts of patterns shared by different civilizations and eras.

If we leave aside temporarily the ironic and negative aspects of the book, *Ulysses* may be seen as a structure of coincidences which transcend time. The two major actions of the book are the meeting of Stephen and Bloom and the cuckolding of Bloom by Molly and Blazes. June 16, the first day Molly has sex with Blazes, is the first time Bloom is aware of being cuckolded while it happens. The fact that he meets Stephen on this day is the major coincidence I will be concerned with. But the meeting of Stephen and Bloom is itself a large coincidence composed of a series of smaller ones. Bloom, who thinks about coincidences all day (using the term twelve times) first crosses Stephen's path when he sees the young man from a carriage in "Hades," and they pass each other in the newspaper office and more closely in the library, where Stephen expresses his abiding notion that we meet in the world what is potential in our minds. They finally meet at the hospital, a scene of birth, and then Bloom loses Stephen thoroughly before finding him in Nighttown by a stroke of luck. But more remarkable than their physical crossings are the interweavings of their minds.

An article by William Walcott, "Notes by a Jungian Analyst on the Dreams in *Ulysses*," discusses the overlapping of dreams and images among Bloom, Stephen and Molly.[4] On Bloomsday eve Stephen dreamed that he flew and came to a street of harlots where a man identified as Haroun al Raschid presented him with a cream-fruit melon and invited him to enter a doorway where a red carpet was spread and someone was waiting: "In. Come" (*U* 47, 217, 571). Bloom's dream opened with an invitation to "Come in" and presented Molly in red slippers and Turkish costume (*U* 370, 381, 397). Molly dreamed "something about poetry" (*U* 775).

Jung regarded dreams as prophetic, and Walcott shows that these dreams by the three characters on the eve of Stephen's meeting with Bloom foretell that meeting. Walcott points out that the sharing by Stephen's dream and Bloom's of the invitation to "come in," reference to the East and the color red demonstrates synchronicity in the form of *participation mystique* or the overlapping of mental content without communication, which implies a collective unconscious. He also points out that the name Haroun al Raschid from Stephen's dream occurs in a hallucination Bloom has in "Circe." Walcott does not observe that references to the East and even the phrase "come in" in both dreams suggest birth.

Other examples of mental content shared between Stephen and Bloom are plentiful. I have shown how Stephen's description of Shakespeare in "Scylla and Charybdis" turns out to describe Bloom. At one much-vexed point Stephen envisions the playwright thusly: "In a rosery of Fetter Lane of Gerard, Herbalist, he walks, greyedauburn. . .One life is all. One body. Do. But do." (*U* 202). These lines depict the bard while his wife is cheating, and in "Sirens," as Bloom's wife is about to cuckold him, his thoughts of Shakespeare lead to the following lines: "In Gerard's rosery of Fetter lane he walks, grayed-auburn. One life is all. One body. Do. But do" (*U* 280). Rather than being interpolated, these lines—followed by "Done anyhow"—fit into Bloom's thoughtstream. In the episode before the Hamlet theory, Bloom recites to himself, "Hamlet, I am thy father's spirit. . ." (*U* 152).

Robert M. Adams, Harry Blamires, French and others have called attention to many coincidences between Stephen's thoughts and Bloom's as when Bloom, who has not heard Stephen's "Parable of the Plums," says of Boylan, "He gets the plums and I the plumstones" (*U* 377).[5] The coincidences are usually attributed to an ironic narrator or cosmic jokester of questionable authority; however, Kenner's attempt to deny their significance in *Joyce's Voices* casts doubt not only on the meaning of *Ulysses*, but on its entire story, its realism.[6] A less skeptical view is suggested by Robert M. Adams, who was the first to discuss coincidence in *Ulysses* in his *Surface and Symbol* (Oxford, 1962). In a piece on "Hades," Adams sees coincidence leading to myth: "In effect, Bloom is a diffused personality. . . In later chapters of the book he will turn transparent, become mythical, and disintegrate. . . When other people's words turn up in Bloom's monologues, or his in theirs, it isn't a 'dropping out of character' but a deliberate dropping of character into some other continuum."[7]

Many more correspondences between Stephen and Bloom could be pointed out. After they see the well-known little cloud that covers the sun, both see "warm running sunlight" reappear (*U* 10, 61). Stephen's urination on the beach, as "widely flowing, floating foampool, flower unfurling" is matched by Bloom's imagining a "pooling swirl of liquor" with "wideleaved flowers" of froth and seeing his penis as "a languid floating flower" (*U* 79, 86).

Bloom tends to substitute the material world for the spiritual word, while Stephen rejects the world for the word. And so Bloom gets from Martha Clifford, the object of his lust, a letter containing the misprint

"I do not like that other world" (*U* 77); and when Stephen asks the spiritual object of his desire for "the word known to all men" (*U* 49, 581), his mother answers contrarily, "I pray for you in my other world" (*U* 581). Stephen reacts to this by hurling at God a traditional bogeyman image used when Bloom remembered working in a slaughterhouse, "raw head and bloody bones" (*U* 171, 581). As J. J. O'Molloy is defending Bloom in a trial which enacts Bloom's feelings, he uses the phrase "of soultransfigured and of soultransfiguring" (*U* 465), which he presented to Stephen in "Aeolus" while Bloom was out (*U* 140). Stephen addresses the straying children of Ireland by the name of Bloom's straying child when he says, "Return. . .Clan Milly" (*U* 393).

After thinking about coincidences in "Lestrygonians," Bloom passes George Russell and overhears him speaking "Of the twoheaded octopus, one of whose heads is the head upon which the ends of the world have forgotten to come while the other speaks with a Scotch accent" (*U* 165). This is unclear, but probably refers to Walter Pater's famous description of *Mona Lisa*: "Hers is the head upon which all 'the ends of the world are come.' " Bloom misunderstands: "What was he saying? The ends of the world with a Scotch accent" (*U* 165). And in "Circe" Stephen seems to use Bloom's unspoken misunderstanding to visualize the end of the world as a two-headed octopus with Scotch accent (*U* 507). This hallucination, like others, may be shared by both men.

Union between the two men is also suggested by a network of supernatural signs which includes every detail of the Homeric and Shakespearean parallels insofar as they imply father and son brought together in art and joined in the act of creation. And there are plenty of paranormal signs outside these frames: linguistic anticipations of the breakdown of boundaries in the *Wake*, as when a note of song joins Simon Dedalus and Bloom as "Siopold" (*U* 276). Even such hard-core hocus-pocus as the stopping of Bloom's watch as Blazes has Molly and a star shooting, as Stephen and Bloom part, from the Lyre (art and Stephen) through the Tress of Berenice (woman) to the sign of Leo (*U* 703).[8] Molly later recalls a prediction of Stephen's advent: "He was on the cards this morning when I laid out the deck union with a young stranger" (*U* 774). The links between these three figures are fully comprehended only by saying that in every detail they are, like star-crossed lovers, made for each other.

These supernatural manifestations define a teleological world in which meaning determines causality. Though Stephen calls God a noise in the street and can't bear the idea of reaching a goal, he must still believe in "the end he had been born to serve" (*P* 165) for he insists we are always moving toward ourselves (*U* 213, 505). At least some of the time history *does* move toward a goal in Ulysses. Stephen says the artist retires like

God behind his creation (*P* 215) and speaks of "the playwright who wrote the folio of this world. . .badly (he gave us light first and the sun two days later)" (*U* 213). If Joyce believes the artist plays God in his work, then he may suspect the characters who inhabit his fiction live in a world in which God exists. But this god, Joyce himself, is ambivalent about his powers.

The various synchronicities of *Ulysses* serve an order which transcends the mutability and separation so prominent in the book, an order of creation that opposes time and chance. The chances that link the major characters contradict mutability, as Joyce emphasizes through the time images examined in my last chapter, such as the elaboration of the factors that render a reunion of Stephen and Bloom improbable: "The irreparability of the past. . .the imprevidibility of the future." Their meeting is opposed by entropy. Any two people in a city might exhibit a similar density of coincidence—and so to present Stephen and Bloom without coincidence would distort reality toward the absurd. Nevertheless, it is no less true for being Romantic that by accepting such coincidences as meaningful, one (or two) can impose an order on life to create something—a relationship that will have value beyond the physical insofar as it gives a sense of being matched beyond probability. (In fact, creation by coincidence obsesses Joyce's heirs Jorge Luis Borges and Thomas Pynchon.)

Conventional science and logic are totally unable to explain creation because they follow irreversible linear models of time in their addiction to causality. But Modernism strives to make the mechanical model of time expand breathing into new possibilities, and in doing so it often turns to prelogical sources. Logic can tell where Coleridge got his phrases or what a baby inherits, but not what gave life to Coleridge's poetry or how the substance of a thirty-year-old person becomes zero years old at birth. Such reversal of time is not comprehensible to science; nor are the humanly created feelings such as happiness and love which make up living value. As Molly says, "I wouldn't give a snap of my two fingers for all their learning why don't they go out and create something" (*U* 782).

Our models for understanding creation come from mythology and center around the idea of death and rebirth or gain through loss.[9] Two primary versions of this pattern are adventure, a passage into the unknown to gain through risk, and coition, a sacrifice of dignity to gain exaltation, of individuality to create life. All versions assume an underlying order of reward for suffering. Such an order, based on the idea of good parenting, is secure only in a small, civilized fraction of life, but without assuming this order exists where it can't be proven, nothing new or creative could be motivated. No one would have reason to venture into the unknown unless he felt his risk would be rewarded.

The condescending Haines asks if Stephen is "a believer in the narrow sense of the word. Creation from nothing and miracles and a personal God" (*U* 19), and Stephen answers, "There's only one sense of the word, it seems to me." Perhaps the only personal God such an anxious young man could bear would be, like his Shakespeare, a very mortal middle-aged cuckold. But one implication of Stephen's answer is that all creation is essentially miraculous "creation from nothing"; for it is precisely the distance between the prior causes and the new thing made that constitutes creation in love, art, thought, biology or any area of life.

In denying creation, Stephen denies the motivation and possibility of life so seriously that the principles for which he makes this denial can't mean much until he changes his view. His suspicion of the sterility of intellectual life emerges when he says, ". . . beware Antisthenes, the dog sage, and the last end of Arius Heresiarchus. The agony in the water closet" (*U* 523). Stephen envisioned Arius's death in "Proteus": "with upstiffed omophorion, with clotted hinder parts" (*U* 38). Upward movement into spirit and downward sinking into matter make up a suitable fate for an intellectual, death by analysis. But the heretic is also a victim of society, and the Croppy Boy, another version of Stephen, repeats the pattern, ejaculating as his body sinks to death by hanging (*U* 594).

If all types of creation have common features, Joyce tends to describe them all in terms of their most concrete form, sex. Thus, Stephen's esthetic theory describes art by analogy to intercourse: a radiant moment of fading glow unites subject and object after the relation of the parts of the object has been studied. The main object of the theory is a beautiful woman, and the enchanted state of union with it leads to artistic "conception. . .gestation and. . .reproduction" (*P* 209). Cosmogony is also seen as sexual: "In woman's womb word is made flesh but in the spirit of the maker all flesh that passes becomes the word that shall not pass away. This is the postcreation" (*U* 391). The *maker* here is theologically God, if esthetically a poet. But biologically, he is a father and his spirit is semen. *Spirit* is semen in Sonnet 129 ("Th' expense of spirit in a waste of shame/ Is lust in action") and in *King Lear* (IV.ii.23), when Goneril says, "This kiss, if it durst speak,/ would stretch thy spirits up into the air."

In the act of sex man becomes god. One reason is that his enthusiasm frees him from the need for authority. Joyce's notes for *Ulysses* refer to "Coition illusion of strength" (*N* 242). Bloom feels rejuvenated by Gerty MacDowell, and Zoe Higgins inspires him to a vision of himself as Messiah. Moreover, the act which transforms a man from son to father also gives him the deific power to make life, as Joyce noted gleefully, "Fucker obliges God to create" (*N* 203). A priestly role, and letters to Nora indicate that for Joyce sex was very much a ritual, with formulas and sacred objects needed to subsidize his organ.

The supreme, crucial eucharist of this ceremony is semen, and Stephen identifies this holy spirit with God because it is capable of transcending time through birth: "Is that then the divine substance wherein Father and Son are consubstantial?" (*U* 38). Despite his scepticism, Joyce was ready to believe that liquid could live forever in ink and sperm, perhaps because liquid is female: ". . .only the plasmic substance may be said to be immortal" (*U* 419). Belief in immortal fluid is only a step from belief in immortal mind, and the *Ulysses* notesheets present "plasmic memory" (*N* 171). This is only a tiptoe from talking like an out-and-out Jungian, and Joyce did so long before publication of the *Wake* in the *Scribbledehobble* notebook of 1922-1923 :"dream thoughts are wake thoughts of centuries ago: unconscious memory: great recurrence: race memorial." [10]

Hermetic science, supposedly descended from Hermes or Thoth and admired by Jung, maintains that the process of creation, "physical, mental or spiritual," is not possible without the interaction of male and female principles.[11] This may take place concretely, as with pen (male) and paper (female) or figuratively, as when the mind plunges into the unknown in the process for which we use the sexual term *conception*. Whether all creation is sexual or not, it is so in Joyce: we have seen Stephen's theories describe creation as coition and *Exiles* shows Richard Rowan as spirit shaping the formless earth of Bertha in a sexual, artistic and deific act of creation. Richard Ellmann describes the creative action of *Ulysses* as based on a sexual model, with the first half of the book leading to "a vision of the act of love as the basic act of art" and the second, to one of "love as the basic act of nature" (*Liffey*, p. 174). Although he realizes the centrality of the image of intercourse to *Ulysses*, Ellmann does not indicate how this idea figures in the plot.

The crux of the plot of *Ulysses* is that Bloom meets Stephen *because* he performs an act of love with Molly on June 16 and this act gives him the psychic power to spiritually father the young man. No point is more central to the novel than this nexus which binds the two main actions into a unified process of creation that transcends time. But these acts of creation are not manifested substantially—partly because they take place in the realm of spirit, partly because Joyce is not sure he believes in them. The novel shows separation while suggesting union, and the active meaning of this ambiguity is that Joyce intends to show a process of connection through separation, a rite of passage like the *Odyssey*. We can see how the dual act of sexual and parental love underlying *Ulysses* functions to inter-animate Bloom, Molly and Stephen by examining the thinking of Jung and *Exiles*.

Joyce said that Bloom was "of the same family" with Richard Rowan (Budgen, *Making*, p. 315). Rowan achieves a complete union with Bertha, who is clearly of Molly's family, by permitting her to commit adultery with Robert Hand. He says he does so because he fears blocking her development by making "her life poorer in love" (*E* 69). By this means he is "united with [her]. . . in utter nakedness" and in "restless living wounding doubt" as he holds her "by no bonds, even of love" (*E* 112). In "Ithaca" Joyce says Bloom feels jealousy because he derives "a fluctuation of pleasure" from "the controlled contemplation" of "a nature full and volatile in its free state. . .alternately the agent and reagent of attraction" (*U* 732). He can only enjoy her vital changes by leaving her free to act.

Rowan and Bloom are heroes in Jung's terms because they both go through ordeals of uncertainty to create new possibilities of life. It is because Bloom has to cope emotionally with the lurking image of Blazes all day that he has the sensitivity to sympathize with Stephen's dispossession. And the reason Joyce called Molly's soliloquy "the indispensible countersign to Bloom's passport to eternity" (Budgen, *Making,* p. 264) is that the gnawing anxiety Bloom constantly endures as he tries to avoid thinking of Blazes ("Today. Today. Not think" *U* 180) is crucially responsible for the flood of vitality that ends the book. As Suzette Henke shows, the beauty and life of "Penelope" are the fruits of Bloom's mental heroism.[12]

Rowan defines love as "to wish her well" (*E* 63). The lover gives life to his beloved as the artist gives lasting life to his object, by a recognition of being, a belief in possibility which involves extending yourself outward to an unknown other. Simony, the selling of grace, is opposed to love in *Stephen Hero:* "Love gives and freedom takes. The woman in the black straw hat [prostitute] gave something before she sold her body to the State. Emma will sell herself to the State but give nothing" (*SH* 203). To sell oneself in prostitution or marriage for advantage is to give nothing. Artist and lover must not think of themselves as they give of their existences. Joyce's heroic love cannot be based on certainty or obligation, must be based on freedom and doubt. Joyce says of Rowan in his notes, "He is jealous, wills and knows his own dishonour and the dishonour of her, to be united with every phase of whose being is love's end, as to achieve that union *in the region of the difficult, the void and the impossible* is its necessary tendency" (*E* 114, my italics). Rowan achieves this union through separation. As with Stephen's Shakespeare, "loss is his gain" (*U* 197).

The curious phrases that describe the "necessary tendency" of Rowan's love echo distinctly in "Scylla and Charybdis" when Stephen describes another kind of love, fatherhood: "It is a mystical estate. . .founded, like the world, macro- and microcosm, upon the void. Upon incertitude, upon unlikelihood" (*U* 207). And this description echoes again at the climax of *Ulysses's* action: in "Ithaca," with its interplanetary atmosphere, Stephen and Bloom are described in parallel terms as moving "between a micro- and a macrocosm ineluctably constructed upon the incertitude of the void" (*U* 697). The universe founded on the void is that of mythology rather than empiricism, a world made by the mind without material support.

These parallel descriptions are behind acts of conjugal love and fatherhood which may be accomplished in accordance with Joyce's conception in "Ithaca," acts of love which take place in a void of incertitude because they take place in a state of freedom. Bloom reaffirms his love for Molly by giving her to Boylan and as a result of his unselfishness; she feels a resurgence of love for him in "Penelope," remembering their passion on Howth Hill and consenting to make his breakfast for the first time in a decade (*U* 738, 780). And by reviving her love he gains the spiritual ability to meet and foster Stephen: his unease on this day, his awakened need, the extension of his psyche beyond himself, these make him notice and follow the young man who leads him out of time.

Bloom may father Stephen successfully because he is a father who does not believe in his own fatherhood, a man who doubts his own manhood, He shows Stephen the sensitive side of paternity as he gives without real hope of reward, offers love but does not try to constrain Stephen, lets him go. As the croppy boy begs the false father who strangles him with the authorities of church and state, *"Bless me, father. . .and let me go"* (*U* 285). Both acts of love, or both parts of the act, may create life, but that life stays free and vital only as long as the results remain uncertain. So the most hopeful indications are outside the physical world of the novel in a teleological sphere, as with the setting of *Ulysses* on the day Joyce fell in love with Nora, the day the original of Stephen was regenerated.

The creation of something new always comes from a meeting of incompatible frames of reference, as Arthur Koestler demonstrates extensively in *The Act of Creation*.[13] Such meeting is made possible by love, a giving of life or belief to what is other than yourself, which changes both you and the other. Because you are aware of the independent existence of another only when her action can't be predicted, love always takes a chance, going into the unknown, the unconscious, the absent realm of spirit or potentiality. This is why Joyce focusses on love that is not merely outside official channels of family contract, but virtually outside the order of conscious discourse. Only by losing yourself, as Odysseus did, can you create something new—a child, a book, a feeling that will reach through time and selfish logic.

Jung's theories describe the "spiritual facts" (*E* 116) adumbrated in Joyce's works from *Exiles* on. These "facts" are processes of regeneration embedded in actions which appear to be defeats typical of the suffering of spirit in the world. In his essay "Concerning Rebirth," Jung defines a form of metempsychosis operating within the life of the individual through psychological activities "beyond sense perception" consisting of "almost invisible. . .and yet vital processes going on in the background."[14] These phrases fit *Ulysses*, especially "Ithaca," with its sometimes eerie unfolding of the void at the foundation of the world, its absurdly detailed physical facts that negate themselves to evoke spiritual needs beneath the surface. For if the uncanny is often mocked in *Ulysses*, it is often felt intensely.

Blake said, "Reason or the ratio of all we have already known. is not the same that it shall be when we know more" (*Poetry and Prose*, p. 2). Therefore, to the eyes of established reason, the act of genuine creation must must appear as an error, a disaster. This idea resounds in the passage of *Ulysses* Joyce read for recording, John Taylor's speech on Moses (*U* 142-143): if Moses had listened to the High Priest who called him a fool for leaving the mighty civilization of Egypt to wander in wilderness, then the new civilizations of the Judeo-Christian tradition would not have come into being. It is a meaningful coincidence that as Stephen and Bloom leave Bloom's house, there is a "secreto" chanting of the psalm about the exodus of Israel from Egypt (*U* 698). Stephen is probably chanting this as an ironic expression of his feeling that Bloom's house was a trap, but at the same time, it has an opposite implication unknown to him: that he has been liberated by Bloom on an unconscious level.

Like the reborn children of Shakespeare's last comedies, who prompt Stephen to say, "There can be no reconciliation if there has not been a sundering" (*U* 193, 195), so the ideas of genius (whose root meaning is fertility) and of love must be lost before they can be found:

Abandonment, exposure, danger, etc. are all elaborations of the "child's" insignificant [i. e. "almost invisible," as in the manger, outside the civilized order] beginnings and of its mysterious and miraculous birth. This statement describes a certain psychic experience of a creative nature, whose object is the emergence of a new and as yet unknown content. In the psychology of the individual there is always, at such moments, an agonizing situation of conflict from which there seems to be no way out—at least for the conscious mind, since as far as this is concerned, *tertium non datur* [no third is given]. But out of this collision of opposites the unconscious psyche always creates a third thing of an irrational nature, which the conscious mind neither expects nor understands.[15]

Stephen and Bloom may be sterile as individuals, but if collision of opposites creates a third thing of an irrational nature, then they share a fertile interface. The area in which they can confront each other without competing or projecting is the unknown or unconscious space in which creative perception can occur. What is created, whether it be a child, a work, an idea or a feeling, is an infusion from the unconscious or spiritual world into the material or known world. If Bloom is extraverted and Stephen, introverted, then Stephen is Bloom's unconscious and Bloom, Stephen's (*PT*, p. 304). Moreover, as Goethe's line about being wary of what you wish for in youth suggests, youth and age or son and father may also serve as embodiments of the crucial unknown to each other. Therefore, the relation of the male pair is parallel to that of man, whose major unconscious element is *anima*, to woman, whose major element is *animus*. In all of these ways Stephen, Bloom and Molly will gain spiritual power, potential to change toward wholeness, as a result of the disorientation connected with their encounters with each other and with the others' needs. And their connections may be fruitful even though they are based on separation, for self-development requires alienation:

The self, regarded as the Counter-pole of the the world, . . .is the *sine qua non* of all empirical knowledge and consciousness of subject and object. Only because of this psychic "otherness" is consciousness possible at all . . .it is only separation, detachment, and agonizing confrontation through opposition that produce consciousness and insight. ("Child Archetype," p. 171)

The creation of personality through opposition is as central as anything Stephen learns in *Portrait,* where he pledges "to err, to fall, to triumph, to recreate life out of life" (*P* 172), says that the soul is born to consciousness in sin, and condemns the good people of Ireland for following their authorities so faithfully that their consciences are uncreated. And in his essay on Wilde Joyce refers to ". . .the truth inherent in the soul of Catholicism: that man cannot reach the divine heart except through that sense of separation and loss called sin" (*CW* , 205).

Jung calls for the stirring up of conflict in personal relations because "there is no consciousness without discrimination of opposites" (*Archetypes,* p. 96) The idea appears in Blake as "Without contraries is no progression" and "Opposition is true friendship" (*Poetry and Prose,* pp. 34, 41). "Relationship is only possible," says Jung, "when there is a certain psychic distance, just as morality must always presuppose freedom" (*CW*, 10, p. 132). This is why Bloom must separate himself from Molly to relate to her again. It is no longer possible for the Blooms "to form by reunion the original couple of uniting parties" (*U* 726), but they can change and discover what is new. In "Marriage as a Psychological Relationship" Jung emphasizes the need of each partner to move toward a conscious individual role by differentiating himself from the other and suggests that infidelity may promote self-development.[16]

Speaking of research, Jung said, ". . .only by going the long way around do we strike the direct road" (*Two Essays*, p. 6), a parallel to Bloom's Odyssean "Longest way round is the shortest way home" and Stephen's "shortest way to Tara. . .via Holyhead" (*U* 377, *P* 250). In terms of physical facts, the idea of connection with others through separation is neurotic or perverse, but Jung was inclined to a more favorable view of neurosis and perversion than Freud. A complex, according to Jung, "can be really overcome only if it is lived out to the full" ("Mother Archetype," pp. 98-99). This formulation encourages perversions, which Freud describes as lived-out complexes or neuroses that find release in action (*SE* XVI, pp. 307-311). Rather than forcing patients to conform to objective realities, Jung recognized that the main realities of life are often subjective and found virtue in peculiarities. He speaks, for example, of the merits of homosexual sensibility ("Mother Archetype," pp. 86-87)—and he finds value in neurosis:

To be neurotic—what good can that do? . . .However stupid this thought is. . . [as] natural science, it may yet be sensible enough from the point of view of psychology. . .Nietzsche. . .acknowledged how much he owed to his malady. I myself have known more than one person who owed his entire usefulness and reason for existence to a neurosis, which prevented all the critical follies in his life and forced him to a mode of living that developed his valuable potentialities. (*Two Essays*, pp. 44-46, 30)

He even implies the neurotic is superior to the normal: "There are vast masses of the population who, despite their notorious unconsciousness, never get anywhere near a neurosis. The few who are smitten by such a fate are really persons of the 'higher' type who, for one reason or another, have remained too long on a primitive level" (*Two Essays*, pp. 182-183). And Jung maintained, "the sick man has not to learn how to get rid of his neurosis, but how to bear it" (*CW* [Jung], 10, p. 170). Bizarre to rational judgment, this view has a solid place in religious tradition, where, as John Donne put it, "Affliction is a treasure."[17]

Art is historically derived from religion, and the religious method of sacrificing rational selfishness to inner drives is consistent with the religion of art founded by Joyce on the void of personal alienation. To give power to your neurosis is even parallel to falling in love in that both involve letting yourself be overcome by an irrational other. Passion is to action as passive to active: "Love gives and freedom takes." In competition, to give authority to another is weakness; but if the other wishes you well, or follows your deepest feelings, it is strength. Most feelings we value in life are based on illusions which derive their power from being shared with others (or denied to others).

In love you reveal your deepest feelings through weaknesses rather than shows of strength. Imperfections are what make us individuals, and therefore, as Brown suggests, neurosis is personality (*Life Against Death*, pp. 6, 11). Bloom and Molly, like all lovers, are bound to each other by need. His connection with her allows him to express his neurotic need for infidelity in such a way that both are satisfied and his indirect act of union with her stirs his imagination to the encounter with Stephen. To this extent, he is capable of love and parenthood even though he is not active enough to practice them directly. Such disfranchised, unrecognized love may occur more frequently in life than the conventional "Rosie O'Grady" ideal Joyce rejects as unreal (*P* 245), and it may play a more creative role than recognized bonds which tend toward stagnation.

The world Joyce depicts combines the reality of alienation with the possibility of communion because he realized that the hang-ups that limit our freedom to behave rationally are the very features that promote the energy of the irrational and the possibility of change. The needs, gaps and flaws which prevent self-sufficiency and entrap us also give access to the creativity of love, art, thought and heroism, all of which are generated by opposition. And the daily passings in which people lose each other are also the contacts in which they find one another. And so it is possible without looking beyond the end of *Ulysses* to see Joyce's characters gaining spiritual potential by being drawn beyond themselves.

Joyce's conception of love is admirable in its attempt to combine connection with freedom, the power of myth with the individual reality of passion. We can gain perspective on how typical Joyce's ideas are of modern literary thought by glancing far afield at André Malraux's existential novel of revolution, *Man's Fate* (1933). Kyo Gisors, Malraux's hero, tells his wife May that she is free to make love to another man and then struggles to overcome his unworthily selfish jealousy when she does so. In contrast, the book's imperialist villain, Ferral, is highly possessive toward women. Kyo's father, who is usually a voice of wisdom, says "The knowledge of a person is a negative feeling; the positive feeling, the reality, is the torment of being always a stranger to what one loves."[18] Old Gisors links knowledge to power elsewhere, and the implication is that insofar as you know, or can predict, someone, you control that person and do not come into contact with life. And a similar attempt to combine love with freedom appears in Rupert Birkin's attempt to relate to Ursula Brangwen in a state of "star equilibrium" in Lawrence's *Women in Love*, while in "*The Rainbow*" Ursula rejected Anton Skrebensky because "She knew him all round, not on any side did he lead into the unknown."

These analogues provide another indication that Joyce believed in ideals of relationship, believed love was a transcendent function. But *Ulysses* portrays a world in which ideal values are unconscious, barely detectable in the background. To understand the role these dreams play in *Ulysses*, one must be fully aware of the forces which oppose them. Most readers of *Ulysses*, including Jung, have been impressed primarily by its skepticism. The recognition of affirmation in the book did not gain critical force until Tindall's work of the fifties, which may well have been prompted by Campbell and Robinson's *Skeleton Key to Finnegans Wake*. The implacability of Joyce's compulsive doubt places these ideals in a world, a mode of life, much more solidly real than the Romantic experiments of *Man's Fate* or *Women in Love*. Unlike Jung, Joyce did not forget the physical facts that the satisfactions of fantasy are less alive than those of actuality, that the transcendent values to which we dedicate most of our lives are approached with such absurd indirection because, as earlier, more direct forms of religion recognized, they are sacrifices to parental ghosts.

XI

SHAME'S VOICE

U1. doublemeaning. (*N* 403)

Designed by Stephen, Bloom has the potential to fulfill Stephen's wishes and give him a solution to his problems in the idea of passivity toward the world based on fetishistic submission to mother. Although he opposes such submission—in fact, because he opposes it so strongly—Stephen shows a need for it. In the library he thinks of infant-mother love as the absolute model for the union of subject and object: "*Amor matris,* subjective and objective genitive, may be the only true thing in life" (*U* 207). The offer Bloom makes Stephen in "Ithaca" seems capable of satisfying the young man's utmost desires and fantasies. This offer of a mother by a father rendered harmless has been in preparation throughout *Ulysses.* Bloom shows Stephen how to reconcile his ambivalent longings for both parents through the image of a union with a castrated father and mother as phallic deity.

In "Circe" Bella immediately recognizes Bloom as the other end of an aggressive woman: "Married, I see. . .And the missus is master" (*U* 527), or Bloom thinks she does, which is almost as bad. When Bloom brings Stephen home, having already enticed him with Molly's picture, Stephen can tell the wife is being served in both senses as Bloom makes various offers of meetings with Molly and then directs Stephen's gaze to the lamp in the "second story (rere)" window.

How did he elucidate the mystery of an invisible person. . ., denoted by a visible splendid sign, a lamp?
With indirect and direct verbal allusions or affirmations: with subdued affection and admiration. . .with suggestion. (*U* 702)

Like the lamp Stephen struck earlier with his ashplant, this one represents virility and deity, but in the window it is something to come home to, and it is here attached to mother. It is the solidity of the material world that Bloom is selling or preaching, the potency of woman. And it has further implications. Giving woman power is indistinguishable for Joyce from letting her encourage competitors, who, as Bloom points out, are always potentially there: ". . .men in the plural, were always hanging around on the waiting list about a lady, even. . .the best wife in the world" (*U* 655). If Stephen were to accept Bloom's offer, each would be supplying the need of the other for a competitor, and when someone competes with you, he tries to be an authority, someone you have to pay attention to, a father with control over your body. This is one reason why a mènage of Stephen, Bloom and Molly would result in sexual union not only between son and mother, but between son and father.

The trinity of Stephen, Bloom and Molly is designed to be a self-sufficient totality, and Fiedler suggests that Joyce intended it as an improvement on the monosexual trinity of the church.[1] On Joyce's schematic chart, Stephen is the brain, Bloom the organs and Molly the flesh ("fat," materially the substance of feminine appeal) of a complete human being. The men complement each other in this "at onement" (Campbell's term): Stephen's intellectual superiority correcting and being corrected by Bloom's materialism, his independence reconciled with Bloom's submissiveness, his selfish introversion confronting Bloom's selflessness, his need for a father he can believe in without being crushed meeting Bloom's for a son who will give him hope for the future.[2] The two set each other off, fulfill each other's wishes and serve as defenses against each other because they are conflicting aspects of the man whose mind created them in its own image. Joyce's object is to be "all in all" through his work, narcissistically to be his own father, as Stephen's Shakespeare and Christ were.

The union of three must take place in arcane terms, for it is not manifested on the lunar "Ithaca" surface of tough-minded irony and failed human communication even though the book is built around it. So it is not adequate to say Joyce's irony is a defense against his desires. The possibility of union is undercut so abysmally, denied so elaborately, that it is necessary to perceive two separate intentions operating. These correspond to Bloom, who accepts and desires the union without reservation, and Stephen, who rejects the possibility of union as false. Neither intention could motivate *Ulysses* by itself.

Jung and Bloom are both essentially religious in that they subordinate the individual to something larger given by nature—natural phenomenon or the collective unconscious—while Stephen and Freud insist the individual find answers in himself. Other points link the pessimistic naturalist Stephen to Freud, who was a psychologist of youth and paternal conflict, and link the optimistic escapist Bloom to Jung, psychologist of middle age and maternal reconciliation. But we must bear in mind the distinctions between the Dubliners and the demi-Germans: Stephen would not find Freud esthetic, while Jung found Bloom grotesque. Freud's system can explain virtually all of Jung's ideas as sublimatory illusions based on the obsessional patterns of religion; while Jung sees Freud's ideas as sterile mechanical overestimation of sex. Similarly, Bloom can easily see what is wrong with Stephen's position: he correctly urges the youth to come down to earth and devote himself to something he can put his hands on. Stephen, in turn, analyzes and demolishes Bloom's regressive prudence before meeting Bloom when he speaks of the Jews hopelessly hoarding to make up for primal dispossession:

> Not theirs: these clothes, this speech, these gestures. Their full slow eyes . . . knew the rancours massed about them and knew their zeal was vain. Vain patience to heap and hoard. Time surely would scatter all. A hoard heaped by the roadside: plundered and passing on. Their eyes knew the years of wandering and, patient, knew the dishonours of their flesh. *(U* 34)

The distance between these two who perceive the falseness of each other's position is the major source of dramatic conflict in the novel. Stephen said in the dramatic form the personality of the artist is submerged as the characters fill with vitality to assume independent esthetic life *(P* 215). How can an artist's characters be distinct from him when they project his mind? By the artistic cultivation of multiple personality. Cancelling each other out as they do, Bloom and Stephen free themselves from Joyce. They are not attached because he does not impose any one idea on them. Bloom is constantly viewed with Stephen's irony, while Stephen is viewed with Bloom's compassion. They have the complexity of living beings freed from any one abstract system through their relation to each other. I have mentioned the occult doctrine that male and female principles must interact for creation to occur. The male and female who interact to create *Ulysses* are the two sides of Joyce represented by Stephen and Bloom.

My last chapter described the acts of love implied in *Ulysses*. This one will examine how *Ulysses* undermines its project by showing the impossibility of the union of its trinity. The energy for this counterforce comes from Stephen's strongest attachment and virtuosity, narcissism. For the youth Joyce kept alive by stubborn adherence to egotistic principles disdained the folly and wisdom of his middle age. "Eumaeus" and

"Ithaca" show how little the two men have in common, how far they are opposed. Bloom advises Stephen at length to make a comfortable situation for himself with his talent, but Stephen, repulsed from woman, views a comfortable place in the world as a trap. After Stephen volunteers the anti-Semitic song about Little Harry Hughes, Bloom is "sad" and "silent" (*U* 692). Bloom and Molly also fail to commune in "Ithaca": their conversation is superficial and leaves out the most important events of the day for both. Whatever real connection takes place is not conscious.

I will focus, however, on one principle obstacle to consummation, the fact that Bloom, who is supposed to fill a paternal place, is less like a father than a son to his wife. He does have a daughter, but Milly never actually appears, and Bloom's thoughts about her are preoccupied with losing her, with her being taken from him and corrupted. She appears to him as another Molly, and his preoccupation with her seduction by Bannon is parallel to his concern with the adultery of his wife, which gives her the unattainability and authority of a mother. Thus, in "Calypso," Milly is brought into his mind by thoughts of Molly and Boylan:

> Milly too. Young kisses: the first. Far away now past. Mrs Marion. . .
> A soft qualm regret, flowed down his backbone, increasing. Will happen [Molly], yes. Prevent. Useless: can't move. Girl's sweet light lips. Will happen too. He felt the flowing qualm spread over him. Useless to move now. Lips kissed, kissing, kissed. Full gluey woman's lips. (*U* 67)

This is striking example of how Joyce's observation of (and with) Bloom is often as physical as it is mental. Bloom's body is shown mixing shame and excitement at the associations which follow Boylan's song. From this unhappy sensuality, Bloom's mind turns to calculating an unlikely plan to visit Milly. Happy love, for the Joycean protagonist, can only be "far away now past," a memory associated unconsciously with memories of infant bliss with mother. Molly's "full gluey woman's lips," remembered from Howth, are here confused with Milly's "sweet light" ones. Bloom frequently sees his daughter, like his wife, as a mother who must be yielded to another. In "Circe" he thinks he sees Molly in her youth with another man until Bello says, "That's your daughter, you owl, with a Mullingar student" (*U* 542). Moreover, Bloom doubts his own paternity. Certainly, others do:

> —Do you call that a man? says the citizen.
> —I wonder did he ever put it out of sight, says Joe.
> —Well, there were two children born anyhow, says
> Jack Power.
> —And who does he suspect? says the citizen.

Gob, there's many a true word spoken in jest. One of those mixed mid-
dlings he is. Lying up in the hotel Pisser was telling me once a month
with headache like a totty with her courses. (*U* 338)

Those who place faith in sensitivity are prone to forget how it suffers
in the eyes of the world. Bloom forgets his suffering too, but not the
doubt that comes from it. In "Sirens" he recalls a saying of Simon
Dedalus, a more authoritative father: "Wise child that knows her father,
Dedalus said. Me?" (*U* 273). Soon after he reflects on his daughter's lack
of interest in good music: "Milly no taste. Queer because we both I mean"
(*U* 278). The trailed-away thought is taken up among Bloom's thoughts
on Milly in "Ithaca": ". . .blond, born of two dark, she had blond an-
cestry, remote, a violation, Herr Hauptmann Hainau, Austrian army, proxi-
mate, a hallucination, lieutenant Mulvey, British navy."[3]

Bloom has also had a son who died after eleven days. In the ten-and-
a-half years since Rudy's death, Bloom has not had full genital sex with his
wife (*U* 736): "Could never like it again after Rudy" (*U* 168). Why
should a baby's death have such extraordinary effect? Fenichel says sexual
pleasure is given up if it is linked to danger founded on the unconscious
idea of injury from the female sex organ (*Theory,* p. 170), and I have
mentioned Freud's point that an infant can symbolize a phallus. The
excessive result of Rudy's death shows that the loss of the baby stands for
destruction of the penis that has been "put out of sight." The event stirs
Bloom's fear of the direct investment of feeling, his lack of belief in the
active function of his own being, his phallus, his ability to extend beyond
himself.

Bloom's mother has given him a potato he carries in his pocket. He lets
a woman, Zoe, take his spud from him in Nighttown, but then he regrets
having given it away when the threats around him, particularly Bella-Bello,
become unbearable, and he asks for it back (*U* 476, 555). Bloom's potato
is equivalent to Stephen's ashplant, and this sequence of events reflects his
uneasiness about entrusting his being to woman. Joyce knows there is
nothing Bloom needs more than to place that trust and is both pained and
amused that he can only do it passively by giving Molly away. It is hard
to imagine a purer form of neurotic anxiety, which Freud defined as fear
without an object to justify it, than fear of the female genitals, for they
must be feared for being receptive. "We have succeeded," Freud said in
1933, "in answering the question of what a person is afraid of in neurotic
anxiety . . . What he is afraid of is his own libido."[4] Since Freud had
already adopted the late theory that the two instincts were life and death,
he must have meant that the neurotic was afraid of his own life.

Bloom's passive, spiritual qualities derive from self-defeat. He is a victim of a social drive toward sacrifice in the repressed, mythically driven society around him. But if he did not negate himself, he would not be a kind person who is good for society and helps others, playing a diffuse but definite parental role. For Joyce agreed with Freud that the expansion of civilization is based on the restraint of the individual: "Altruism saves race, anarchy individual, half & half" (*N* 395). Bloom's anxiety must have sources more immediate than social mores. Little is given of his early childhood, but it seems that like Stephen and Joyce, who called his father an Irish suicide, he had a father who tried to be patriarchal, but was weak and left him with a dread of male authority. Like his fellow compulsive Stephen, he must have had a strong attraction to mom which came to be overshadowed by male threat until female genitals fused with anxiety in his mind.

Confirmation for such a hypothesis exists in that the threats confronting Bloom which appear to have female sources often turn out, on closer examination, to be masculine threats in drag. In "Circe" Joyce indicates that the aggressive, horsey women Bloom prefers and Martha, whose threats excite him, are essentially men by turning Bella into Bello. The root fantasy of submission to father, both attractive and terrifying, is exposed here without its usual disguise. Bloom himself is transformed into a female slave, ridden by Bello and told "she" will be offered to Bello's male friends. Even the vitally sexy Zoe appeals to Bloom for perverse reasons as an aggressive mother figure surrounded by fetishes. After he hails her as "The hand that rocks the cradle" and she calls him "Baby," he breaks into counting the bronze buckles on her slip in baby talk. Then she captures him with her talon, "luring him to doom":

(*He hesitates. . . She leads him. . . by the odour of her armpits, the vice of her painted eyes, the rustle of her slip in whose sinuous folds lurks the lion reek of all the male brutes that have possessed her.*)

THE MALE BRUTES
(*Exhaling sulphur of rut and dung and ramping in their loosebox, faintly roaring, their drugged heads swaying to and fro.*) Good! (*U* 500–501)

He is attracted by thoughts of her men, and the male threat is always in the background of Bloom's relations to women, as is the tendency to associate with them. Bloom's apparent menstrual pains were just cited; he gives birth to eight children in "Circe." In "Penelope," itself a monument to the ability of man to empathize with woman, Molly reveals that Bloom dwells on her ties to other men while making love to her bottom (*U* 780), encouraging her thoughts of competitors:

. . .who are you thinking of who is it tell me his name who tell me who the German Emperor is it yes. . .think of him can you feel him trying to make a whore of me what he never will he ought to give it up. . .simply ruination for any woman and no satisfaction in it pretending to like it till he comes and then finish it off myself anyway and it makes your lips pale. . .(*U* 740)

This passage indicates that Bloom wants to enter Molly's rectum. Her conviction that such an act is strictly for prostitutes is an artificial social distinction that shows her repression; and Joyce's references to the English preoccupation with water closets suggest that he may recognize a link between social elevation and the quality of being up-tight. But even if Bloom had access to this last resort, it would lose its excitement as he found himself accommodated by it. He is oriented toward the side of his wife that leads to death rather than creation by the same inner restriction that makes him dread the extension of his own life. Sultan uses the passage in the course of demonstrating that Bloom doesn't so much lose Molly as actively give her away (*Argument*, 132-133, 331, 407). The degradation of adoring the adulterous rump is compounded by the degradation of making love to a woman who doesn't enjoy it. One reason Bloom spends so much time urging himself to "keep my mind off" (*U* 280) is that he must avoid putting together the isolated components in his mind which add up to a desire for self-negation. Whether or not he traces such self-negation back to infantile "crimes," Joyce shares with Freud the liberating insight that we spend much of our lives expressing guilt for things we shouldn't feel guilt over, if we knew what they were.

When Bloom evades thoughts of Boylan for fingernails, statues or correspondence with Martha, his self-distraction is also a reversion to anality: he busies himself accumulating symbols of time and matter to escape genital problems. This is one respect in which he is what he is often called, the average sensual man; for many men in middle age subordinate the freedom of love to work or success. Economy starts with the realization that you don't have what you want. Bloom's economic plans culminate in his ultimate ambition in "Ithaca," a seven-page daydream of wealth and property in which he envisions himself as "Bloom of Flowerville." When the daydream is over, the text asks why he meditates "on schemes so difficult of realization" and answers

It was one of his axioms that similar meditations or the automatic relation to himself of a narrative concerning himself or tranquil recollection of the past when practised habitually before retiring for the night alleviated fatigue and produced as a result sound repose and renovated vitality.

His justifications?

As a physicist he had learned that. . .of complete human life at least 2/7ths. . . passed in sleep. As a philosopher he knew that at the termination of any allotted life only an infinitesimal part of any person's desires has been realized. As a physiologist he believed in the artificial placation of malignant agencies chiefly operative during somnolence.

What did he fear?

The committal of homicide or suicide during sleep by an aberration of the light of reason, the incommensurable categorical intelligence situated in the cerebral convolutions. (*U* 720)

This suggests nothing less than that all of Bloom's materialism and daydreaming, virtually all of his life, is compulsion motivated by anxiety, an effort to repress "malignant agencies chiefly operative during somnolence." This explains his constant shifting from thoughts of Boylan and time to those of business and reason. The chief thing Bloom takes an interest in to placate these unconscious forces is Molly, who, like matter, attracts or distracts Bloom because of her tendency to change. But what are the agencies placated by Bloom's pursuit of the two *M*s? Of the "homicide or suicide" they threaten, homicide seems to carry little weight: Bloom is incapable of it. Freud says (*Totem*, p. 154n.) that suicide is generally a turning inward of murderous wishes. We see little of Bloom's childhood or his aggression, but if he fulfills Stephen's wishes, it may be that Stephen's constant patricidal hostility represents Bloom's other side.

Suicide, at any rate, is a considerable presence in Bloom's thought. At the chemist's he thinks, "Poisons the only cures" (*U* 84); of his father's suicide in "Hades," "No more pain" (*U* 97); on O'Connell Bridge, "If I threw myself down?" (*U* 152). In "Circe" he harbors fantasies of dying: "To be or not to be. Life's dream is o'er. End it peacefully. They can live on. . . I am ruined. A few pastilles of aconite. The blinds drawn. A letter. Then lie back to rest. (*He breathes softly.*) No more. I have lived" (*U* 499). Bello says, "Die and be damned to you if you have any sense of decency. . . We'll bury you in our shrubbery jakes. . ." (*U* 543). In other passages, such as Bloom's observation of his cat, an interest in death mingles masochism and suicidal tendencies: "Cruel. Her nature [a comforting explanation]. Curious mice never squeal. Seem to like it" (*U* 55).

"Lotus Eaters" presents Bloom's absorption in the correspondence with Martha, in other fantasies and in "the stream of life" (*U* 86) as a self-negation through drug addiction. This idea is reiterated in "Ithaca" after a passage listing memories which Bloom's father narrated to his son. Time is father time here, an active, threatening force:

Had time equally but differently obliterated the memory of these migrations in narrator and listener?

In narrator by the access of years and in consequence of the use of narcotic toxin: in listener by the access of years and in consequence of the action of distraction upon vicarious experiences. (*U* 724–725)

The years have a parallel function here to both *narcotic* and *distraction*, and so Bloom's "distraction upon vicarious experiences," the entire body of his life, is equated with drug induced suicide. I do not mean that Bloom is about to kill himself, but that the only reason this couldn't happen is that he is perpetually engaged in artificially placating malignant agencies, in warding off the paternal threat at the back of his mind by involvement in material concerns and submission to his wife-mother. Everything he values, even in himself, comes from outside, and so he has given up his own life.

While it is not always easy to measure Joyce's awareness of the psychological material he presents, the passage on Bloom's bedtime meditation shows Joyce's amazing penetration into Bloom's psyche. It is the ironic detachment of Stephen which allows Joyce to dive below the surface play of compulsion and evasion in Bloom's mind, just as it is the recognition of human needs and limits shown in Bloom that allows Joyce to delineate Stephen's egotism with dramatic power. As a result of the complexity of Joyce's perspective, both are characterized with stereoscopic depth and richness. Moreover, it is because the world of Bloomsday is depicted through so many techniques and contradictory viewpoints that it has the living complexity of reality.

If we look at Bloom with the sensibility of Stephen, who sees all male conversation as contest, Bloom loses all day to a line of men longer than the list of Molly's imagined lovers. Leaving aside obvious abusers like Blazes, the citizen, Myles Crawford, John Henry Menton, Mulligan and Stephen, I'd like to turn to a subtle example to show how thoroughly Bloom's experience is conditioned by his passivity. A remarkable passage in "Sirens" shows how the threat and attraction which lurks in the background of Bloom's life can insinuate itself under his defenses to generate a wave of feeling which inundates the text. It occurs as Bloom is listening to Simon Dedalus as Lionel singing "M'Appari" from Flotow's *Martha,* eight pages after Blazes has left for his assignation (*U* 267). As Bloom listens to Simon's singing, he thinks of the adulterous couple and of "loves old sweet song," which they will sing. He also thinks of the virility of singers such as Simon: "Tenors get women by the score" (*U* 274). Earlier Simon said to Ben Dollard, "Sure, you'd burst the tympanum of her ear. . .with an organ like yours," and Father Cowley added, "Not to mention another membrane" (*U* 270). Now, as Simon sings, Bloom imagines Blazes in his carriage jingling up to Molly's female door, imagines it briefly from Molly's point of view:

Jing. Stop. Knock. Last look at mirror always before she answers the door. The hall. There? How do you? I do well. . .Hands felt for the opulent.

Alas! The voice rose, sighing, changed: loud, full, shining, proud.

—*But alas, 'twas idle dreaming*. . .

Glorious tone he has still. . .Wore out his wife: now sings. But hard to tell. Only the two themselves. . .(*U* 274)

Here Stephen's image of his father killing his mother is presented and then partially retracted. It reflects the tendencies of Joyce and Bloom to see all active masculinity as aggressive and destructive, for Bloom is impressed by the magnificence of Simon's organ, which is given much more solidity than the facts of the scene might suggest:

Tenderness it welled: slow, swelling. Full it throbbed. That's the chat. Ha, give! Take! Throb, a throb, a pulsing proud erect.

Words? Music? No: it's what's behind.

. . . . . .

Bloom. Flood of warm jimjam lickitup secretness flowed to flow in music out, in desire, dark to lick flow, invading. Tipping her tepping her tapping her topping her. Tup. Pores to dilate dilating. Tup. The joy the feel the warm the. Tup. To pour o'er sluices pouring gushes. Flood, gush, flow, joygush, tupthrop. Now! Language of love.

Bloom is certainly enjoying the manly vigor Simon is thrusting at him, and as he does so, he mentally dirfts into the sensations of sexual intercourse. The sex must be mainly that of Blazes and Molly, the wedding of the second that kills the first. After this there is an interlude of less than a page during which Bloom reflects on Lydia Douce, Martha Clifford and Molly, unattainable objects of his longing as Martha is the object of Lionel's in the aria; then the song sweeps to its climax in powerfully orgasmic rhythms, which I can only quote in part:

Come!

It soared, a bird, it held its flight, a swift pure cry, soar silver orb it leaped serene, speeding, sustained, to come, don't spin it out too long long breath he breath long life [length is salient], soaring high, high resplendent, aflame, crowned, high in the effulgence symbolistic, high, of the ethereal bosom, high, of the high vast irradiation everywhere all soaring all around about the all, the endlessnessnessness. . .

—*To me!*

Siopold!

Consumed. (*U* 275-276)

Joyce seems to recognize here how esthetic elements of form and content serve as a screen under which psychosexual feelings may be unconsciously admitted, a point developed fifty years later by Norman Holland (*Dynamics*, pp. 104-133). Bloom's thoughts of Boylan blend with thoughts of Simon's virility to produce an intense vicarious experience of sexual energy which unites Simon with Leopold as "Siopold." Harry Blamires refers to this experience as "Bloom's one completely satisfying emotional fulfillment today" (*Bloomsday*, p. 185). In mixing the overwhelming of Bloom by the prolific father Simon with the violation of Molly by Boylan, Joyce seems to recognize the need to be cuckolded as a need to derive sexual satisfaction from submission to paternal authority.

Tradition has provided for such needs in most people by such devices as the *droit du seigneur*. The role of manhood is to avoid submitting to another man except under certain ritual conditions based on fatherhood, such as teaching and sport. One of these is performance, and performers as idols or subjects of adoration are granted the overvaluation of passion. By the submission involved in recognizing their excellence, the audience gains the power of having an ideal to aim at. Joyce recognizes audience passivity as degrading and has Stephen insist that the man of genius avoids every model but himself. Bloom, however, is no genius, and the energy of Simon's longing stirs the energy of his need, which draws him to possibilities of communion.

If the idea of singing as sex seems far-fetched, it is confirmed in later works. From 1929 on Joyce befriended and promoted the aging Irish tenor John Sullivan, a large, robust, aggressive man who may well have served as a father figure. Another tenor named John was meanwhile growing increasingly ill back in Ireland, and after the death of Joyce's father in 1931, his support of Sullivan intensified (*JJ* 632-641, 653-654). In 1932 Joyce published a piece in a style resembling that of the *Wake*, "From a Banned Writer to a Banned Singer," which describes Sullivan in various operatic roles, lavishly praising his vocal ability and his manliness. As Arnold in Rossini's *William Tell*, singing to an audience that includes Joyce, the tenor reaches one of his famous notes: "Pass auf! Only four bars more! He draws the breathbow: that arrownote's coming. Aim well, Arnold, and mind puur blind Jemmy in the stalls!" (*CW* [Joyce], 263). A metaphor from the opera provides a striking example of Joyce's phallic valuation of language. He himself is passive, castrated, feminine, "puur blind Jemmy." And of course this leads to a thundering conclusion which includes tea, a fetish for Joyce, and an exploding apple: "Half a ton of brass in the band, ten thousand throats. . .Libertay. libertay lauded over the land (Tay!) And pap goes the Calville!" The parallel between this and the scene of Bloom listening to Simon enhances the impression of homosexuality in the earlier passage, for Joyce grew progressively freer to recognize this aspect of himself.

The consummation of Simon and Leopold illustrates a key psychological problem in *Ulysses*. The intention of the book to illustrate love and parenthood is compromised because Bloom, who occupies the paternal position in the novel's structure, is not psychologically a father at all, but a son—and a perverse son. If Stephen and Bloom are both sons, the theme of paternity in the novel loses its authority and the heterosexuality the book glorifies seems like subterfuge. If Stephen, Bloom and Molly were to unite, they would soon find themselves in need (and in danger) of a third man who would act as father to them. The Freudian may conclude love is impossible for the Joycean hero because his compulsion always seeks relation to a paternal authority, but he can never bear to remain in such relation because it reminds him that he desires to suffer.

Joyce's attempt to differentiate the two protagonists of *Ulysses* so that each can relate to the other as meaningful complement seems to founder on the fact that the pair have essentially identical complexes. Both men are obsessed with the idea of father taking away mother from them and violating her (God taking May Dedalus, Blazes taking Molly). Both regard mother as having betrayed them, view sex as a violent activity that threatens their manhood, are horrified at the thought of woman's castrated genitals and tend to associate with mothers and feel tempted by fathers. Both incline toward fetishism and other strategies of perversion, though Bloom is more deeply entrenched in submission to mother as placation of father. The principle difference between Stephen and Bloom on this level is that Stephen takes a rebellious attitude toward the situation they are in, while Bloom has submitted, but both are in the same neurotic situation, aspects of the same man fixed in this situation by his mind.

On the other hand, Bloom's acceptance and devotion embody psychological values for which Freud has not made adequate provision; and this is also true of Molly's even less critical acceptance and devotion. Molly is Bloom's idea that "love loves to love love" (*U* 333) personified: even her aggressive moments are titillating. Freud's scientific world view sees all phenomena determined by what preceded them and all energy and matter perpetually using themselves up. But such causality, as I've explained, is notoriously at a loss to account for the creative side of life and Molly knows this. She is free to make her own world, freed from the rack of causality and its machinery of time and demarcation by her deified position as the object of Bloom's anxious labor. Her version of neurotic compromise is to give up, as a woman, the real world of power for the dream world of love.

Lionel Trilling said that Freud had access to two concepts of reality—a deeper one and a more shallow one:

. . .the essentially Freudian view assumes that the mind, for good as well as bad, helps create its reality by selection and evaluation. In this view, reality is malleable and subject to creation. . .a series of situations which are dealt with in their own terms. But. . .the conception which arises from Freud's therapeutic-practical assumptions . . . deals with a reality which is quite fixed and static. . ."given" and not. . ."taken." In his epistemological utterances, Freud insists on the second view, although it is not easy to see why. . .For the reality to which he wishes to reconcile the neurotic patient is. . ."taken". . .It is the reality of social life and of value, conceived and maintained by the human mind and will. Love, morality, honor esteem— these are. . .created reality. If we are to call art an illusion then we must call most of the activities and satisfactions of the ego illusions. . .[5]

Trilling was no Jungian, but his criticism of Freud has parallels in the work of Jung, who said that Freud's instinctive psychology forgot "the creative instinct," was too much concerned with "yesterday" and not enough with "tomorrow," and neglected "value." Joyce was centrally concerned with the creative relation of the mind to experience and the world of mind-made values. He saw intangible forces operating every day to make life possible in ways that could not be explained in empirical terms. As I have suggested, many of the miracles Joyce believed in were based on love and art, which employ common principles of relationship.

Though Bloom has difficulty living with his desire for self-negation, he is able to do so with Molly's help. A grand virtue of marriage is that it allows each mate to live with his faults by blaming them on the other. Thus, Bloom emphasizes Molly's responsibility for her adultery, giving her the inevitability of nature; but when we get to Molly's thoughts, she sees him as driving her to it. Bloom's painful need to deny himself becomes a virtue insofar as it allows her to expand in the area of her propensity, while her vice gives Bloom satisfactions, including the chance to meet Stephen. Though our individual needs may be pathological, we can become capable of transcending ourselves if we invest them in others, if only because we don't know their weakness and they don't know ours. And this is why Joyce was no keyless citizen: as those scandalous letters show, Nora was willing to share his fantasy life. However much she gave in bed (or bath), she at least gave him what the Virgin gave and what his readers still give—her ear.

The scene in which Bloom hears Simon sing, while it is a typical indication of Bloom's weakness, can also, like every part of *Ulysses,* be read in terms of spiritual deliverance. It unites Dedalus and Bloom because they share the universal feeling of desire for the distant, lost woman (*anima* or mother) the song evokes. Bloom has a sense after the song that he and Simon have participated in human continuity which extends beyond them: "Thou lost one. All songs out that theme" (*U* 277). The sense of loss may be the thing people share on the deepest level, the ultimate eucharist of communion. But sharing can make this void a source of life, and the "Siopold" transfer of fatherhood seems to regenerate Bloom and to prefigure and celebrate by ritual Bloom's spiritual fatherhood of Stephen, Bloom uniting with Stephen's father. Thus the communion at the Ormond is one of the coincidences that indicate the psychic order underlying the novel.

Ulysses then, consists of two different narratives, simultaneous and congruent in the same way that matter and spirit coexist in every living being: one story shows three isolated individuals drifting through a wasteland, the other sets forth a trinity of fulfillment and fertility. Joyce used the weakness of his inability to make up his mind as a tool to recognize and recreate reality. Only through fruitful self-conflict can he include all that he gets into *Ulysses* in living human form and filled with personality. Only by keeping both sides going can he achieve the fullness of unreduced, unmediated vision. But *Ulysses* is not only balanced; it also shifts from its Stephen side to its Bloom side.

The movement from Stephen to Bloom, which is partly analogous to movement from Freud to his disciple Jung, shifts from hopeless conflict based on defiantly facing the truth to a reconciliation based on self-delusion and from an independence that is not really free to subjugation that is not really trapped. This movement is typical in many ways of the transition from youth to middle age. It seems to be triggered in this case, by the death of Stephen's mother, which makes the earlier position too painful to be tenable, impelling Stephen to seek a substitute. Glancing at biography, I suspect that it was this death that made Joyce find Nora when he did as much as any quality of Nora's. Mother's death may also promote heterosexuality by showing mom weaker and less to be feared than dad (as loss of father is sometimes thought to promote homosexuality).

The truth, the reality, the world which disturbs both men, generating bitter anxiety for Stephen and rationalization for Bloom, is built on a primal scene of father violating mother, God devouring matter. In the earlier phase the crime that father or Father committed is an absolute one that cannot be forgiven: murder. In the later one, not father but mother is responsible for a crime now seen as relative, just another phenomenon "neither first nor last nor only nor alone in a series originating in and repeated to infinity" (*U* 731), not individual, but archetypal. The early phase is apocalyptic: Stephen, student rebel, predicates the "ruin of all space, shattered glass and toppling masonry, and time one livid final flame" (*U* 24). The later phase is cyclical: Bloom expects nothing new: "The year returns. History repeats itself" (*U* 377). The early phase corresponds to the period of growth and development in any historical movement, when individualism struggles to find God in itself. The later phase features consolidation, contraction and the acceptance of external authority. In this sense they are Romanticism and Classicism—and therefore it is ironically logical that Stephen yearns to be a Classicist and Bloom a Romantic.

The earlier phase is transfixed with dread of a squalid physical world in conflict with its abstract ideals. The later one increasingly finds its ideals present and accomplished in that same world by transmuting actuality into a dreamy swarming of symbolic values. So Bloom strives persistently for the solid authority of matter by hoarding bourgeois paraphernalia, but he is an outcast trapped in spirit because he can never really possess the material things he lusts after. He has a considerable interest in mythology, but does not realize that his devotion to science is part of it, and in these respects he resembles Jung. On the other hand Stephen, oppressed by his parents and social connections, strives for freedom. The Stephen phase predominates in *Dubliners* and *Portrait:* stories of people trapped ineluctably in time and society and a novel which, despite its cycles, is infused with a sense of final deliverance, climactic truth, absolute division. The ultimate expression of the Bloom phase is the *Wake,* in which all conflicts are blurred by endless repetition and there is no sense or question of entrapment though no one has the slightest choice about anything he does.

Ulysses, standing between *Portrait* and *Wake,* moves from Stephen to Bloom, from anxious rebellion against the father to fetishistic submission to the mother. While working on *Ulysses* Joyce remarked to his friend Budgen that he was no longer as interested in Stephen as he was in Bloom (*Making,* p. 105), and Stephen progressively fades from the novel as it proceeds, not appearing physically on the last eighty pages as Bloom did not on the first fifty. With the departure of Stephen, an element of individuality leaves Joyce's fiction never to return; yet the universality of the Bloom phase could not have been realized without passing through the Stephen phase. Stephen's needs motivate Bloom—and Bloom's ignorance of the needs he answers reflects an escape from self-consciousness through self-division which is pathological in the real world and sublime where Joyce finally settled, in the world of art.

Ulysses ends with the ascendency of Molly as "Gea-Tellus," earth mother (*U* 737): "God a woman" (*N* 421). Tindall says, "By her existence and her position at the end Mrs. Bloom resolves the tensions of the book . . .her irrationality. . .reconciles all rational conflicts. Stephen and Bloom, conflicting opposites, become one in her" (*His Way,* p. 37). "Greater love hath no man" is an understatement in regard to Molly, for Joyce accepted the traditional view that women are more capable of giving love than men.

This belief enabled him, like many believers in heterosexuality, both to glorify women and to debase them as the source of love's powers and its problems. A relationship which is not based on overvaluation of the object may be fair, but it's not love.

Molly is a powerful *anima* figure, the purest archetype in the novel, and one of the conditions of her adoration is her lack of responsibility. Supporting her in her pampered state gives Bloom something to believe in, a sense of being he could not support in himself. Jung observes that archetypes are not individuals: "There is nothing in their behavior to suggest that they have an ego-consciousness . . . They show, on the contrary, all the marks of fragmentary personalities. They are masklike, wraithlike, without problems, lacking self-reflection with no conflicts, no doubts, no sufferings; like gods, perhaps, who have no philosophy. . ." (*Archetypes,* pp. 283-286). This applies not only to Molly, but to the whole cast of *Finnegans Wake* for the resolution of *Ulysses* by Molly leads to an attempt, in the *Wake,* to vest ultimate authority in the mother deity A. L. P.: "In the name of Annah the Allmaziful, the Everliving, the Bringer of Plurabilities, haloed be her eve, her singtime sung, her rill be run, unhemmed as it is uneven!" (*FW* 104). Northrop Frye says of the *Wake,* ". . .the central figure is female because the containing form is ironic and cyclical."[6]

XII

ONANYMOUS LETTERS
THE *WAKE* AS CONCLUSION

Stephen, who longs to pass into the future, is caught in cyclical repetition, but Bloom, hurt by linear time, wants to believe in cycles. In *Finnegans Wake* cyclical time eclipses linear time. The book takes place in a world of eternal return in which everything is repeated. The mental structuring which seemed an obstacle to reality in earlier works now becomes a substitute for it. In the absence of linearity none of the dichotomies caused by time—such as spirit and matter, inner and outer, past and present—are serious. They are temporary illusions in a new context, the cosmic perspective. This dream world ruled by primary process thinking is like the world of primitive, prerational men, "The Eternal Ones of the Dream." [1] Jung saw the primitive world as one of mere archetypes, of men absorbed in their collective unconscious who have not yet risen into individuation and consciousness.

Wholly contained by their group system, such men are not aware of their minds and perceive mental forces as external, supernatural powers (*Two Essays*, pp. 144ff.). Molly, in her irresponsibility—or responsibility to her unconscious—is such a primitive.

The *Wake* is inhabited not by mortal beings, but by eternal principles. Joyce recognized that these principles only exist in particular entities, but his references to individuals are so widespread and glancing that they extend vastly beyond themselves in transindividual identity. The book is supposed to center on a tavern keeper of the Dublin suburb Chapelizod named Humphrey Chimpden Earwicker (H. C. E.), and his family; but these facts are merely a sporadic series of hints in the text, and critics disagree on such points as the protagonist's name, the date of the book's action and who (singular or plural) dreams it. In fact, questions about the *Wake* seem to be increasing. The book often suggests that its action is shared by everyone and its time and place are always and everywhere. Characters and settings shift and multiply identities because they are states—gestures or impulses that may appear in any number of individuals—or several such states might appear in the same "individual" at various times.

Thus, H. C. E. as "Bygmester Finnegan" (*FW* 4.18) is both the Celtic Finn MacCool and Halvard Solness, the Norwegian master builder of Ibsen's play *Bygmester Solness*. Moreover, he is "mester," the brogue for *mister* Finnegan, the stage Irish bricklayer of the song "Finnegans Wake." And here at the start of the book he is also an infant ironically called *master*. All of these figures embody a common element of endangered aspiration and Joyce does not distinguish the dancer from the dance, the principle from its bearer.

When he "lived in the broadest way immarginable" (*FW* 4.19), Finnegan fit the Cabalistic concept of Adam Kadmon (*U* 38) or Blake's Albion. This ancient mythological giant united all of humanity in one being who filled all time and space before the fall into selfishness, negative reason, sin and individuation, "before joshuan judges had given us numbers or Helviticus committed deuteronomy" (*FW* 4), that is, in the time of "guenneses" (*FW* 4). His "immarginable" life embodied the limitless power of the imagination. He was a pagan living in the freedom before the imposition of Old Testament morality and repression, suggested by the references to Genesis, Leviticus, Numbers, Deuteronomy, Joshua and Judges. He felt the lack of division between self and universe that egoless babies and mystics feel. And he was also an Irishman filled with Guinness and carrying on outrageously. The outrageous Celt feels like the mystic giant, the mirthful babe or the noble savage, and the expansive feeling they share is immortal and universal, archetypal. Anyone participates in this feeling and embodies this form when he enjoys himself freely or reaches outward with his imagination.

Are such composite beings of shifting identity and perspective real? They have no more physical reality than a neurotic fantasy or an angel, yet their spiritual reality must be recognized because it springs from the basis of all meaningful human values beyond sustenance. Such beings were around before we came and will be here after we are gone, like gods or ideals. They reside in their most solid form in literature and culture, which record and shape the forces circulating through life. Blake's *Jerusalem* insists that states must be seen as more important than individuals for the sake of ideal values: "As the Pilgrim passes while the Country permanent remains / So Men pass on: but States remain permanent for ever" (Plate 73, *Poetry and Prose*, p. 227). The texture of the *Wake*, being about as abstract as *Jerusalem's*, seems to express Blake's position that particular, passing identities are mere selfishness, though they must be respected as primary because they are all we perceive directly. What is important, what art ultimately aims at, is immortal.

When Blake wrote, "Mental Things are alone Real. . ." in "A Vision of the Last Judgment," a competent scientist could have hoped that such notions would soon be eradicated by reason. By the time Robert Duncan chose "Mental things alone are real" as one subject of "Variations on Two Dicta of William Blake," most ideas held by the scientist of 1810, including belief in something called matter, had grown scientifically doubtful. Duncan, as he developed Blake's thought, fused with him: ". . . we are men/ who are of one mind." [2] For a significant moment he was Blake, and the record of this union is intended to make the reader join it. In "Proteus" Stephen worried about the identity shift which occurred when he used the gestures and words of others. But Joyce came to realize, as Shakespeare did, that just as his life combined inside and outside, so he could order and absorb his sources to fit structures resulting from the interaction of his personality and tradition so that his life would go on in his work. He is present with astonishing vitality in the *Wake*, constantly tipping his fedora to us and nudging our ribs with nuances of his thinking. No other work presents as much author.

The definition of life not in terms of discrete individuals, but of transpersonal states of feeling solves the problem of time by archetypal thought. It achieves victory in the world of art, creating new possibilities of reconciliation, warmth and love in Joyce's most affirmative, inspirational book. In clinical terms, however, the breakdown of the ego into disembodied states shows a new extreme of pathological inner division and distance from objective reality. Blake and Jung maintain that the ultimate reality is made up of mental images, the ideas and dreams of the psyche, and the *Wake* world is as real as these images.

Joyce believes these dreams remain the same throughout history, though their outer clothing changes. In designing his five-member family quincunx of elemental figures, Joyce synthesizes all cultures to delineate eternal patterns, thus formulating a universal religion based on psychology, as Jung and Blake do. But he emphasizes the role of language as the medium men use to record and organize the dreams that make up reality, as Vico and Lacan's Freud do. Recognizing that every language and literary work is a system for interpreting the world, Joyce breaks down conventional categories of reality to find the essential patterns common to all—a psychic "root language" (*FW* 424.17). This process extends the principle of Stephen's esthetics theory in *Portrait*, which sought beyond local and temporary ideas to find a universal pattern for beauty in the mind. The *Wake* is meant to include all reality and every system, to show the absolute truth.

Margot Norris's fine study *The Decentered Universe of Finnegans Wake* seems to contradict such a view by demonstrating that the *Wake* argues there is no single truth, that it undercuts every truth presented.[3] This is sound if truth is meant in the ordinary (giving orders), proprietary sense of a particular formulation with one center. It is consistent with Jung's warnings that archetypes as such can never be expressed in definite form. But Norris's valuable emphasis on the book's skepticism is not meant to cover such qualities as delight, pathos and beauty. The spiritual things that give it the life to succeed in creating its own genre—slapstick scripture—to accommodate most subsequent writers from Barth to Wilder. It is because Joyce denies that any one truth is final that he is able to accept without guilt the life force they embody. The old pattern of words for deeds—substitute satisfaction made possible by primary abdication of the threatening position of centrality—has now become as universal as a pattern can be.

To transform the world into art, one must withdraw from it and promote spirit at the expense of matter. For Jung this withdrawal is creative, for Freud, neurotic. Freud saw religion as a perversion of sex, neurosis acted out, while Jung regarded most Freudian sexuality as a perversion of spiritual principles. Both views have validity, for, as Denis de Rougemont observes, the strongest metaphors of mystics are sexual, while the strongest feelings of sex are mystical.[4] Acceptance of the value of physical perversion is one way Jung corrected Freud's narrowness by turning back to tradition. The *Wake* completes by its range the process begun in *Ulysses* of seeing every feeling of love as love for a fantasy even while recognizing that people not only interact, but give and take all of life across these dreams. In a shift typical of post-modernism, the conscious range of possible lives increases as the authenticity, the intensity of commitment decreases for each possibility.

When I told a gay student that homosexuals tend to be unhappy, she replied that heterosexuals tend to be unhappy. Because human drives seek different paths to satisfaction, reality can take many forms whose truth can be judged only relatively, according to how they fit into the overall context. The artist must see many sides of life, but as he builds contradictory views, his confrontation of reality may be subordinated to confrontation between forces within him. Turning from external to internal experience, Joyce used the myth of artistic creation to harness his masochistic tendencies or weaknesses to a sacrifice of the world and the self that would yield power on an internal level. He used the concentrating, analyzing power of compulsive cognition to dismember and reshape established codes in order to communicate new life, new images to his readers. His influence, sometimes working at second or third hand, has had an enormous generative effect on virtually everyone's perception of life, ranging from his early dissemination of William James's "stream of consciousness" to the latest use being made of his work by Lacan and Jacques Derrida.

The near-blind exile who spins out elaborate variations on his inner vision of a primal quincunx to make the *Wake* is like a holy man who has given up the material world to meditate on a cross or mandala. Joyce himself saw similarities between the *Wake* and the *Book of Kells.* Having abandoned worldly power, he gained awesome spiritual power, and it may long be too soon to foretell the ultimate influence of his scripture of united humanity. The *Wake,* then, is Joyce's most Jungian book, and the Jungian *Skeleton Key* has remained the best commentary on it for thirty-five years.[5] But Joyce does not forget the physical roots and connections of spiritual impulses. His root language is also rude, and his awareness of psychosexual mysteries and morsels is most extended and penetrating in his last, most shameless work.

Joyce probes the childhood roots of neurosis and art in the ninth chapter of the *Wake,* "The Children's Hour" or "The Mime of Mick, Nick and the Maggies." Here H. C. E.'s sons, Shem and Shaun, are seen playing with sister Iseult and her girl friends. The girls ask Shem a riddle, and if he gets the answer, heliotrope, he wins the right to chase a girl.[6] Among the various meanings of heliotrope, all centering on his knowledge of her nature, are the color of her panties, her vagina ("In the house of breathings lies that word, all fairness," *FW* 249.6) and intercourse: "the monthage stick in the melmelode jawr. . .Up tighty in the front, down again on the loose, drim and drumming on her back and a pop from her whistle. What is that, O holytroopers? Isot givin yoe?" (*FW* 223). Joyce believes that women incessantly confront men with this question and that the pattern of a man's reaction is formed in childhood. The artistic, autobiographical Shem, who is called Glugg here, is unable to answer correctly or make contact. Shaun, here called Chuff, "is really the rapier of the two though thother brother can hold his own. . ." (*FW* 224.33). Shem-Glugg is a masturbator and incontinent pervert, as well as being a pacifist with no respect for social status: "Ni, he make peace in his preaches and play with esteem" (*FW* 225.6). And the reasons for Glugg's inhibition from active genital life and competition center around guilt over his mother and fear of his father and of some terrible injury sustained by mother:

This poor Glugg! It was so said of him about of his old fontmouther . . . O dire! And all the freightfullness whom he inhebited after his colline born janitor. Sometime towerable! With that hehry antlets on him. . .So that Glugg . . . in that limbopool which was his subnesciousness he could scares of all knotknow whither his morrder had bourst a blabber. . .(*FW* 224)

This is his response to an especially gross version of the girl's riddle given in the ellipses: "How do you do that lack a lock and pass the poker, please?" (compare 21.18). This fear makes Shem regress from forward movement into a backward movement which is typical of him and linked to incontinence. Joyce indicates that a similar (but retentive) recoil from sex is promoted by society when he later has Shaun, the voice of conservative authority, advise his female followers to hold in their desires: "A hemd in need is aye a friendly deed" (*FW* 440.26). He orders them to regress from genital to anal satisfaction, from incestuous free action to stealth and acquisitiveness: "Put off the old man at the very font and get right on with the nutty sparker round the back" (*FW* 435.17). The key sex difference between the brothers is that Shem is perverted while Shaun is repressed—Shem expresses forbidden desires while Shaun denies them, thereby allowing himself to secretly satisfy them. And Shaun demonstrates by his popularity and success how society favors repression over self-consciousness.

Alison Armstrong, in "Shem the Penman as Glugg as the Wolf Man," argues that images associated with Glugg's "angskt" are derived from "From the History of an Infantile Neurosis" (1918), Freud's famous account of the obsessed "Wolf-man." She cites such lines as "Warewolff! Olff! Toboo!" (*FW* 225.8).[7] Whether based on Freud or memory, Glugg certainly shows obsessive characteristics. Having failed with the girls, he sits on his toilet reading Aquinas autoerotically: "With his tumescinquinance in the thight of his tumstull. . .Experssly at hand counterhand" (*FW* 240.8).[8]

Glugg's first reaction to his frustration is violence, but he then turns his aggression inward to divide himself into an artist and chase himself into exile: "He would split" (*FW* 228.5). The main purpose of his art is to expose to the world the genitals and the primal sin of his parents, which are depicted in ambiguous images of castration immediately after a paragraph containing modified versions of the names of twelve episodes of *Ulysses:*

He would bare to untired world. . .how wholefallows, his guffer, . . . he too had a great big oh in the megafundum of his tomashunders and how her Lettyshape, his gummer, . . .she had never cessed at waking malters. . . since the cluft that meataxe [his tomahawk] delt her made her microchasm as gap as down low. . .He would jused sit it all write down. . . (*FW* 229)

He sees his mother's chasm or gap as a product of father's brutality and insists that the flawed father "too" has a hole, emasculating him to the level of filial passivity. This is an accurate account of the purpose of

Joyce's work. And it includes an element of maturity, for the realization that your father has the same weakness you have leads to the possibility of fatherhood through the realization that your children will see you as a behemoth even though you are still a boy inside. Fatherhood and manhood are illusions, "founded on the void" (*U* 207) of infantile ignorance which glorifies the father. The myth of manhood is real primarily to the family of external believers to whom it is passed on, "a mystical estate, an apostolic succession, from only begetter to only begotten" (*U* 207). A man who fully believes he has the independence to fill the traditional role of manhood is fooling himself from the point of view of Joyce's century.

Father Dolan, Blazes, Shaun and other aggressors in Joyce's work are cardboard figures not only because Joyce can't empathize with active aggression, but because he believes action to be unreal, subhuman. The *Wake* word "manmichal" (340.21) associates the man of action (Michael) with the animal. As Stephen's theory of stasis suggests, only the passive attitude perceives reality: when you harden and narrow yourself to thrust forward, you lose part of your consciousness, yet this is the male role. And so the first riddle of the universe is that a man is not a man when he understands himself: "the farst wriggle from the ubivence, wherom is man, that old offender, nother man, wheile he is asame" (*FW* 356.12-14; compare 170.4-5). Recognition of the superiority of passivity, expressed in Yeats's famous lines "The best lack all conviction, while the worst/ Are full of passionate intensity," is a modernist doctrine prominent in Joyce's successors. It is implicit in all of Faulkner and explicit in Pynchon:

. . .as long as you are passive you can remain aware of the truth's extent but the minute you become active you are somehow, if not violating a convention outright, at least screwing up the perspective of things, much as someone observing subatomic particles changes the works, data and odds, by the act of observing.[9]

If Glugg's writing is a therapeutic unveiling of what his passivity allows him to see, art also covers up glimpses of disturbing psychosexual truths with formal defenses: "the best and schortest way of blacking out a caughtalook of all the sorrors of Sexton" (*FW* 230.10). The sorrows of Satan that are written up and blocked out are the female aspects of sexuality, *soror* being Latin for sister. This image is an extension of those in the "Shem the Penman" chapter showing Shem using his fecal ink as a squid does to obscure himself with purple prose, "cloaked up in the language of blushfed porporates" (*FW* 185-186). One can hardly bear to look into one's underside for more than one "monolook interyerear" (*FW* 182.20), but art, by deflecting attention onto technique, makes it possible to explore the unconscious and reality without imposing one's mind on them.

If this is Joyce's view of childhood and art in the *Wake,* his depiction of social responsibility is just as perversely informed with analytic concepts. The major scene of social intercourse between men in the *Wake* is the eleventh chapter, "Tavernry in Feast," which presents H. C. E. as public man. The two big narratives of this long chapter, the story of the Norwegian captain and the tailor and the recounting of how Buckley shot the Russian general, both based on stories told by John Joyce,[10] deal with the two principle obligations of manhood. The Captain's story depicts through the image of clothing the taking on of responsibility. It is primarily about marriage, though most of the story shows relation between two men; and Joyce anticipates here an idea developed in the story of Charles Eitel in Mailer's *Deer Park* and expanded in the story of Franz Pökler in Pynchon's *Gravity's Rainbow,* the idea that most men end up being married mainly to their businesses. The notion actually harks back to feudalism. Buckley's story presents violence and reflects Joyce's belief that virtually all significant social action is based on the model of violent conflict between men, a belief expressed earlier in the phrase, "the joust of life" (*U* 32).

The Buckley story, perhaps the most detailed version of a series of male encounters that punctuate the book, is especially dense with Freudian material. A pair of comedians known as Butt (Shem) and Taff (Shaun), playing before an audience of bar patrons who represent society, narrate the shooting of a Russian general by a British private in the Crimean War. Swarms of allusions to the Russian Revolution, the Napoleonic Wars and a host of other military engagements indicate that this patricidal act stands for all conflict between men. And most of the conflicts in the world may be interpreted as oppositions between established powers and newcomers.

In *Totem and Taboo* (1913), which seems to have been written partly in response to the final break with the restless disciple Jung, Freud presented a theory that made father-son conflict the basis of almost all religion and social organization. According to this theory, which was first formulated by Charles Darwin, the earliest society of men was a primal horde ruled, like animal herds, by a patriarch who held all the other men in subjection by arrogating to himself first choice of all women in the group (*SE* XIII, pp. 125-126). In the *Wake* this primal father is associated with a famous example of political patricide as "Sire Jeallyous Seizer" (*FW* 271.3). At a crucial point the men of the tribe or sons kill the father and eat him; this act joins them together, changing the nature of their society from patriarchal to fraternal. After this the brothers are bound by a shared guilt which subjects them to a series of inhibitions and rituals— such as the prohibition against marrying any woman of the group, the women, according to Freud, remaining linked to the patriarch. This is the proto-religion of totemism—a stage, in Freud's view, which every group goes through—and at its center is the sacred animal of the tribe.

The totem animal is thought of as the tribe's progenitor, and Freud argues that he is a disguised version of the slain father who haunts the band of brothers: "with their familiar, making the toten" (*FW* 389.33). The junction in Freud's theory when the sons kill the father and join together is depicted in the *Wake* when Butt and Taff fuse after the shooting of the general:[11]

BUTT AND TAFF (*desprot slave wager and foeman feodal unsheckled, now one and the same person, their fight upheld to right for a wee while being baffled and tottered, umbraged by the shadow of Old Erssia's magisquammythical mulattomilitiaman, the living by owning over the surfers of the glebe whose sway craven minnions had caused to revile, as, too foul for hell, . . . he falls . . .*) (*FW* 354).

The fact that the tribal animal is both sacred and demonic or unclean, both mythical and foul, both totem and taboo, like all the dead, reflects the ambivalent attitude of the sons toward their father, a combination of love and hate which generates guilt.[12] Thus, for example, the minions not only had cause to revile his sway, but they caused his sway to be vile by their own craven need for his authority. Such ambivalence is always shifting between men in the *Wake*, which carries its implications beyond Freud.

As Buckley is about to shoot the general from his hiding place, the officer lets down his pants and defecates. In the story received by Joyce, the sight of the general in such a human position makes the soldier hesitate, but when the general picks up a piece of the turf they are fighting for to wipe himself, Buckley shoots him. Taking the turf represents violation of mother earth, and all male conflict in the *Wake* is understood to be over a female. But the victory of one man over another is also a sexual conquest of the second by the first. Thus, Tristan the symbolic son, screws King Mark:

Hohoho, moulty Mark!
. . . . . .
. . .Tristy's the spry young spark
That'll tread her and wed her and bed her and red her
Without ever winking the tail of a feather
And that's how that chap's going to make his money and mark!
(*FW* 383)

As Buckley hesitates to shoot the exposed Russian, Joyce presents images of the general's underside as landscape which imply homosexual connection between the two men (*Geomater*, pp. 43-49). The Russian is referred to by a quasi-Japanese pun on Pukkelson, one of H. C. E.'s names, because the Japanese fought the Russians and the general is a target:

> BUTT ... Sehyoh narar, pokehole sann! Manhead very dirty ...
> TAFF ... Say mangraphique ...!

> BUTT...Come alleyou jupes of Wymmington that graze the calves of man!. . .Warful doon's bothem Here furry glunn. Nye? Their feery pass. Tak! With guerrillaman aspear aspoor to prink the pranks of primkissies. (*FW* 339.2-340.11)

The act of violence is also an act of love. The mixing of the two instincts, which is prominent in the *Wake*, moves in Jung's direction. In the essay "On Psychic Energy," Jung argued for one instinct, a life energy which was not innately directed toward any goal, but operated in a variety of ways, depending on internal and external situation. This solution (at the expense of differentiation) to Freud's struggle to define two instincts corresponds to the shift from the conventional logic of exclusive categories to a Hermetic or Brunonian conception of life as a unity made up of conflicting but inseparable opposites—as virtually every word of the *Wake* is.

But in order to take action, it is necessary to deny the other side of one's motivation, so the son must deny his love even as he is portrayed as Oscar Wilde with a sunflower in his buttonhole:

> BUTT (*with a gisture expansive of Mr Lhugewhite Cadderpollard with sunflawered beautonhole pulled up point blanck by mailbag mundaynism* [Shaun] *at Oldbally Court though the hissindensity buck far of his melovelance tells how when he was fast marking his first lord for cremation the whyfe of his bothem was the very lad's thing to elter his mehind*). (*FW* 350)

What he claims to be the last thing to enter his mind (or body) is not only A. L. P., the wife of H. C. E.'s bosom for whom he kills, but the whiff (or wipe) of H. C. E.'s bottom and the "lad's thing." The sinflawed beautonhole that inverts forward movement and causes the hesitancy behind his malevolent lovelance may be equated with another crime, "his rent in his rears" (*FW* 47.11). Butt's name belies his role as man of action, for every man's authority is undermined by the side of him that corresponds to the female or bad son, "haunted always by his ham" (*FW* 49.22).

As Stephen said in "Scylla and Charybdis," the secret which must be suppressed most completely is sexual attraction to father. This desire generates the crucial weakness of Freud's totem sons and is the source of the guilt which drives them to sacrifice. Moreover, it is the temptation to submit to father that makes it necessary to strike out at him in the form of enemy. Butt says, "He deared me to it and he dared me do it" (*FW* 353.10).

The moral import of this scene lies in its insistence on the sexual nature of violence. The terrible inhumanities of history have usually been perpetrated by people with well-developed rationalizations and myths. During our last war in Asia, it was common for soldiers to repeat that they were only doing their jobs. Men who carry out wars dismiss as preposterous any claim that they enjoy violence; but whatever external factors were involved, they took their roles as the most satisfying ones possible. Joyce was concerned with analyzing the function of culture as a system of reasons designed to separate people from the psychic meanings of their actions.

He recognizes in *Dubliners* how society uses people's psychological needs to entrap them, and in Chapter III of *Portrait* he details parallels between religious doctrine and the psychological guilt which supports it. "Scylla and Charybdis" aligns original sin with oedipal passivity and *Ulysses* as a whole equates cuckoldry with mortality because the impossibility of union with parents ushers in the sufferings of mutability and dispossession. The equation of original sin with the oedipal complex through cuckoldry is clarified in the *Wake,* where the cuckold-wife-lover triangle causes the trials of man's fallen state because of boyhood mutilation: "The wittold, the frausch and the dibble! How this loosefair brimsts of fussforus! And was this treemanangel on his soredbohmend because Knockout, the Knickknaver, knacked him in the knechtschaft?" [*German* knighthood or boyhood] (*FW* 505). Paternal authority protects its own parts by cutting off Lucifer's:

Such was a bitte too thikke for the Muster of the hoose so as he called down on the Grand Precurser who coiled him a crawler of the dupest dye and thundered at him to flatch down off that erection and be aslimed of himself for the bellance of hissch leif. (*FW* 506.4-8)

Original sin and the oedipal complex both explain why man is "ashamed for the beauty of his love" by ascribing his lack of freedom to a mysterious crime in a past which cannot be remembered. The need for authority which was explained theologically for thousands of years is explained psychologically by reason, and Joyce sees religion and psychology as sides of the same truth.

Members of the totem clan find authority in worship of their group's animal and cannot kill or eat it except at communal sacrificial rituals called totem feasts. With time after the death of the patriarch, however, hatred of him declines and longing for him increases, causing the totem animal to change into a god, the surrogate to regain human form. Freud (p. 156) sees the paternal totem in all communal sacrifices, including the imaginary one of tragedy. The Russian general, though mainly human, is also a bear, "Bruinoboroff" (*FW* 340.20), a deer, a goat, a sabre tooth and a bull. H. C. E. as bartender parallels the general in being destroyed by the hostility of his customers, and he is fish (316.30), goat (360.36) and bull (358.31).

As publican, H. C. E. serves the people a communion of his own substance. The "host of a bottlefilled" (*FW* 310.26) says, "Trink me dregs!" (321.29). When, as part of his sacrifice, he is hung and married, "crucifixioners" throw lots (377.23), and as Roderick O'Connor," he "greatly" gives a "last supper" (380.15). Like Bacchus, he is a slain and eaten god: "We could ate you, par Buccas, and imbabe through you. . .One fledge, one brood till hulm culms everdyburdy" (378.3). Christ was sacrificed to atone for the crime against the father, but every man is Christ through the sacrifices society and his mind impose on him. And that makes this a realistic representation of the feelings an average person might have while making the concessions of business or social dealings, including embarrassment at his marraige as a function of lost freedom. This self-sacrifice holds society together at points where individual pride would break it down. Anyone who wills to sacrifice himself gains authority which joins him to the father.

Joyce believed that morality is based on masochism, though he must have realized, after all he put Nora through to make himself suffer, that all masochism is not moral. Joyce must have seen Christ, the prime model of self-sacrifice, as a masochist insofar as he chose his role and was a god rather than a mere victim. As Bloom is flagellated by three ladies of social elevation, "He offers the other cheek" (*U* 468). One moral point of Joyce's emphasis on Christ's masochism is that if people realize how essential self-sacrifice is both for society and for the self, they can avoid the righteousness of Shaun and the shame of Shem. A man who believes that all his sacrifice is for the good of others and not for himself—and this describes the traditional noble warrior—will feel ready, if not obligated, to strike down those who disagree with him. The other extreme is the sensitive person who blames himself for qualities which could be virtuous. Freud observed that really bad people seldom feel guilty, while good ones often do so (*SE* XIX, pp. 170-171).

H. C. E.'s defense, when accused of his breach by the public, is that if he has a flaw, so does everybody: "Guilty, but fellows culpows" (*FW* 363.19). The irony is that the softness he confesses to may be his best feature. Even on the lowest physical level his weak spot is creative, for creation is linked to defecation in the *Wake*. Ultimately, Joyce believes that the naked truth literature reveals to us is that everyone is innately bisexual, man and woman as well as parent and child, and he indicates this in naming a source: "their old one page codex book. . .by his fellow girl, the Mrs. Shemans. . .her *totam in tutu*, final buff noonmeal edition" (*FW* 397.29). The letter that is the book of life expresses both a "feminine libido" and the control of a "male fist" (*FW* 123.8-10). Effort to relate to life exclusively through one of these sides or any other category or system will miss the vital reality that can only be perceived by combining opposed views.

But the truth of the ambivalent perspective which catches a full range of possibilities is sundered from the practical concerns of what we usually call reality—a system of power built on the logic of exclusive categories. And Freud's account of religion as obsessive ambivalence applies to the glorification of hermaphroditism found in Hermetism, Romanticism, Symbolism and the Modernism of Joyce, Mann, Proust, Lawrence and Woolf.[13] If, in the progress of compulsion, more and more use is made of "substitutes for the forbidden sexual act and. . .imitations of it" (*Totem*, p. 88), then the mind, as self-sufficient hermaphrodite, may increasingly satisfy itself mentally. This tendency shifts Joyce's work from naturalism to symbolism, from bitterness to play, from external to internal, from reality to dream. Late in his career he came to believe his work could predict the future (*JJ* 611, 742); the external world tended to dwindle to material for his system, a field upon which his interpretative power could play, with his major opposition coming from his own skepticism.

Freud says "universalization" is characteristic of compulsion, with object relations marked by "looseness" and "displaceability" (*Anxiety*, p. 158). Nowhere are these features as evident as in the *Wake*, where characters are not individuals, but tissues of reference to ongoing patterns: "any filly in a fog" (*FW* 415.21). These archetypal figures "reamalgamerge" (*FW* 49.36) with each other often, changing identity and even number.

Freud's precision blade can be aimed to fall sharply on such a dreamy fabric: ". . .under the guise of obsessional acts, the masturbation that has been suppressed approaches ever more closely to satisfaction" (*Anxiety*, p. 115). The texture of Joyce's great word-hoard is markedly compulsive: puns and portmanteau words combine with conceptual framework to provide endless ambiguity. The ritual use of language, piling up of words, regressive playfulness, concern with time, magic symbols and numbers, painstaking systematization, egregious intellectualism and preoccupation with what may be called sexcrement appear on almost every page.

Neurotic behavior uses the logic of dreams while awake. The dream techniques of isolation, undoing and displacement of feelings onto small details, which the *Wake* evidently derives from Freud, characterize the waking life of the obsessive. Analysis must conclude that Joyce was playing verbal games with himself in the *Wake*. The "ideal reader suffering from an ideal insomnia" (*FW* 120.13) to whom Joyce addresses himself evidently does not have sexual intercourse often enough—but who does?

The *Wake* is both Joyce's least repressed and most repressed work, as it is his most and least serious. The final product of Joyce's tendency to be increasingly unrestrained in dealing with sex throughout his career, it wallows in incest, particularly the latest permutation of Joyce's attachment to his mother, an unhealthy, polarized love of father for daughter. The book also indulges itself outrageously in patricide, scatology, homosexuality and other taboos. And yet, grotesquely bemired with scandal as the *Wake* is at times, the book is more careful than anything else Joyce wrote except the imitative *Chamber Music* in avoiding real conflict or threat. Aggression is always enveloped in a dense swarm of defenses which render it harmless. When a character strikes another, it turns out that the aggressor and the victim are the same or separated only by time. Confrontations generally end with one antagonist changing identities with or fusing with the other.[14] Violence is transformed into a puppet show or comedy routine, seen from a distance, recounted by a scholar, isolated from feeling or associated with mythological rebirth: "Phall if you but will, rise you must" (*FW* 4.14). No one really gets hurt; and the painful aspect of sex is also censored, as the benign harmlessness of father H. C. E. indicates.

As Joyce's works move steadily away from the harshness of reality, they increasingly avoid the paternal threat which enforces that harshness. *Dubliners* begins with a series of terrible men: the sinister Father Flynn of "The Sisters," the old sadist of "An Encounter," Eveline's brutal father, the apelike Corley of "Two Gallants," Polly Mooney's bully of a brother in "The Boarding House," the swaggering Gallaher of "A Little Cloud" and the violent father Farrington of "Counterparts." All confront us in the first hundred pages, inflicting pain and humiliation. Moving on from this horrendous opening, we find Simon Daedalus considerably more unpleasant in *Stephen Hero* than in *Portrait;* and no one as cruel as Father Dolan or the God of the third chapter of *Portrait* registers in *Ulysses* because the threats of the *dio boia*, Mulligan, Boylan and Bello are ameliorated by irony, humor or evasion.

H. C. E., the patriarch of the *Wake*, could be called as mild and emasculated as Bloom: he spends most of his time dying or being victimized. His grand copulation with A. L. P. late in the book, which cannot take place until she goes upstairs to comfort son Jerry (Shem), is sometimes festive, but never passionate. Though this weary early morning grind of the old couple "tickled her innings to consort pitch" (*FW* 584.2), she does not register satisfaction: "You never wet the tea! And you may go rightoway back to your Auntie Dilluvia, Humphrey, after that!" (*FW* 585.32). The *Wake* has a few glorious invocations of sexual union, but they take such forms as campy dream fantasy (395-396) and buried memory (547–548). The communion of love, opposed by selfishness and neurotic limitations, is finally no more present than the communion of the Church. And the failure of H. C. E. to continue strongly satisfying A. L. P. is a failure of forward thrust connected with the cyclical structure of the novel.

Man tends to be inadequate to the threat of his own expansion posed by woman in the *Wake*, a pattern firmly established by the tale of Jarl Van Hoother and the Prankquean (*FW* 21-23). A. L. P., "annadominant" (*FW* 14.7), assumes much of the power of the deity in her roles of destroyer, preserver and motivator: ". . .Anna was at the beginning lives yet and will return. . ." (*FW* 277.12). When male authority is invoked to preside or punish, it either appears in the clownish form of Shaun or it is rendered impersonal and associated with magic numbers by being divided into four evangelists or twelve jurors. Virtually the only aggressive acts which originate with H. C. E. himself are his thunderclaps, which frighten his family. These noises of defecation are a regressive, neuter disguise for H. C. E's phallic power and fertility.[15] Each of the ten thunderclaps ends a phase of a cycle, but begins a new one; thus, it is not only apocalypse, but creation, and does as much good as harm.

The portrayal of H. C. E. shows that Joyce can take the necessary step of associating with a father provided that the father's powers are severely limited and elaborately circumscribed. This arrangement was prefigured in *Ulysses*, where Stephen was potentially able to associate with Bloom because Bloom was balanced, father and no father, between Joyce's compassion or empathy and his satire. Since association with father is essential to resolving the oedipal complex, it seems Joyce has made progress toward health, either through the self-analysis of his work or through the experience of parenthood. But does association with Bloom or H. C. E. constitute association with a father?

Joyce thought so. *Ulysses* and the *Wake* show that most fathers and men, at least insofar as they have the unselfishness to transmit civilized moral values, are aware of being no more than keyless on an inner lever, no matter how they may strut. One of H. C. E.'s names is "god at the top of the staircase, carrion on the mat of straw" (*FW* 131.17). And A. L. P. says she once thought him great and glittering, but after years of marriage she has come to loathe his smallness and dishonesty: "You're but a puny"

(*FW* 627.24). The exalted patriarch is born in the eyes of the wife or child who does not realize that the mind of the supposed father is still that of a boy; he is an illusion resting on the infantile ignorance which perceives parents as omnipotent.

A father uses the authority of his position to make his sons strong by resisting them, but they develop themselves by defeating him: "we go into him sleepy children, we come out of him strucklers for life" (*FW* 132.8). The defeat of the father is not merely a singular event, but an archetypal pattern. The shooting of the general by Buckley corresponds to all the scenes in which the soldiers see the crime of H. C. E. and to all occurrences of the everyday situation of a follower recognizing a weakness in his leader. A typical version, "the treepartied ambush was laid (. . .near Stop and Think, high chief evervirens and only abfalltree in auld the land)" (*FW* 87-88). As Norris suggests, the fall is also the creation in the *Wake* (*Decentered*, pp. 33ff.). Just as realism begins as a reaction against myth, so the striking down of the father, demolishing an ideal, confronts the sons with the realities of the world and themselves, as eating the tree of knowledge would. After this the soldiers list his vices, some of which form a sequence beginning with the letters HERECOMESEVERYBODY (*FW* 88). While they do not see their own guilt consciously, the knowledge of human weakness they take from him binds them together. Because every victim tends to take on paternal qualities, this pattern makes virtually every defeat creative.

I have shown that Joyce conceives of the operations of creativity, fatherhood and love as based on the mythic principle of death and rebirth or losing in order to gain, sinking to rise. Because such processes must go into the unknown, the creative impulse must aim at something which is illusory in empirical terms. This aim is exemplified by the unknowable target of another person's mind, which can only be manifested in an illusory form. But when two minds share an illusion, it gains psychological reality as both affirm themselves by contact with each other through the intermediate object.[16] A cardinal point of Joyce's vision from "The Dead" on is that men derive their being and vitality from the image they project to women, while women gain being by presenting themselves to the devotion of men. This exchange is founded on the way in which parents expand the powers of their children by investing emotion in them, having a faith in their ability which goes beyond reductive logic. A person is equal to the sum of love people give him. Molly is free to love because Bloom worries about her and Bloom gains the spiritual power to confront and release Stephen by earning the gratitude he gives her the freedom to feel. If each person transcends his own limits by partaking of the faith of the opposite sex and projecting that faith into undeveloped extensions of himself, then heterosexuality has a powerful religious function:

Prospector projector and. . .giant builder of all causeways woesoever, . . .zeal whence to goal whither, wonderlust, in sequence to which every muckle must make its mickle. . ., being the only wise in a muck's world to look on itself from beforehand; mirrorminded curiositease and would-to-the-large which bring hills to molehunter, . . .prick this man and tittup this woman, our forced payrents, . . .we beseech you, down their ladder-case of nightwatch service. . .(*FW* 576)

This deeply felt prayer uses the Freudian image of a ladder to hail the erotic drive "wonderlust" as the first cause and the only real motivation people have for getting outside themselves, the "mirrorminded curiositease" that leads them to know themselves and others by reflection and the "only wise" toward transcendence. Though forced to pay rent or obliged to make a place for their children by their effort of consideration, man and woman should grow erect with confidence. For the conflict-free area they generate by wishing each other well is what Winnicott calls the play space; and only within this space can one expand creative perception and see new reality because one feels no need to think of self-interest or any other imposed system. Only within the matrix of good wishes which is love can one enlarge molehills to mountains. And so every muckle makes his mickle in wanderlust, in the freedom of "zeal whence" or desire.

But just as Christian prayer sees the world filled with temptation (*P* 18), so this invocation as it goes on grows preoccupied by the distractions of fantasy, neurosis and narcissism that surround the true path: "guide them through the labyrinth of their samilikes and. . .pseudoselves, hedge them bothways from all roamers. . .,from loss of bearings deliver them; so they keep to their rights and be ware of duty frees. . ." In making love absolute, elevating it to deity, Joyce makes it unattainable, and in making it the reservoir of potential, he puts it beyond fact.

Whether or not it is true that love and fatherhood are illusions and the world a "mystical estate" founded on the void (*U* 207), the idea has at least the virtue that made Jesus speak in paradoxes, the power of poetry to undermine authoritarianism. Many critics have found Bloom and H. C. E. typical or average figures representative of modern civilized man—and so Joyce intended them to be. Their rampant obsessions and perversions help make them so. What sort of man reads *Playboy*? Perhaps a very common sort whose strongest emotional attachment is to fantasy.

The emasculated fathers of Joyce's last novels are intended to be complete men, but these keyless citizens are, perhaps to their credit, no more complete than most of us. *Totem and Taboo* says the civilized father fails to fill a space left by a primitive father remembered from individual and racial infancy: ". . . the gulf between the new fathers of a family and the unrestricted primal father of the horde was wide enough to guarantee the persistence of an unappeased longing for the father" (p. 149).

The threatening absolute father, though subsided from the surface, must be avoided and contained by strategies of defense all through the book. He arises awesomely at the end as Neptune: "sad and weary I go back to you, my cold. . .mad feary father, till the near sight of the mere size of him . . . makes me seasilt saltsick and I rush, my only, into your arms. I see them rising! Save me from those therrble prongs!" (*FW* 628). At crucial points in our lives we are confronted with the need to submit to authority in order to advance. This is what makes them crucial, as the cross was Christ's submission to father. The apparition of father Ocean is so overwhelming that it brings the book and the career to a fitting climax. The only place Joyce can go from this point is back to the beginning.

NOTES

INTRODUCTION

1. Arthur Power, *Conversations with James Joyce,* ed. Clive Hart (New York: Harper and Row, 1974), pp. 54, 74, 89.
2. Hayman, *Ulysses: The Mechanics of Meaning* (Englewood Cliffs, N.J.: Prentice-Hall, 1970), pp. 78ff.
3. *Joyce in Nighttown: A Psychoanalytic Inquiry into Ulysses* (Berkeley: Univ. of California Press, 1974). Inner life is equated with fantasy on p. 123.
4. *The Classical Temper: A Study of James Joyce's Ulysses* (London: Chatto and Windus, 1961), pp. 69-70.
5. Hugh Kenner, *Dublin's Joyce* (London: Chatto & Windus, 1956); Harry Levin, *James Joyce: A Critical Introduction* (New York: New Directions, 1941, 1960); Richard M. Kain, *Fabulous Voyager: James Joyce's Ulysses* (Chicago: Univ. of Chicago, 1947); Darcy O'Brien, *The Conscience of James Joyce* (Princeton, 1968).
6. Goldberg, *Temper;* William York Tindall, *James Joyce: His Way of Interpreting the Modern World* (New York: Scribner's, 1950); Richard Ellmann, *Ulysses on the Liffey* (New York: Oxford, 1972). I have had to confine myself to the most important works.
7. *Temper,* pp. 139-143, 257-259 *et passim.* Goldberg rejects all of the *Wake* on pp. 103-114.
8. *Liffey,* pp. 125, 133, 139.
9. (Univ. of Chicago, 1961), pp. 323-336.
10. *The Joyce Paradox: Form and Freedom in His Fiction* (Evanston, Ill.: Northwestern Univ. Press, 1966), pp. 9-11, 43-50, 107, 161 *et passim.*
11. Louis A. Murillo, *The Cyclical Night: Irony in James Joyce and Jorge Luis Borges* (Cambridge: Harvard Univ. Press, 1968); Hayman, *Mechanics;* Marilyn French, *The Book as World: James Joyce's Ulysses* (Cambridge: Harvard, 1976); C. H. Peake, *James Joyce: The Citizen and the Artist* (London: Edward Arnold, 1977); James H. Maddox, Jr., *Joyce's Ulysses and the Assault upon Character* (New Brunswick, N.J.: Rutgers Univ. Press, 1978).
12. *Exile,* trans. Sally A. J. Purcell (New York: David Lewis, 1972), pp. 437-595. Originally *L'Exil de James Joyce ou l'art du remplacement* (Paris: Grasset, 1968).
13. *A Scrupulous Meanness: A Study of Joyce's Early Work* (Urbana: Univ. of Illinois Press, 1971).
14. *Book as World,* pp. 169ff.
15. *Liffey,* pp. 86, 174.
16. *The Consciousness of Joyce* (New York: Oxford, 1977), p. 74.
17. Leonard Albert, *Joyce and the New Psychology,* Dissertation, Columbia Univ. (DA 58-1329). Support comes from Chester G. Anderson, "Leopold Bloom as Dr. Sigmund Freud," *Mosaic* 6, no. 1 (1972), 23-43.
18. *My Brother's Keeper: James Joyce's Early Years* (New York: Viking, 1958), p. 181.
19. Frederick J. Hoffman gathered analytic references in the *Wake* into "Infroyce," *Freudianism and the Literary Mind* (Baton Rouge: Lousiana State Univ. Press, 1945), reprinted in *James Joyce: Two Decades of Criticism,* ed. Seon Givens (New York: Vanguard Press, 1948, 1963). Anderson, "Bloom as Freud," finds *Ulysses* referring to all twelve chapters of *The Psychopathology of Everyday Life* as well as other early works of Freud.
20. *Consciousness,* pp. 54ff., 109, 114, 115.
21. Glover, *Freud or Jung?* (Cleveland: World, 1956), pp. 35-88.

22. "On Psychic Energy," *CW* [Jung], 8, pp. 23-25. This essay is one of Jung's best metapsychological defenses.
23. Reik, *Of Love and Lust: On the Psychoanalysis of Romantic and Sexual Emotions* (New York: Bantam, 1967), p. 11.
24. Richard Wollheim, *Sigmund Freud*, Modern Masters (New York: Viking, 1971), pp. xix, 5.
25. Joseph Campbell, "Editor's Introduction," *The Portable Jung* (New York: Viking, 1971), pp. vii-ix.
26. Cited in Arthur Koestler, *The Roots of Coincidence: An Excursion into Parapsychology* (New York: Vintage, 1973), pp. 54-55.

1. THE GRAVE OF BOYHOOD

1. *Citizen and Artist*, pp. 69ff.
2. *JJ* 27-28; Ulick O'Connor, ed. *The Joyce We Knew* (Cork: The Mercier Press, 1967), pp. 7, 15-59. Little is invented in *Portrait*, and what is rearranged serves Joyce's interpretation of his life. See *JJ* and Edmund Epstein, *The Ordeal of Stephen Dedalus: The Conflict of Generations in James Joyce's A Portrait*. . .(Carbondale: Southern Illinois Univ. Press, 1971), pp. 36ff.
3. "The Seven Lost Years of *A Portrait*. . . ," *Approaches to Joyce's Portrait: Ten Essays*, ed. Thomas F. Staley and Bernard Benstock (Univ. of Pittsburgh Press, 1976), p. 34.
4. Stephen's oedipal pattern has been pointed out by Tindall, *His Way*, p. 47; Richard Wasson, "Stephen Dedalus and the Imagery of Sight: A Psychological Approach," *Literature and Psychology*, 15 (Fall 1965), 195-209; Evert Sprinchorn, "A Portrait of the Artist as Achilles," *Approaches to the Twentieth Century Novel*, ed. John E. Unterecker (New York: Thomas Y. Crowell, 1965), pp. 17-21; Sheldon Brivic, "James Joyce: From Stephen to Bloom," *Psychoanalysis and Literary Process*, ed. Frederick Crews (Cambridge, Mass.: Winthrop, 1970), pp. 118-142; and Suzette A. Henke, *Joyce's Moraculous Sindbook: A Study of Ulysses* (Columbus: Ohio State Univ. Press, 1978), pp. 226, 245.
5. Robert S. Ryf, *A New Approach to Joyce: The Portrait of the Artist as Guidebook* (Berkeley: Univ. of California Press, 1962), p. 113.
6. *Viking Critical Library* edition of *Portrait*, ed. Chester G. Anderson (New York: Viking, 1968), pp. 267-268.
7. Fenichel, *The Psychoanalytic Theory of Neurosis* (New York: Norton, 1945), p. 78. Hereafter cited as *Theory*.
8. Freud, "Fetishism" (1927), *SE*, XXI, pp. 152-157. *Selected Letters of James Joyce*, ed. Richard Ellmann (Viking, 1975), pp. 180-192, presents the least expurgated texts of the letters.
9. Budgen, *James Joyce and the Making of Ulysses* (Bloomington: Indiana Univ. Press, 1960), p. 319.
10. Epstein, *Ordeal*, pp. 38-39, sees some of these patterns.
11. *The Complete Dublin Diary of Stanislaus Joyce*, ed. George Harris Healey (Ithaca: Cornell Univ. Press, 1971), pp. 5-6. Stanislaus describes James as extraordinarily devoted to his father in *My Brother's Keeper*, pp. 32, 57, 238 *et passim*.
12. Cited in *James Joyce: The Critical Heritage*, ed. Robert Deming (London: Routledge & Kegan Paul, 1970), p. 225.
13. The "Wolf Man" is in "From the History of an Infantile Neurosis" (1918). *SE* XVII, pp. 1-121; the "Rat Man," in "Notes upon a Case of Obsessional Neurosis" (1909), *SE* X, pp. 155-250.
14. *SE* X, p. 245n.; *Inhibitions, Symptoms and Anxiety* (1926), *SE* XX, pp. 113ff.
15. Holland, *The Dynamics of Literary Response* (New York: Oxford, 1968), p. 46.
16. "A Child Is Being Beaten: A Contribution to the Study of the Origin of Sexual

Perversions" (1919), *SE* XVII, pp. 179-204; "The Economic Problem of Masochism" (1924), *SE* XIX, pp. 161-170.
17.   *Theory,* pp. 358-362. See Shechner, *Nighttown,* pp. 102-109, 145-148.
18.   Wilhelm Reich, *The Function of the Orgasm* (New York: Farrar, Straus and Cudahy, 1942), p. 223.

2. CORK

1.   Freud says some men court other men's women to satisfy oedipal fixation; see "A Special Type of Choice of Object Made by Men (Contributions to the Psychology of Love, I)" (1910), *SE* XI, pp. 166-176.
2.   *Two Essays on Analytic Psychology, CW* [Jung], 7, pp. 165-188.
3.   "(Contributions to the Psychology of Love, II)" (1912), *SE* XI, pp. 177-190.
4.   *Playing and Reality* (Harmondsworth, Middlesex: Penguin, 1974), p. 115. This idea resembles Jung's concept of individuation.

3. CIRCLES OF SUPEREROGATION

1.   "Obsessive Actions and Religious Practices" (1907), *SE* IX, pp. 117-127.
2.   *Joyce among the Jesuits* (New York: Columbia Univ. Press, 1958), pp. 128ff.
3.   Hugh Kenner, "The Portrait in Perspective," Seon Givens, ed., *James Joyce: Two Decades of Criticism* (New York: Vanguard Press, 1948, 1963), pp. 163-169.
4.   (New York: Vintage, 1955), p. 316.
5.   "Identity and Sexuality: A Study of Their Interrelationship in Man," *Journal of the American Psychoanalytic Association,* 9 (1961), 211 ff.
6.   "On the Universal Tendency. . . ," pp. 179-186. Darcy O'Brien discusses the pattern in "Some Psychological Determinants of Joyce's View of Love and Sex," *New Light on Joyce from the Dublin Symposium,* ed. Fritz Senn (Bloomington: Indiana Univ. Press, 1972), pp. 15-26.
7.   Fenichel, *Theory,* p. 288. See discussion of obsessive cognitive patterns in David Shapiro, *Neurotic Styles* (New York: Basic Books, 1965), pp. 26-53.
8.   *Life Against Death: The Psychoanalytic Meaning of History* (Middletown, Conn., 1959), particularly "Part Three: Death," pp. 77-134, and Chapter XV, "Filthy Lucre," pp. 234-304. Brown speaks not of compulsion, but of anality.
9.   "By and About Joyce," *Hudson Review,* 21 (Summer 1968), 383.
10.   *The Stream of Consciousness and Beyond in Ulysses* (Pittsburgh: Univ. of Pittsburgh Press, 1973), pp. 13-27.
11.   Sprinchorn, "Achilles," pp. 27-33, and Diane Fortuna, "The Labyrinth as Controlling Image in Joyce's *A Portrait . . . ,*" *Bulletin of the New York Public Library,* 76 (1972), 120-180.

4. ART

1.   He mentions confessing to Davin (*P* 202) and Cranly (*P* 178, 232, 247), while the presentation of the esthetic theory shows him in the habit of opening his mind to Lynch.
2.   See Simon O. Lesser, *Ficton and the Unconscious* (New York: Vintage, 1962), pp. 59-144 and the first four chapters of Holland, *Dynamics.*
3.   *A Reader's Guide to James Joyce,* (New York: Farrar, Straus, 1959), pp. 95ff.
4.   Robert Scholes and Richard M. Kain, *The Workshop of Daedalus: James Joyce and the Raw Materials for A Portrait. . .*(Evanston, Ill.: Northwestern Univ. Press, 1965), pp. 247-248.

5. FLIGHT

1.   Chester Anderson traces references that associate Stephen and Christ in "The Sacrificial Butter," *Accent*, 12 (Winter 1952), 3-13.
2.   See Daniel A. Weiss, *Oedipus in Nottingham: D. H. Lawrence* (Seattle: Univ. of Washington Press, 1962), pp. 32ff. Epstein, *Ordeal*, pp. 2-4, suggests Joyce derived the idea of father-son conflict from Ibsen, Samuel Butler, Meredith, Dickens, et al.
3.   *Symbols of Transformation*, CW [Jung], 5, p. 294.
4.   "The State of Psychotherapy Today," *CW* [Jung], 10, pp. 167-170; *Two Essays*, p. 182.
5.   Frank O'Connor, "Joyce and Dissociated Metaphor," *Viking Critical Portrait*, p. 376, says, "The soul. . .is born in males only with mortal sin."
6.   *The Masks of God: Creative Mythology* (New York: Viking, 1968), pp. 27ff.
7.   "State of Psychotherapy" (1934) argues that Freud sees a negative unconscious because the Jews, as an ancient race, have used up the positive potential of their unconscious. Analytic psychology, in contrast, is seen as an expression of the positive psychic power of the newer German race.
8.   The Signet *Hamlet*, ed. Edward Hubler (New York: New American Library, 1963), glosses the *conscience* that "does make cowards of us all" (III.i.83) as "self-consciousness." Stephen would be aware that *conscious* and *conscience* have the same etymology.
9.   Introductory Lectures on Psychoanalysis (1917), *SE* XVI, pp. 376-377.

6. "THE DEAD"

1.   Don Gifford, *Notes for Joyce: Dubliners and A Portrait* . . . (New York: Dutton, 1967), p. 80.

7. *EXILES:* LIVING WOUNDING DOUBT

1.   Aitken, "Dramatic Archetypes in Joyce's 'Exiles,'" *Modern Fiction Studies*, 4 (Spring 1958), 43. I am indebted to Aitken's study of the imagery of the play.
2.   *The Poetry and Prose of William Blake*, ed. David V. Erdman (Garden City, N.Y.: Doubleday, 1965, 1970), p. 39.
3.   Robert Martin Adams, "Light on Joyce's Exiles?: A New Manuscript, A Curious Analogue, and Some Speculations," *Studies in Bibliography*, 17 (1964), p. 86.
4.   Dante Alighieri, *The Divine Comedy*, trans. John A. Carlyle, Thomas Okey and P. H. Wicksteed (New York: Modern Library, 1932, 1950), Canto XXX, p. 373. My italics.
5.   Frances A. Yates, *Giordano Bruno and the Hermetic Tradition* (New York: Vintage, 1969).
6.   *Psychological Types*, CW , [Jung], 6, p. 332.
7.   *Ego and Id*. p. 33n. The letter is dated January 8.
8.   *The Art of Courtly Love*, trans. John Jay Parry (New York: Norton, 1969), p. 28.
9.   Letter to George and Thomas Keats, December 21, 1817, *Selected Letters of John Keats*, ed. Lionel Trilling (New York: Doubleday, 1951, 1956), p. 103.

8. FROM STEPHEN TO BLOOM

1.   A. Walton Litz, *The Art of James Joyce: Method and Design In Ulysses and Finnegans Wake* (New York: Oxford, 1964), pp. 132-137.

2. Schutte, *Joyce and Shakespeare: A Study of the Meaning of Ulysses* (New Haven: Yale, 1957), pp. 104-120.

3. Weldon Thornton, *Allusions in Ulysses: An Annotated List* (Chapel Hill: Univ. of North Carolina Press, 1968), p. 332.

4. *Ham.* II.ii.405-406. Cited by Schutte, *Shakespeare,* p. 111.

5. Lecture on Joyce and Shakespeare at Fifth International Joyce Symposium, Paris, June 19, 1975.

6. Identified in Tindall, *Reader's Guide,* p. 213.

7. Von Abele, *"Ulysses:* The Myth of Myth," *PMLA,* 69 (June 1954), 358-364.

9. JOYCE'S SYSTEM AND JUNG'S TYPES

1. "'Ulysses': A Monologue," *CW* [Jung], 15, p. 114.

2. Lewis, *Time and Western Man* (New York: Harcourt Brace, 1928), pp. 75-118.

3. The most complete of many versions of this diagram is Ellmann, *Liffey,* pp. 188ff.

4. *CW* [Jung], 6, p. 330. Future references to pages of this work will appear in parentheses preceded by *PT.*

5. Lifton, "Protean Man," *Partisan Review,* 35 (Winter 1968), 13-27.

6. Stanley Sultan, *The Argument of Ulysses* (Columbus: Ohio Univ. Press, 1964), pp. 407, 43ff., was first to indicate how thoroughly responsible for his cuckoldry Bloom is.

7. *One Hundred Middle English Lyrics,* ed. Robert D. Stevick (Indianapolis, Ind.: Bobbs-Merrill, 1964), p. 134.

10. LOVE AS CREATION IN *ULYSSES*

1. *The Book as World: James Joyce's Ulysses* (Cambridge: Harvard Univ. Press, 1976), p. 43.

2. "Synchronicity: An Acausal Connecting Principle" and "On Synchronicity," *Structure and Dynamics,* pp. 419-519 and 520-531 respectively. Also see "Richard Wilhelm: In Memoriam" (1930), *CW* [Jung], 15, pp. 53-62.

3. "Synchronicity," pp. 486-495, includes all of my references.

4. *James Joyce Quarterly,* 9 (Fall 1971), 37-48.

5. Adams, *Surface and Symbol: The Consistency of James Joyce's Ulysses* (New York: Oxford, 1962), pp. 95-98; Blamires, *The Bloomsday Book: A Guide Through Joyce's Ulysses* (London: Methuen, 1966), pp. 116, 148; French, *Book as World,* pp. 188-194, Maddox, *Assault,* pp. 148ff.

6. (Berkeley: Univ. of California Press, 1978), pp. 53, 78-80, 87ff.

7. "Hades," *James Joyce's Ulysses: Critical Essays,* ed. Clive Hart and David Hayman (Berkeley: Univ. of California Press, 1974), pp. 109-110.

8. Mark E. Littmann and Charles A. Schweighauser, "Astronomical Allusions, Their Meaning and Purpose in Ulysses," *JJQ,* 2 (Summer 1965), 238-246.

9. An outstanding exposition of these Jungian ideas is Joseph Campbell, *The Hero with a Thousand Faces,* Bollingen Series XVII (Princeton: Bollingen, 1949).

10. *James Joyce's Scribbledehobble: The Ur-Workbook for Finnegans Wake,* ed. Thomas E. Connolly (Chicago: Northwestern Univ. Press, 1961), p. 104.

11. Three Initiates, *The Kybalion: A Study of the Hermetic Philosophy of Ancient Greece and Egypt* (Chicago: Yogi Publication Soc., 1912, 1940), p. 40.

12. *Moraculous Sindbook,* pp. 86-87, 127. I had these ideas before reading Henke; see "Joyce in Progress: A Freudian View," *JJQ,* 13 (Spring 1976), 322.

13. (New York: Macmillan, 1964), pp. 27-49 *et passim.*

14. (1940, 1950), *Archetypes,* pp. 116, 142, 146.

15. "The Psychology of the Child Archetype," *Archetypes,* p. 167.

16. "Marriage as a Psychological Relationship," *The Development of Personality,* *CW* [Jung], 17, pp. 191-201. Compare Winnicott, *Playing,* p. 105.

17. "Meditation XVII, Now, this Bell tolling softly for another. . ."

18. *Fate,* trans. Haakon M. Chevalier (New York: Random House, 1934, 1961), p. 224.

11. SHAME'S VOICE

1. My source is Philip W. Kenny's summary of Fiedler's address in "James Joy-symposium, Hawaii 1974," *JJQ* , 12 (Spring 1975), 208-209.

2. Maddox, *Assault,* pp. 145ff., develops the complementarity of Stephen and Bloom.

3. The doubtfulness of Bloom's paternity is discussed in Alan Dundes, "Re: Joyce—No In at the Womb," *Modern Fiction Studies,* 8 (Summer 1962), 137-147.

4. *New Introductory Lectures on Psychoanalysis* (1933), *SE,* XXII, p. 84.

5. "Freud and Literature," *The Liberal Imagination: Essays on Literature and Society* (New York: Anchor Books, 1953), p. 42.

6. "Quest and Cycle in *Finnegans Wake,*" *Fables of Identity: Studies in Poetic Mythology* (New York: Harcourt, Brace and World, 1963), p. 263.

12. ONANYMOUS LETTERS: THE *WAKE* AS CONCLUSION

1. Title of Geza Roheim's study of aborigines, subtitled *A Psychoanalytic Inter-pretation of Australian Myth and Ritual* (New York: International Universities Press, 1945).

2. Duncan, *Roots and Branches: Poems* (New York: Scribners, 1964), p. 50. Blake, *Poetry and Prose,* p. 555.

3. *The Decentered Universe of Finnegans Wake: A Structuralist Analysis* (Balti-more: Johns Hopkins, 1976), particularly pp. 73-97.

4. de Rougemont, *Love in the Western World,* trans. Montgomery Belgion (New York: Pantheon, 1956), pp. 153ff.

5. Joseph Campbell and Henry Morton Robinson, *A Skeleton Key to Finnegans Wake* (New York: Harcourt, Brace, 1944), contains some points later shown to be erroneous, but no other guide to the *Wake* is nearly as readable, helpful or popular.

6. Joyce explained this chapter in a letter of November 22, 1930, to Harriet Shaw Weaver, *Letters, I,* 295.

7. *A Wake Newslitter,* New Series, 10 (1973), 51-59.

8. I am indebted for interpretation of sexual symbolism to Margaret C. Solomon, *Eternal Geomater: The Sexual Universe of Finnegans Wake* (Carbondale: Southern Illinois Univ. Press, 1969), in this case, pp. 21-33.

9. "Low Lands," *New World Writing 16* (Philadelphia: J. B. Lippincott, 1960), p. 100.

10. *JJ* 411 and Dounia Bunis Christiani, *Scandinavian Elements of Finnegans Wake* (Evanston: Northwestern, 1965), p. 40.

11. Norris, *Universe,* pp. 41, 50, sees reference to *Totem* here.

12. *Totem,* pp. 4-7, 140-146. Joyce, of course, was also influenced by Sir James George Frazer, Lucien Lévy Bruhl and other anthropologists.

13. Coleridge, for example, said, "The truth is, a great mind must be androgy-nous." Cited in Caroline G. Heilbrun, *Toward a Recognition of Androgyny* (New York: Harper Colophon Books, 1974), p. xx.

14. E.g., *FW* 92, 153-159, 161, 187, 193, 252, 259, 354, 487-490 and 617.

15. Adaline Glasheen, *A Second Census of Finnegans Wake: An Index of the Characters and Their Roles (*Northwestern, 1963), p. xxiv.

16. See Winnicott, *Playing and Reality*, pp. 2ff., 112.

INDEX

ABOUT THE AUTHOR

Sheldon Brivic is an assistant professor of English at Temple University in Philadelphia. He has specialized in Joyce for fifteen years and his articles on modern writers have appeared in *Novel, Massachusetts Review, James Joyce Quarterly,* and Frederick Crews's collection *Psychoanalysis and Literary Process.* He has appeared and presided at the International James Joyce Symposia in Paris, Dublin, and Zürich.